SPIDER-MAN
DOCTOR OCTOPUS
YEAR ONE

SPIDER-MAN/DOCTOR OCTOPUS: YEAR ONE. Contains material originally published in magazine form as SPIDER-MAN/DOCTOR OCTOPUS: YEAR ONE #1-5. Second edition. First printing 2018. ISBN 978-1-302-91545-2. Published by MARVEL WORLDWIDE, INC., a subsidiary of MARVEL ENTERTAINMENT, LLC. OFFICE OF PUBLICATION: 135 West 50th Street, New York, NY 10020. Copyright © 2018 MARVEL No similarity between any of the names, characters, persons, and/or institutions in this magazine with those of any living or dead person or institution is intended, and any such similarity which may exist is purely coincidental. **Printed in Canada.** DAN BUCKLEY, President, Marvel Entertainment; JOHN NEE, Publisher; JOE QUESADA, Chief Creative Officer; TOM BREVOORT, SVP of Publishing; DAVID BOGART, SVP of Business Affairs & Operations, Publishing & Partnership; DAVID GABRIEL, SVP of Sales & Marketing, Publishing; JEFF YOUNGQUIST, VP of Production & Special Projects; DAN CARR, Executive Director of Publishing Technology; ALEX MORALES, Director of Publishing Operations; DAN EDINGTON, Managing Editor; SUSAN CRESPI, Production Manager; STAN LEE, Chairman Emeritus. For information regarding advertising in Marvel Comics or on Marvel.com, please contact Vit DeBellis, Custom Solutions & Integrated Advertising Manager, at vdebellis@marvel.com. For Marvel subscription inquiries, please call 888-511-5480. **Manufactured between 12/7/2018 and 1/8/2019 by SOLISCO PRINTERS, SCOTT, QC, CANADA.**

10 9 8 7 6 5 4 3 2 1

WRITER: **ZEB WELLS**
ARTIST: **KAARE ANDREWS**
COLOR ARTIST: **JOSÉ VILLARRUBIA**
LETTERER: **VC'S DAVE SHARPE**
EDITOR: **WARREN SIMONS**
EXECUTIVE EDITOR: **AXEL ALONSO**

COLLECTION EDITOR: **JENNIFER GRÜNWALD**
ASSISTANT EDITOR: **CAITLIN O'CONNELL**
ASSOCIATE MANAGING EDITOR: **KATERI WOODY**
EDITOR, SPECIAL PROJECTS: **MARK D. BEAZLEY**
VP PRODUCTION & SPECIAL PROJECTS: **JEFF YOUNGQUIST**
SVP PRINT, SALES & MARKETING: **DAVID GABRIEL**
BOOK DESIGNER: **CARRIE BEADLE**

EDITOR IN CHIEF: **C.B. CEBULSKI**
CHIEF CREATIVE OFFICER: **JOE QUESADA**
PRESIDENT: **DAN BUCKLEY**
EXECUTIVE PRODUCER: **ALAN FINE**

SPIDER-MAN CREATED BY **STAN LEE** & **STEVE DITKO**

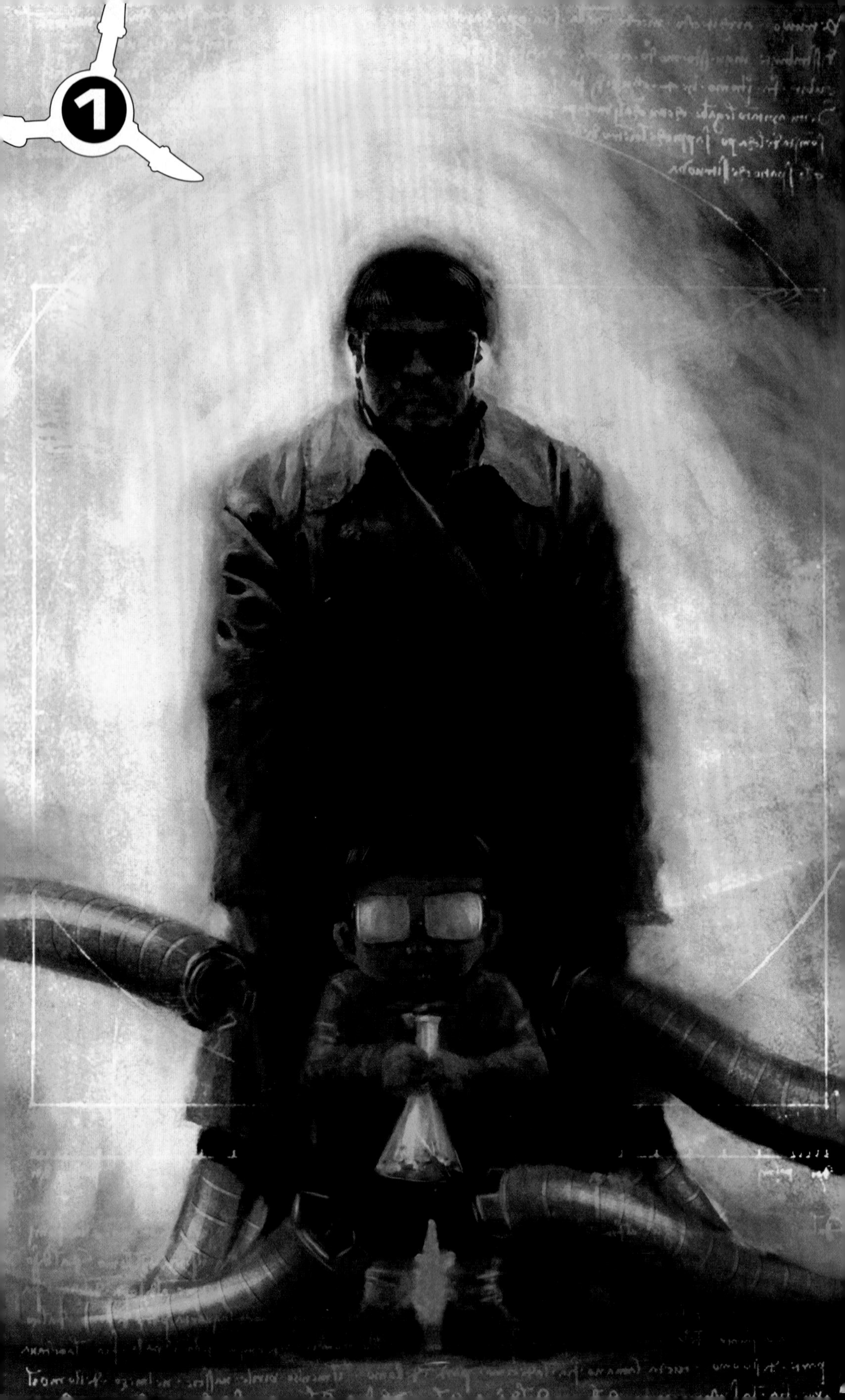
1

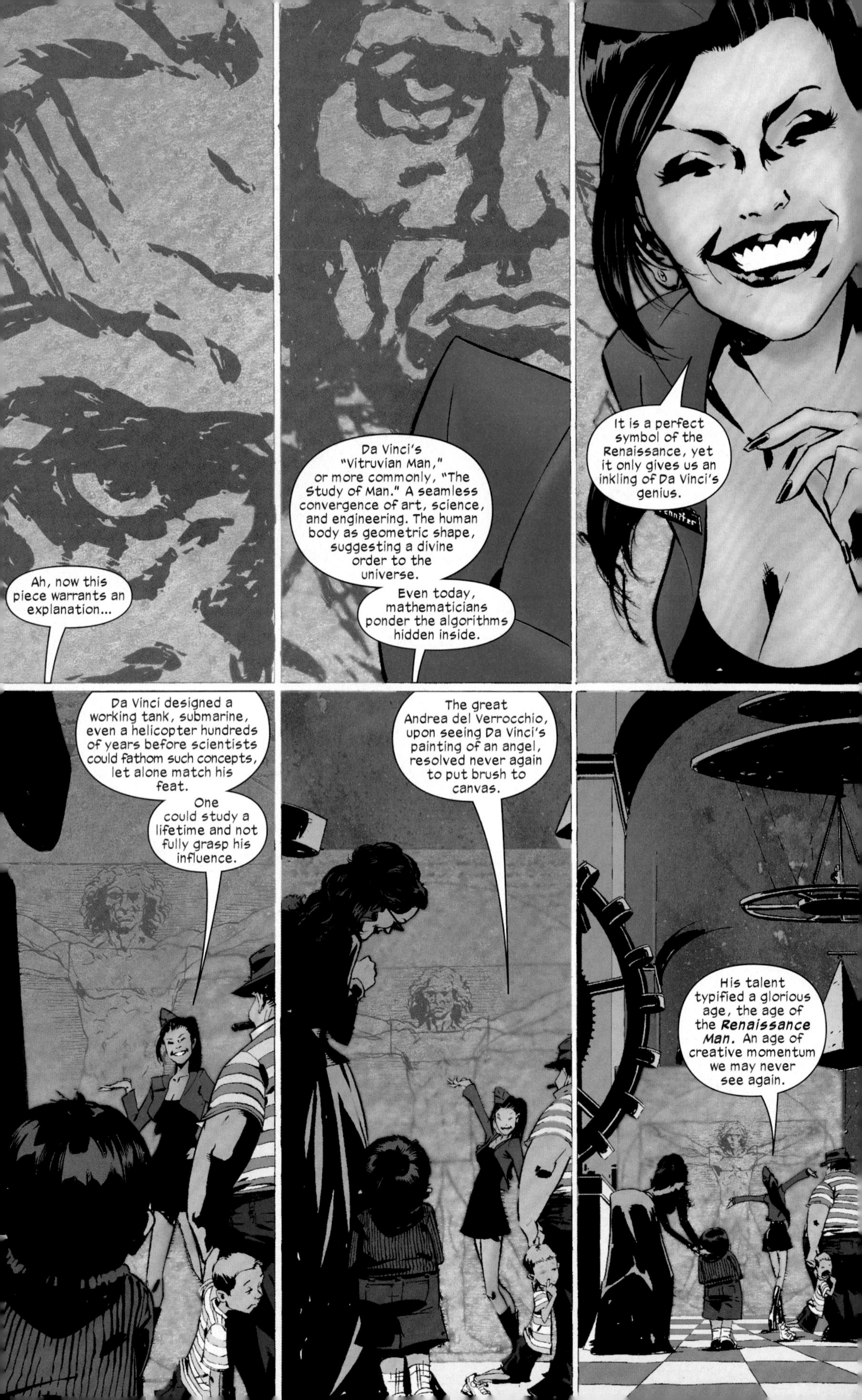

Ah, now this piece warrants an explanation...
Da Vinci's "Vitruvian Man," or more commonly, "The Study of Man." A seamless convergence of art, science, and engineering. The human body as geometric shape, suggesting a divine order to the universe.
Even today, mathematicians ponder the algorithms hidden inside.
It is a perfect symbol of the Renaissance, yet it only gives us an inkling of Da Vinci's genius.
Da Vinci designed a working tank, submarine, even a helicopter hundreds of years before scientists could fathom such concepts, let alone match his feat.
One could study a lifetime and not fully grasp his influence.
The great Andrea del Verrocchio, upon seeing Da Vinci's painting of an angel, resolved never again to put brush to canvas.
His talent typified a glorious age, the age of the *Renaissance Man.* An age of creative momentum we may never see again.

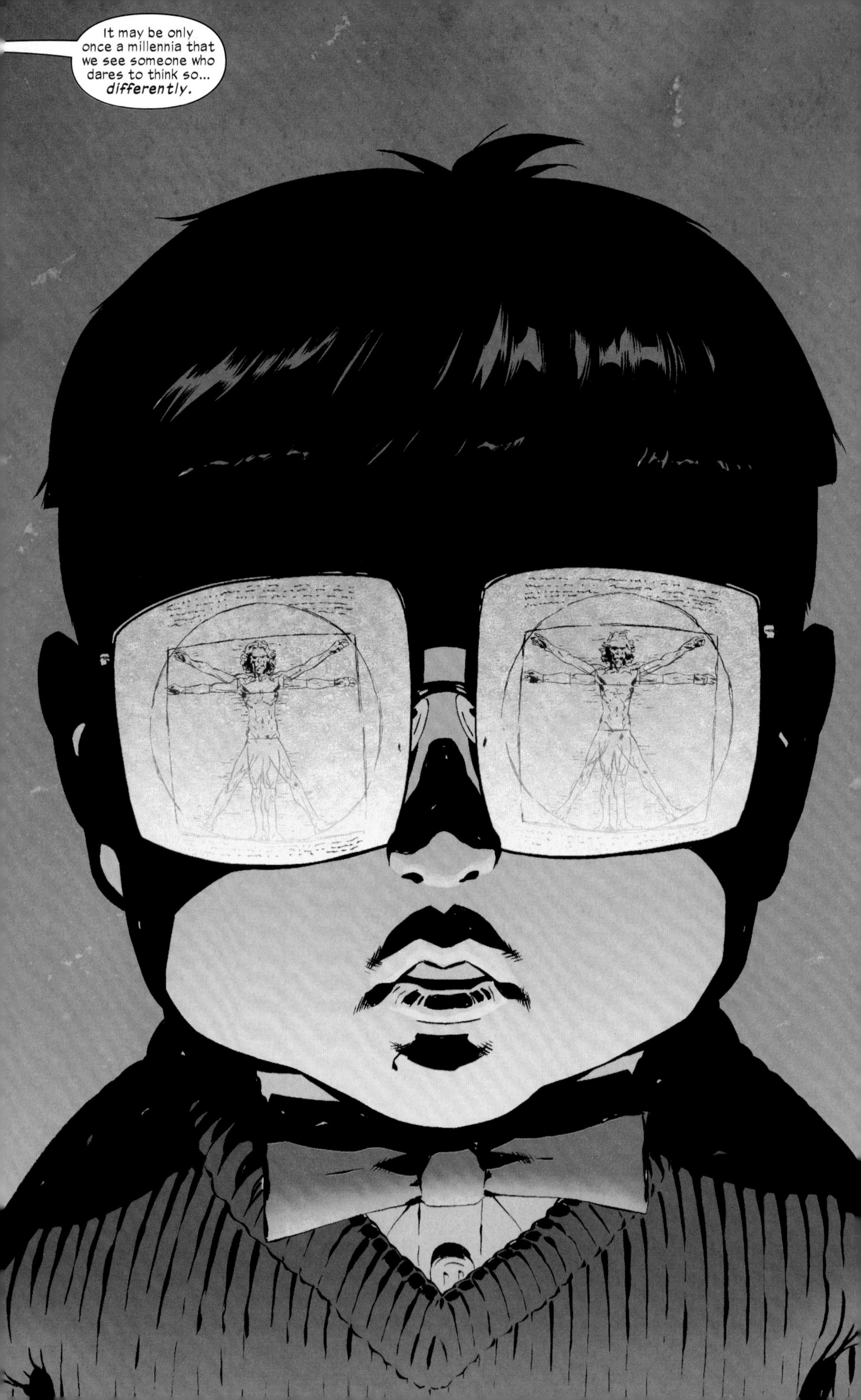
It may be only once a millennia that we see someone who dares to think so... *differently*.

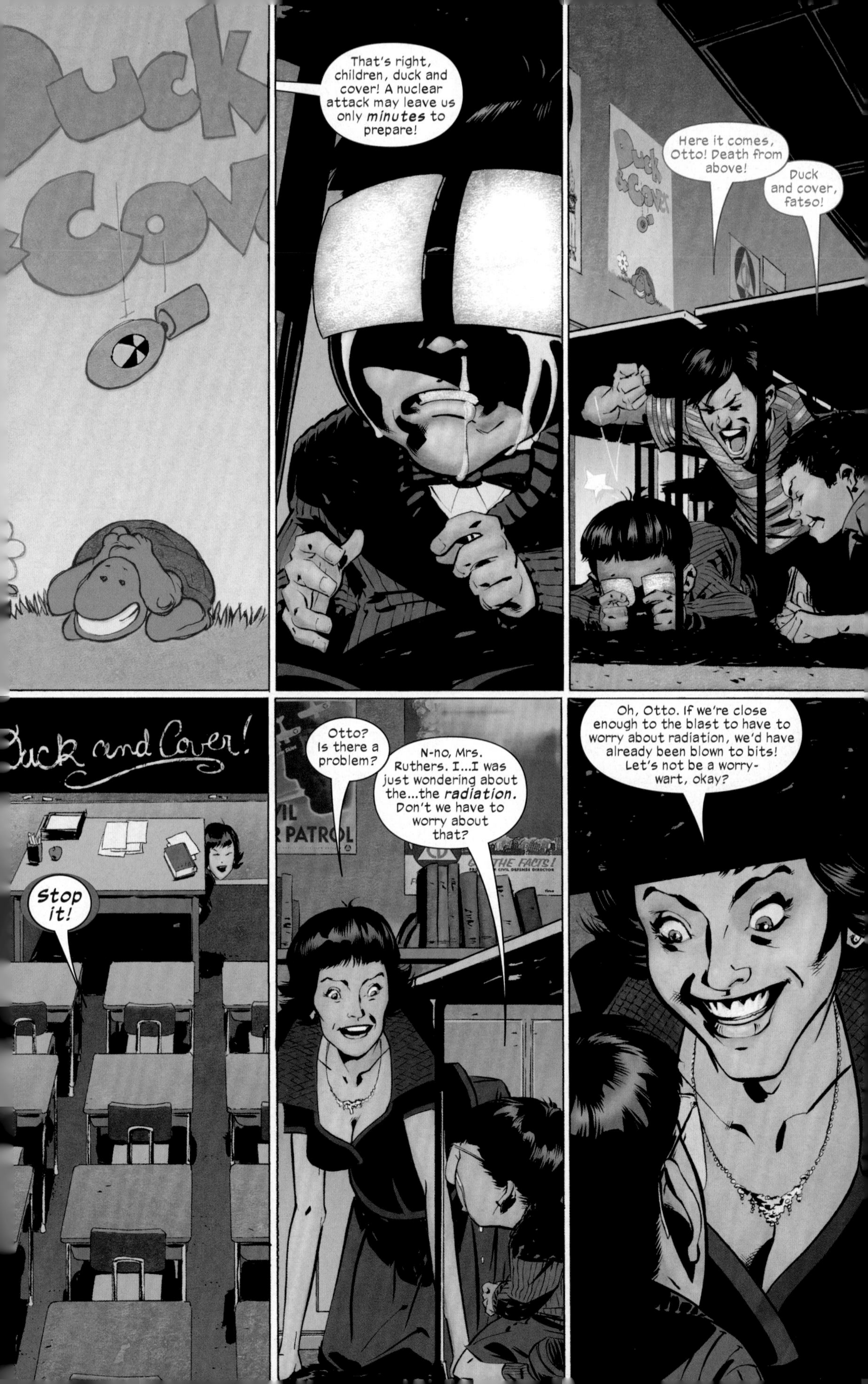
Duck & Cover
That's right, children, duck and cover! A nuclear attack may leave us only *minutes* to prepare!
Duck & Cover
Here it comes, Otto! Death from above!
Duck and cover, fatso!
Duck and Cover!
Stop it!
Otto? Is there a problem?
N-no, Mrs. Ruthers. I...I was just wondering about the...the *radiation.* Don't we have to worry about that?
CIVIL AIR PATROL
THE FACTS!
Oh, Otto. If we're close enough to the blast to have to worry about radiation, we'd have already been blown to bits! Let's not be a worry-wart, okay?

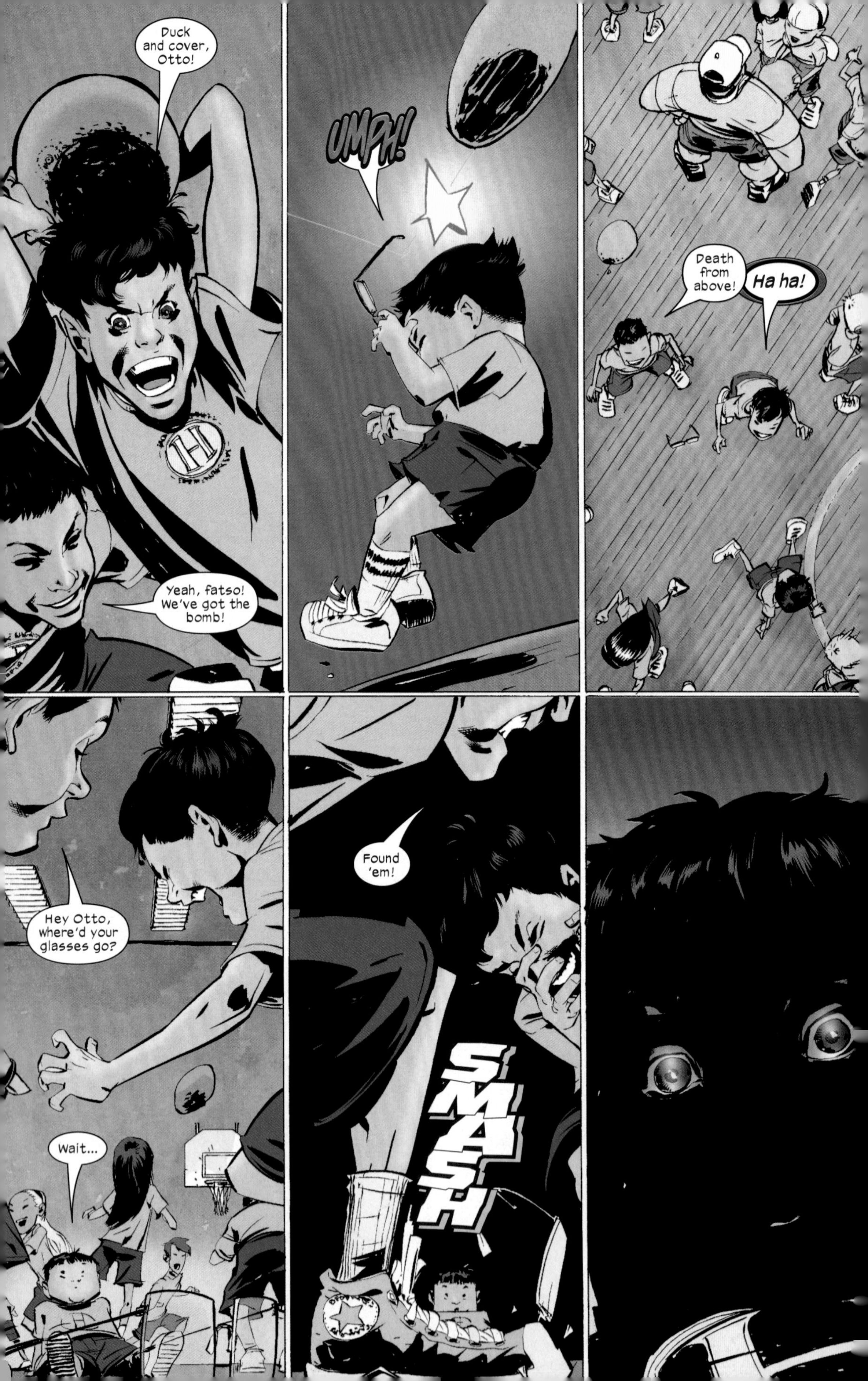
Duck and cover, Otto!
Yeah, fatso! We've got the bomb!
UMPH!
Death from above!
Ha ha!
Hey Otto, where'd your glasses go?
Wait...
Found 'em!
SMASH

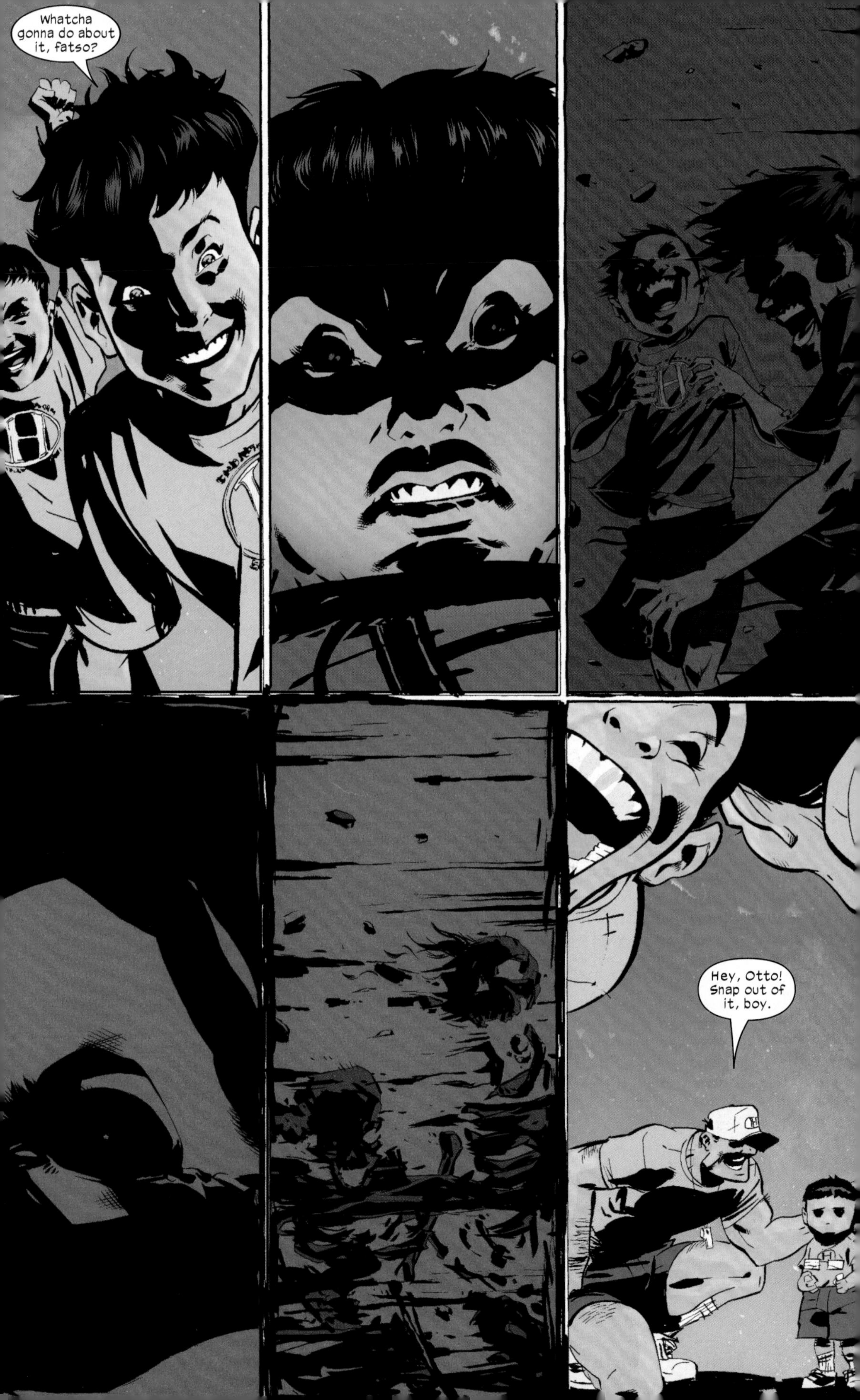
Whatcha gonna do about it, fatso?
Hey, Otto! Snap out of it, boy.

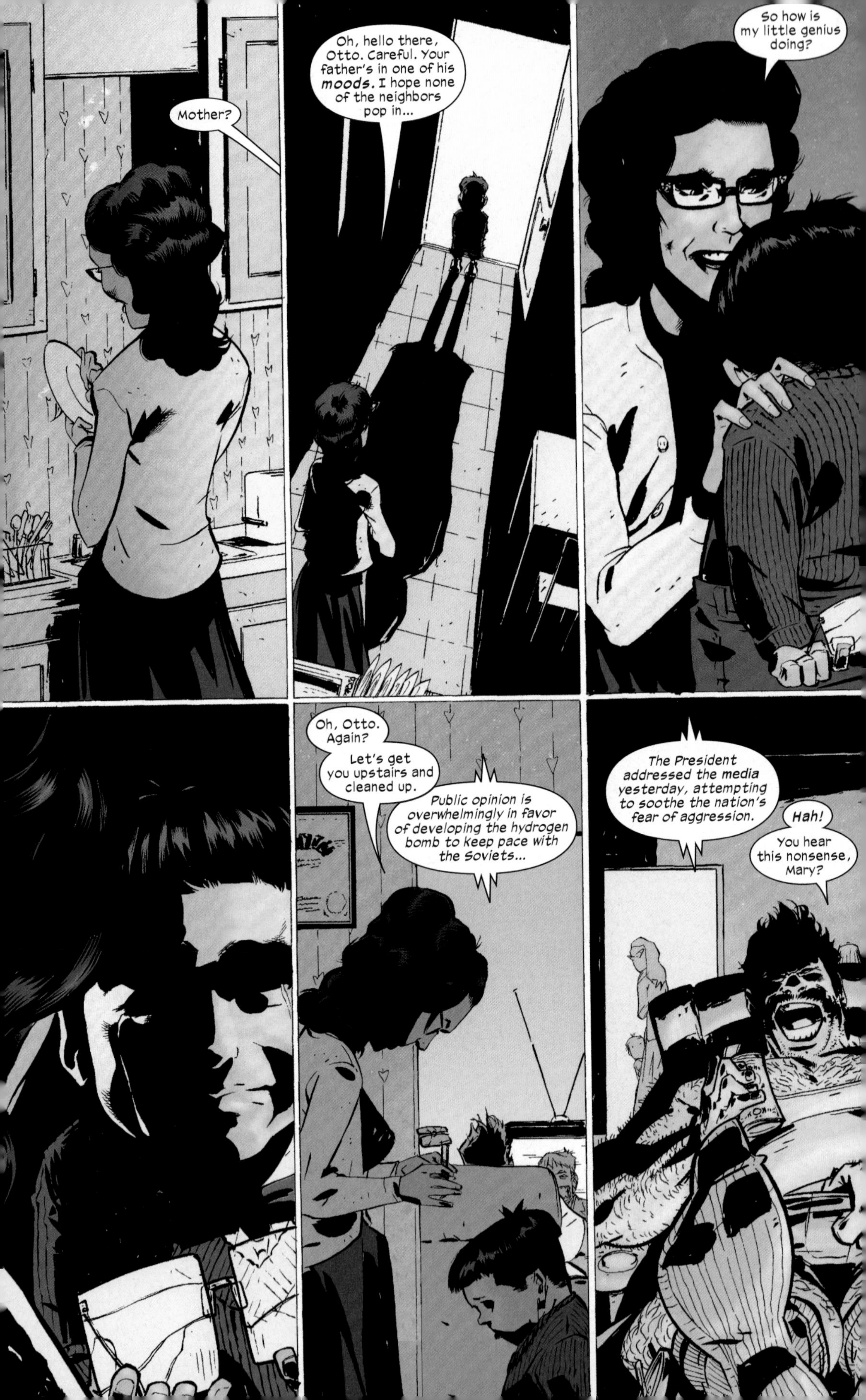
Mother?
Oh, hello there, Otto. Careful. Your father's in one of his moods. I hope none of the neighbors pop in...
So how is my little genius doing?
Oh, Otto. Again?
Let's get you upstairs and cleaned up.
Public opinion is overwhelmingly in favor of developing the hydrogen bomb to keep pace with the Soviets...
The President addressed the media yesterday, attempting to soothe the nation's fear of aggression.
Hah!
You hear this nonsense, Mary?

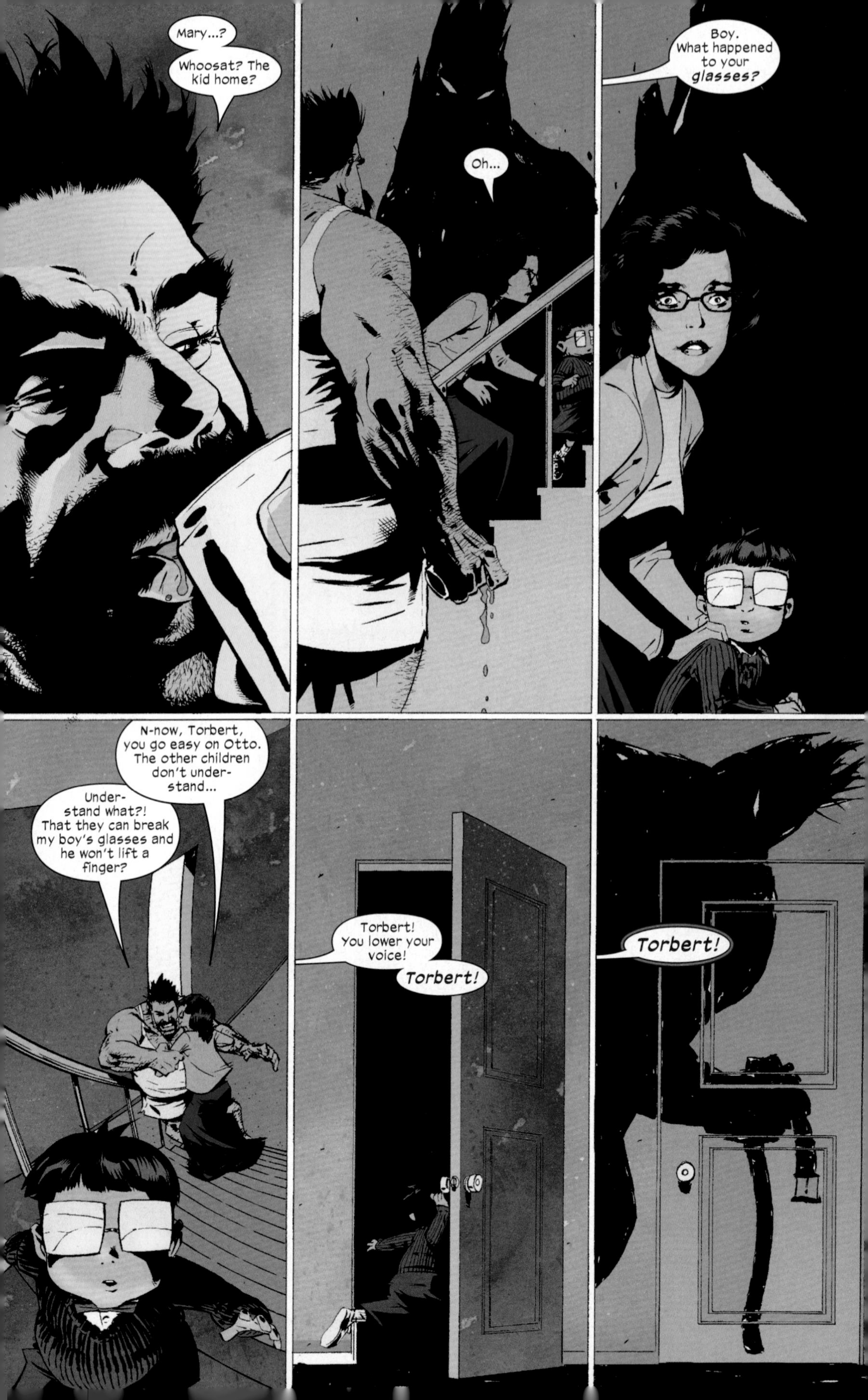
Mary...?
Whoosat? The kid home?
Oh...
Boy. What happened to your glasses?
N-now, Torbert, you go easy on Otto. The other children don't under-stand...
Under-stand what?! That they can break my boy's glasses and he won't lift a finger?
Torbert! You lower your voice!
Torbert!
Torbert!

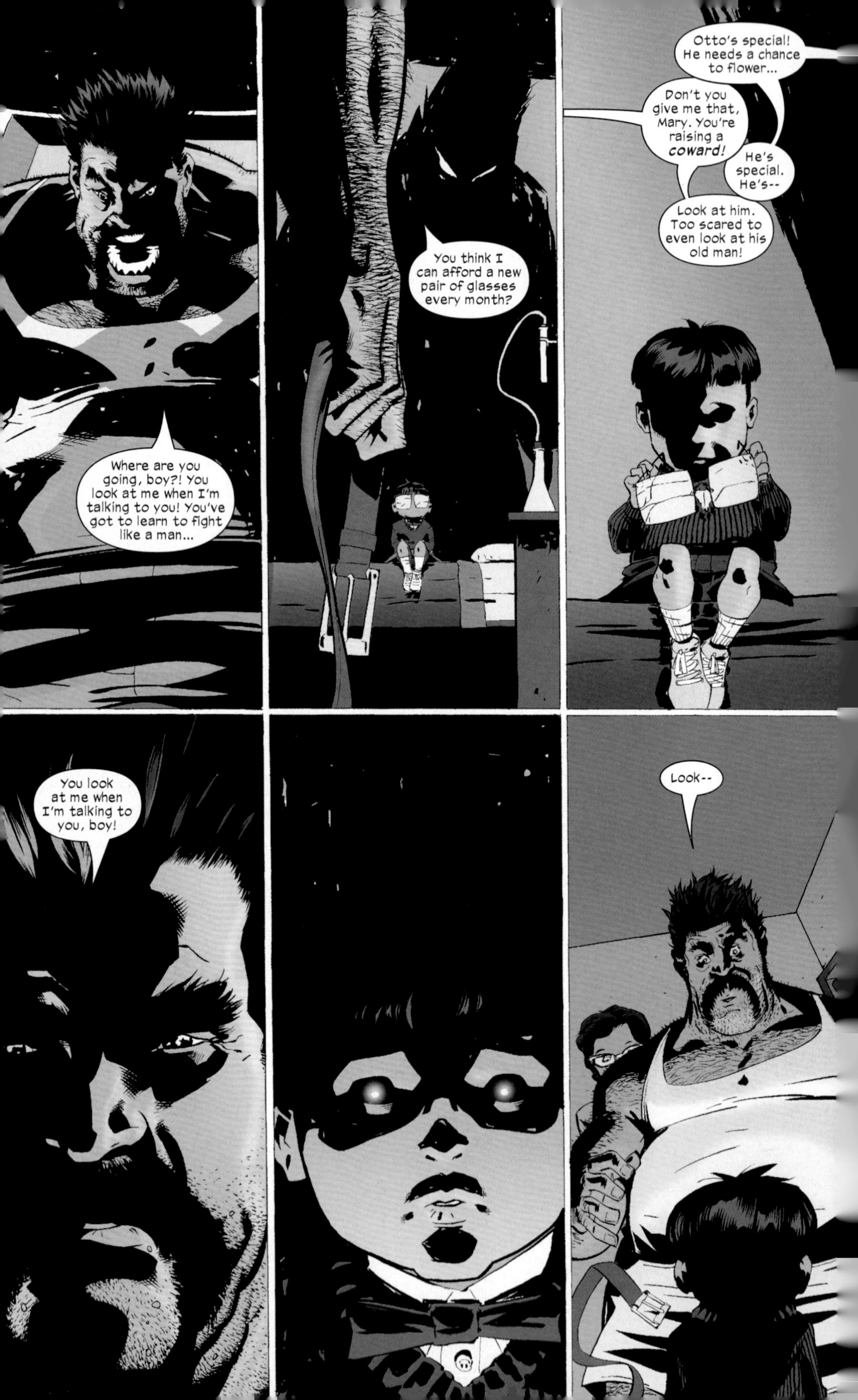
Where are you going, boy?! You look at me when I'm talking to you! You've got to learn to fight like a man...
You think I can afford a new pair of glasses every month?
Otto's special! He needs a chance to flower...
Don't you give me that, Mary. You're raising a *coward!*
He's special. He's--
Look at him. Too scared to even look at his old man!
You look at me when I'm talking to you, boy!
Look--

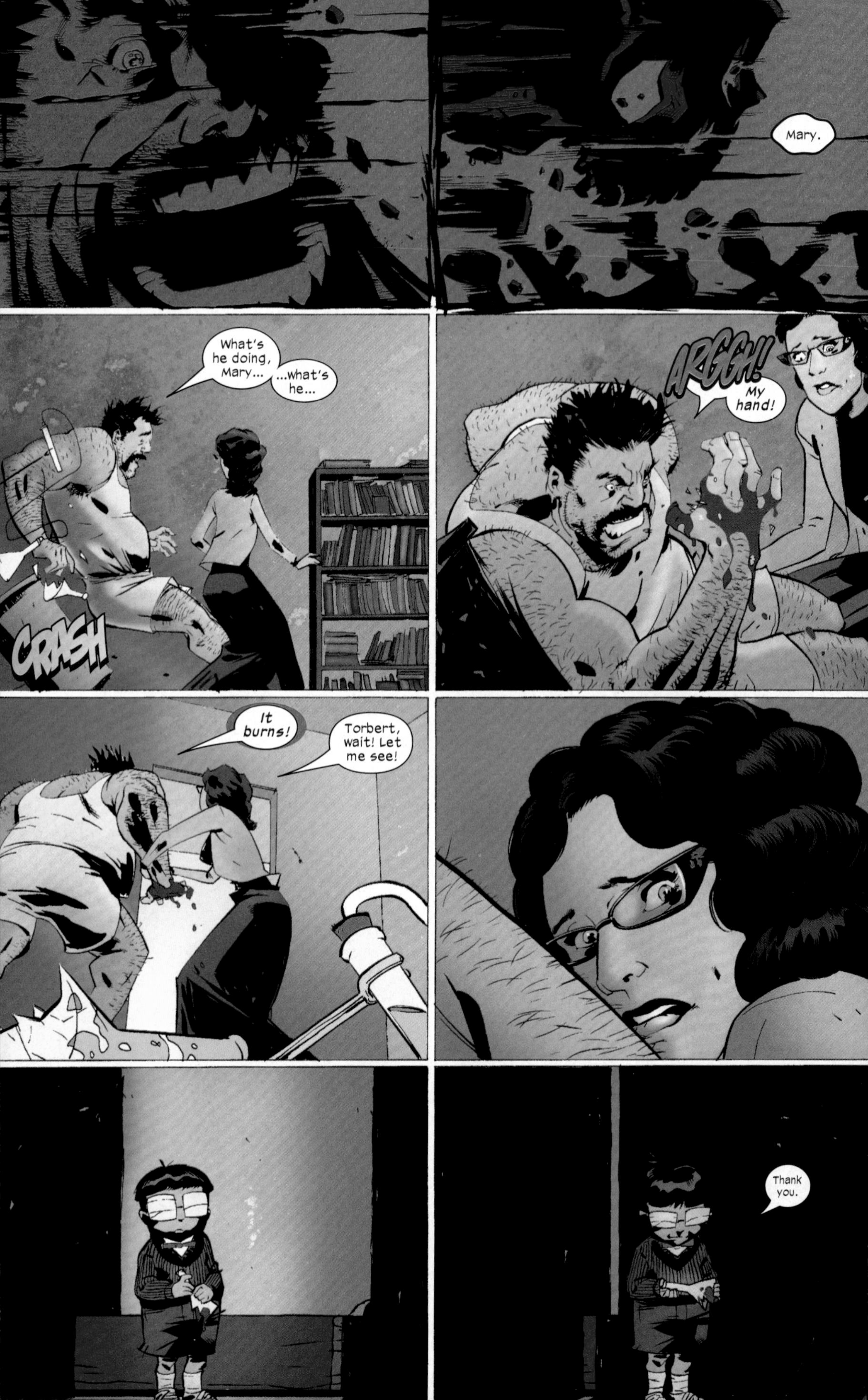
Mary.
What's he doing, Mary...
...what's he...
CRASH
ARGGH!
My hand!
It burns!
Torbert, wait! Let me see!
Thank you.

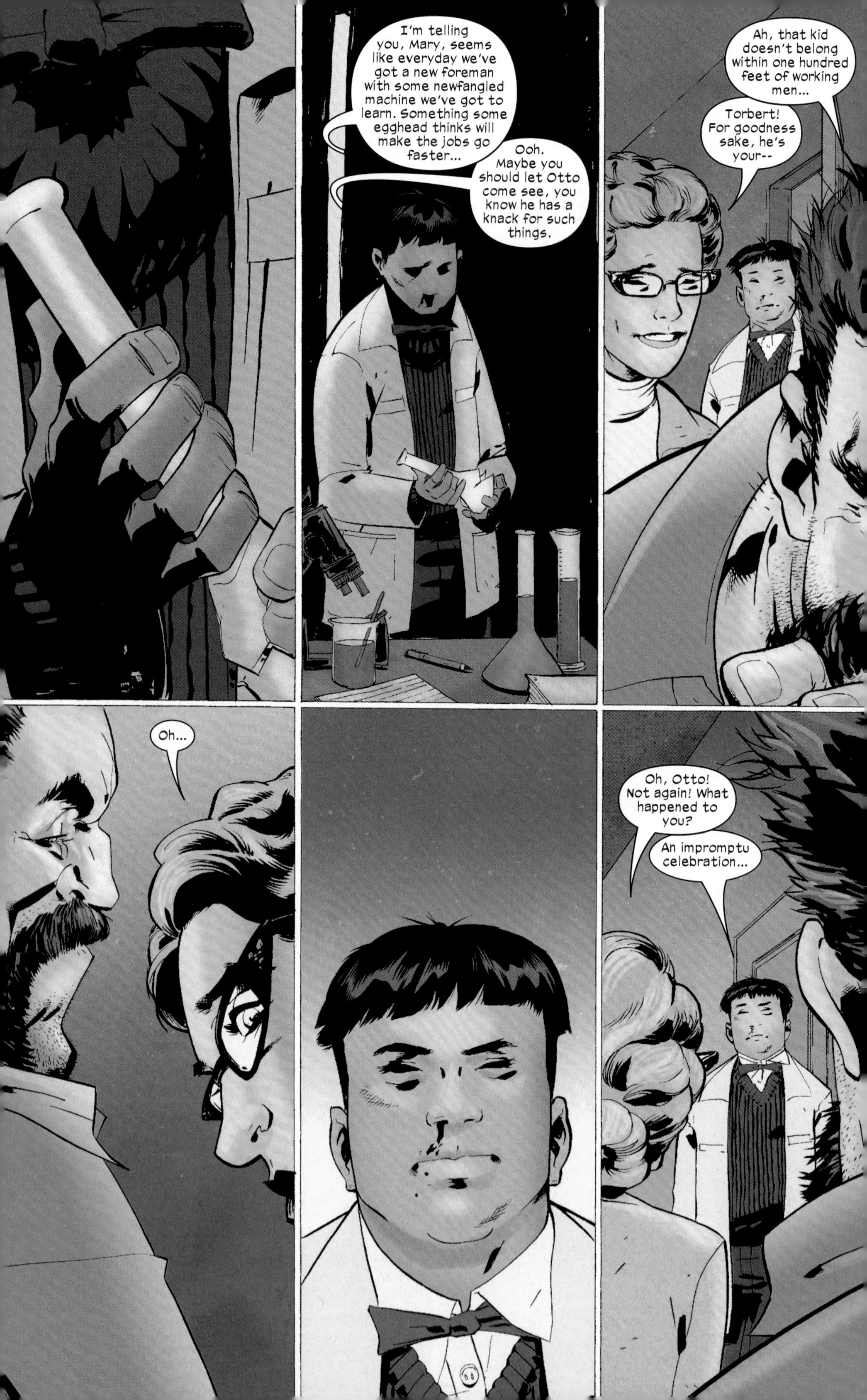
I'm telling you, Mary, seems like everyday we've got a new foreman with some newfangled machine we've got to learn. Something some egghead thinks will make the jobs go faster...
Ooh. Maybe you should let Otto come see, you know he has a knack for such things.
Ah, that kid doesn't belong within one hundred feet of working men...
Torbert! For goodness sake, he's your--
Oh...
Oh, Otto! Not again! What happened to you?
An impromptu celebration...

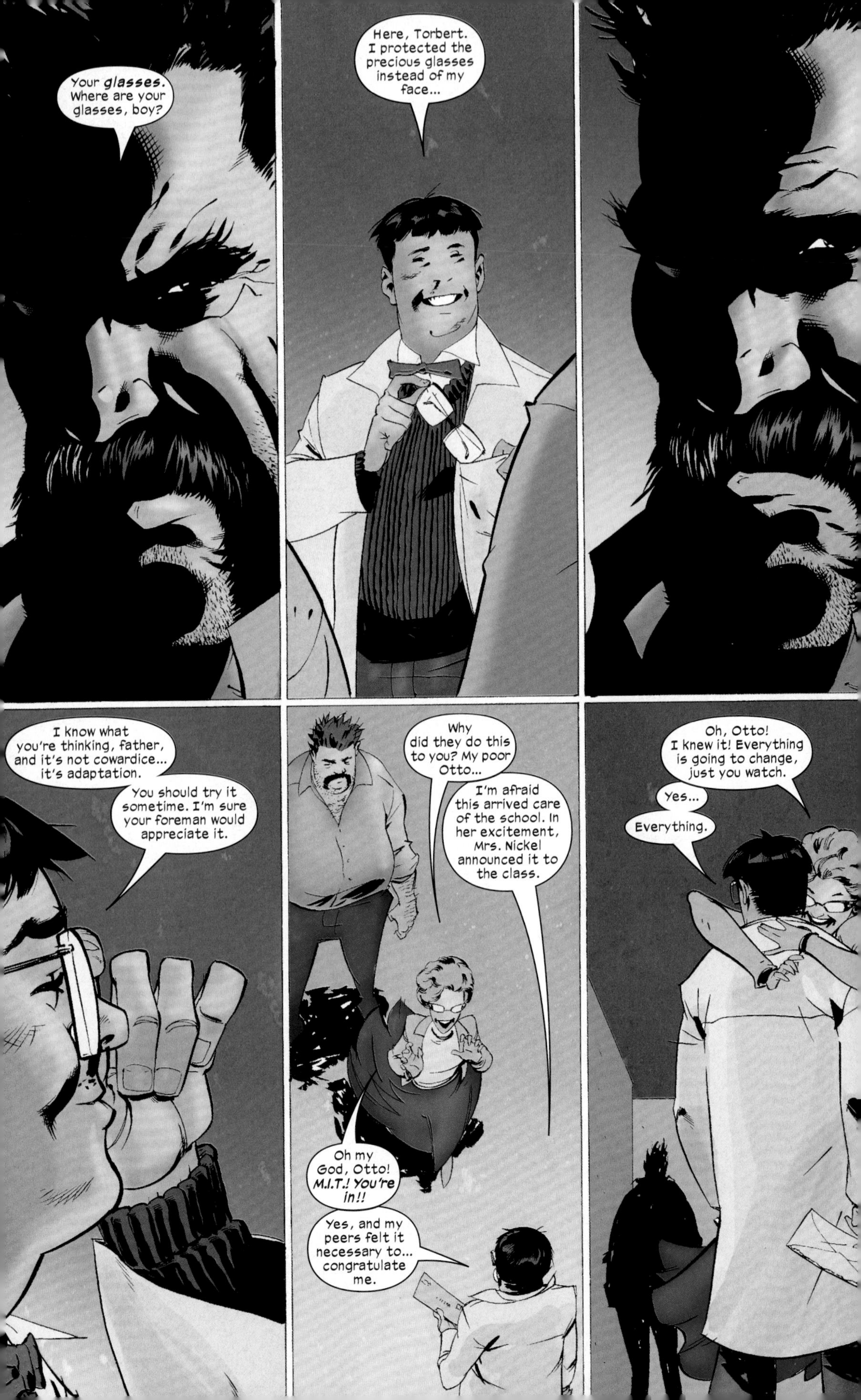
Your *glasses.* Where are your glasses, boy?
Here, Torbert. I protected the precious glasses instead of my face...
I know what you're thinking, father, and it's not cowardice... it's adaptation.
You should try it sometime. I'm sure your foreman would appreciate it.
Why did they do this to you? My poor Otto...
I'm afraid this arrived care of the school. In her excitement, Mrs. Nickel announced it to the class.
Oh my God, Otto! *M.I.T.! You're in!!*
Yes, and my peers felt it necessary to... congratulate me.
Oh, Otto! I knew it! Everything is going to change, just you watch.
Yes...
Everything.

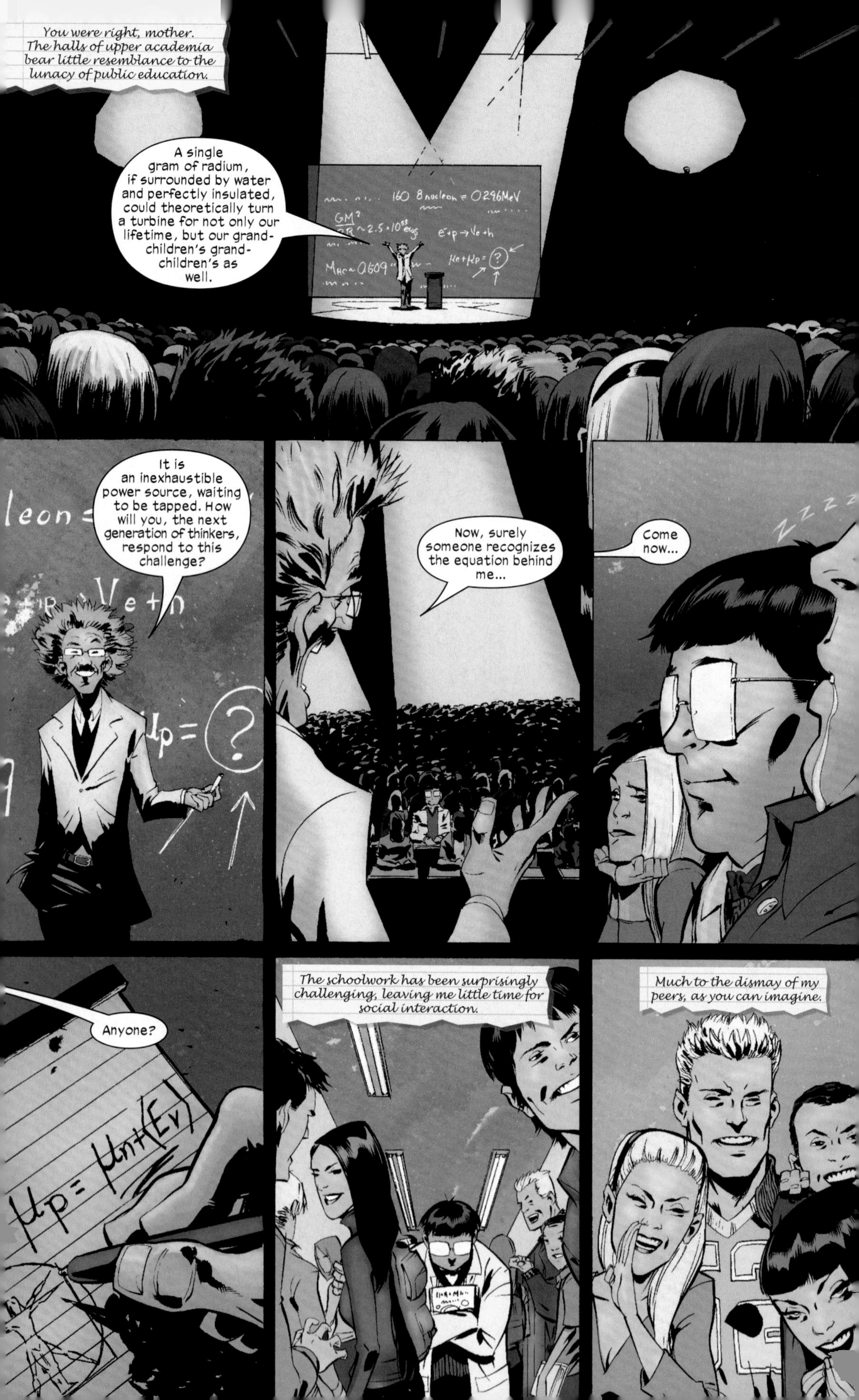
You were right, mother. The halls of upper academia bear little resemblance to the lunacy of public education.
A single gram of radium, if surrounded by water and perfectly insulated, could theoretically turn a turbine for not only our lifetime, but our grand-children's grand-children's as well.
It is an inexhaustible power source, waiting to be tapped. How will you, the next generation of thinkers, respond to this challenge?
Now, surely someone recognizes the equation behind me...
Come now...
Anyone?
The schoolwork has been surprisingly challenging, leaving me little time for social interaction.
Much to the dismay of my peers, as you can imagine.

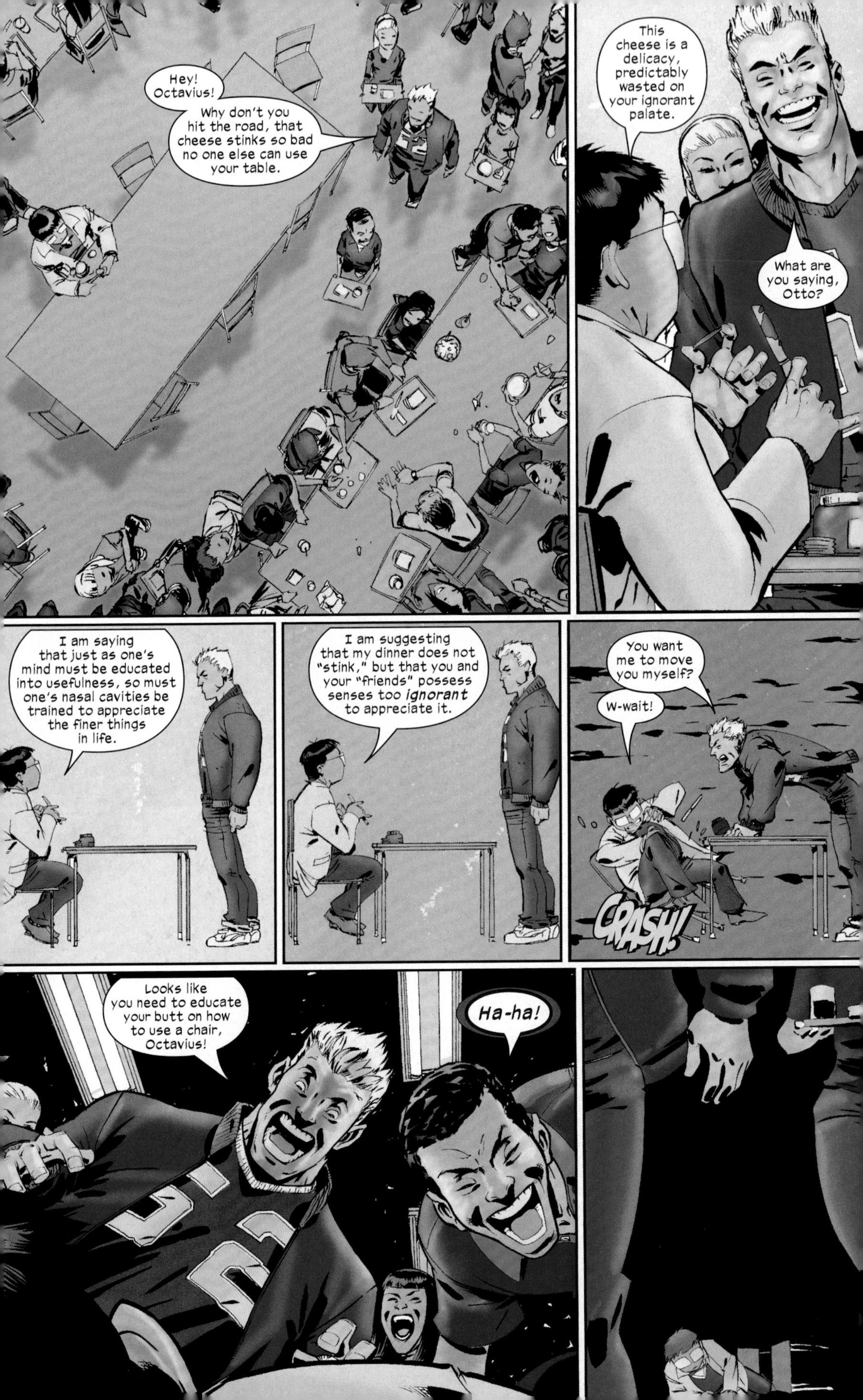
Hey! Octavius!
Why don't you hit the road, that cheese stinks so bad no one else can use your table.
This cheese is a delicacy, predictably wasted on your ignorant palate.
What are you saying, Otto?
I am saying that just as one's mind must be educated into usefulness, so must one's nasal cavities be trained to appreciate the finer things in life.
I am suggesting that my dinner does not "stink," but that you and your "friends" possess senses too ignorant to appreciate it.
You want me to move you myself?
W-wait!
CRASH!
Looks like you need to educate your butt on how to use a chair, Octavius!
Ha-ha!

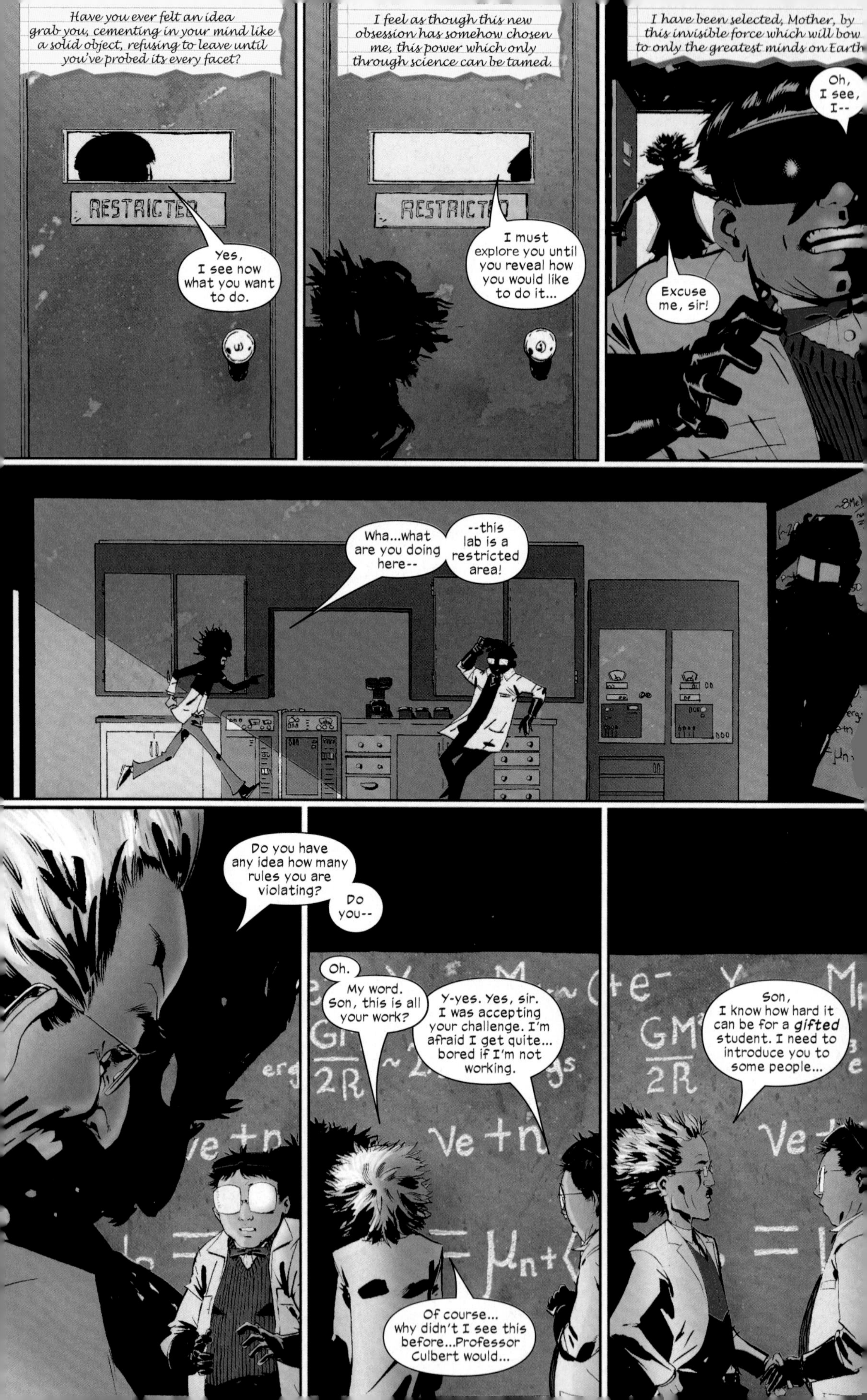

Have you ever felt an idea grab you, cementing in your mind like a solid object, refusing to leave until you've probed its every facet?
RESTRICTED
Yes, I see now what you want to do.
I feel as though this new obsession has somehow chosen me, this power which only through science can be tamed.
RESTRICTED
I must explore you until you reveal how you would like to do it...
I have been selected, Mother, by this invisible force which will bow to only the greatest minds on Earth
Oh, I see, I--
Excuse me, sir!
Wha...what are you doing here--
--this lab is a restricted area!
Do you have any idea how many rules you are violating?
Do you--
Oh.
My word. Son, this is all your work?
Y-yes. Yes, sir. I was accepting your challenge. I'm afraid I get quite... bored if I'm not working.
Of course... why didn't I see this before...Professor Culbert would...
Son, I know how hard it can be for a *gifted* student. I need to introduce you to some people...

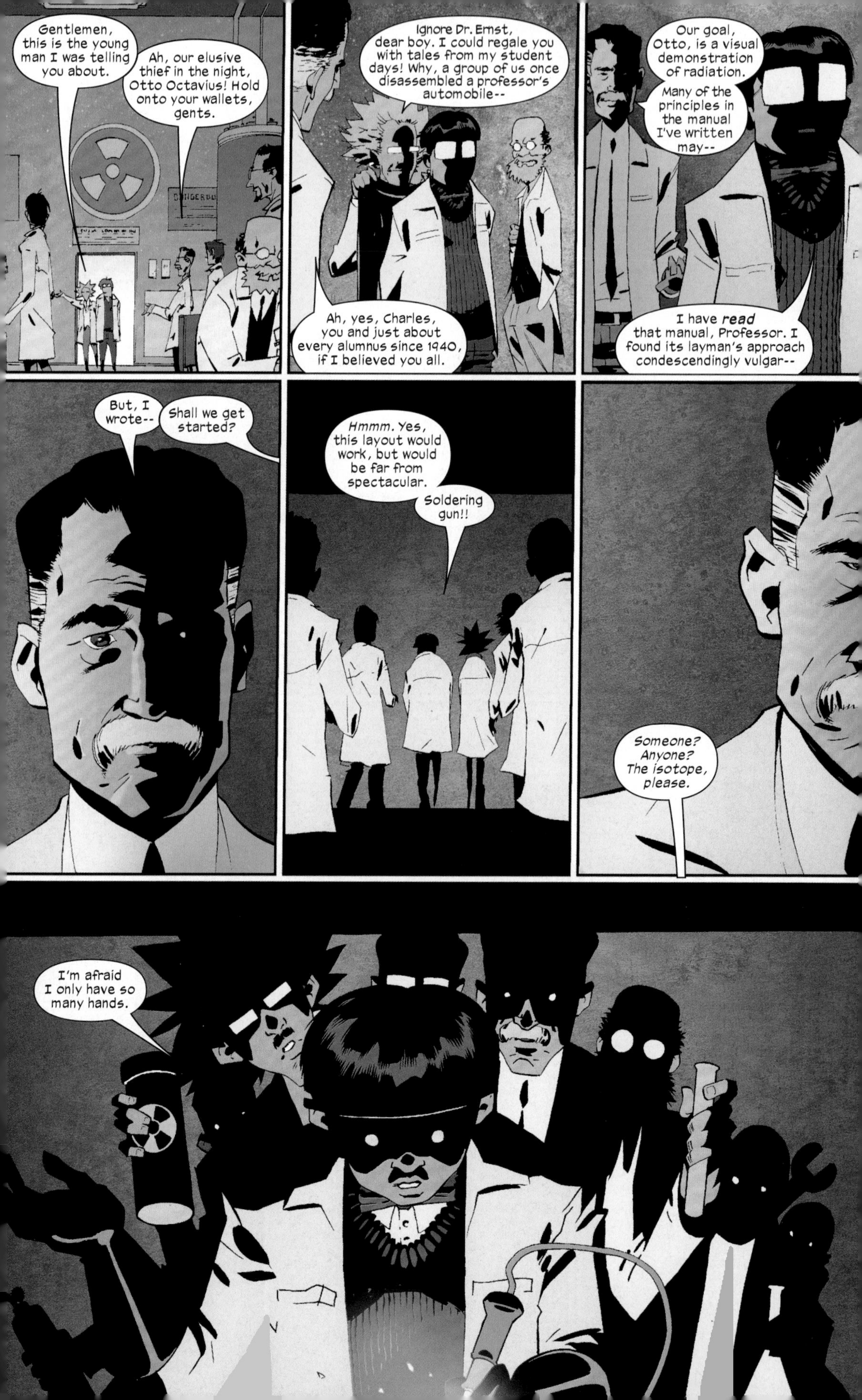
Gentlemen, this is the young man I was telling you about.
Ah, our elusive thief in the night, Otto Octavius! Hold onto your wallets, gents.
Ignore Dr. Ernst, dear boy. I could regale you with tales from my student days! Why, a group of us once disassembled a professor's automobile--
Ah, yes, Charles, you and just about every alumnus since 1940, if I believed you all.
Our goal, Otto, is a visual demonstration of radiation.
Many of the principles in the manual I've written may--
I have *read* that manual, Professor. I found its layman's approach condescendingly vulgar--
But, I wrote--
Shall we get started?
Hmmm. Yes, this layout would work, but would be far from spectacular.
Soldering gun!!
Someone? Anyone? The isotope, please.
I'm afraid I only have so many hands.

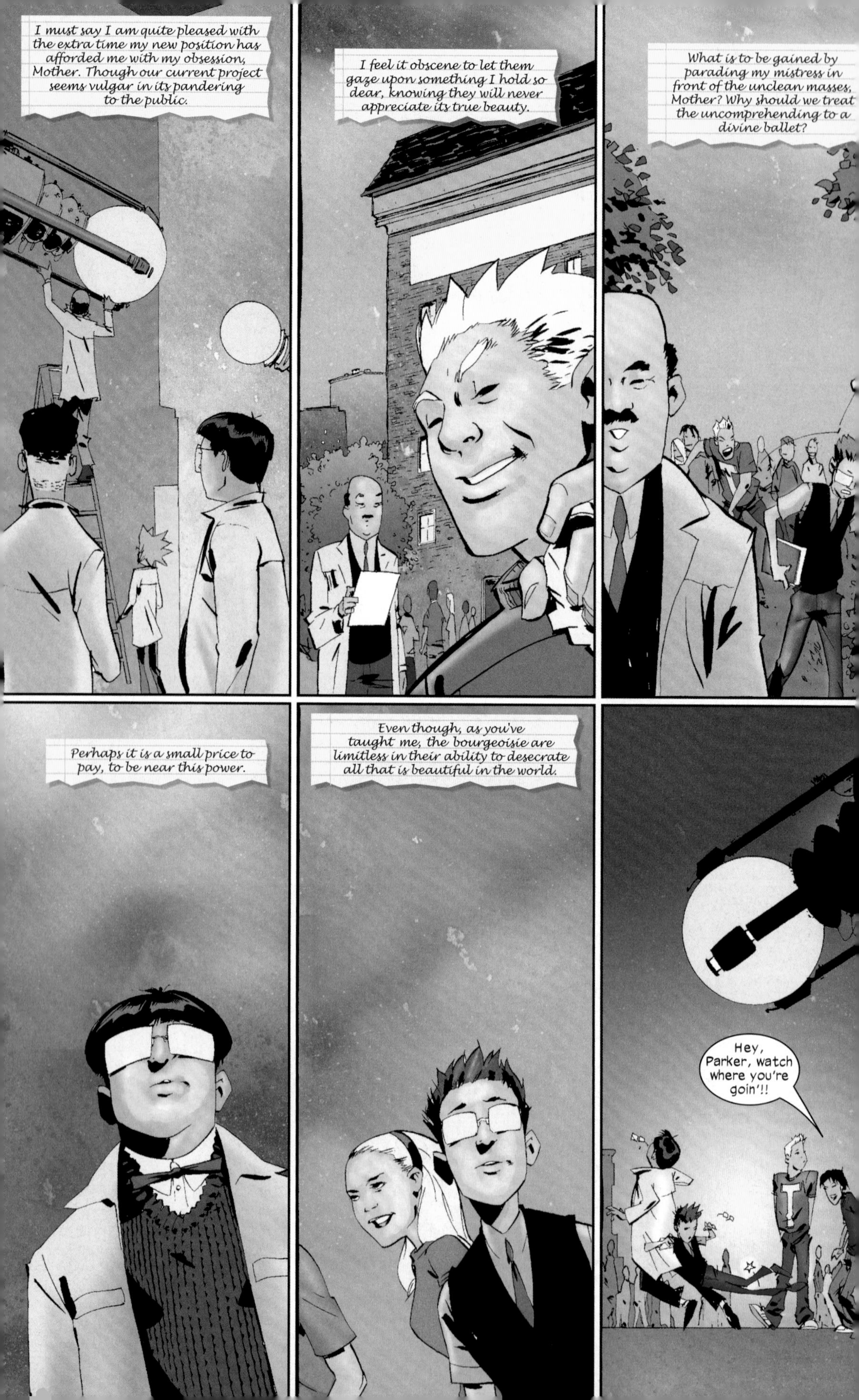
I must say I am quite pleased with the extra time my new position has afforded me with my obsession, Mother. Though our current project seems vulgar in its pandering to the public.
I feel it obscene to let them gaze upon something I hold so dear, knowing they will never appreciate its true beauty.
What is to be gained by parading my mistress in front of the unclean masses, Mother? Why should we treat the uncomprehending to a divine ballet?
Perhaps it is a small price to pay, to be near this power.
Even though, as you've taught me, the bourgeoisie are limitless in their ability to desecrate all that is beautiful in the world.
Hey, Parker, watch where you're goin'!!

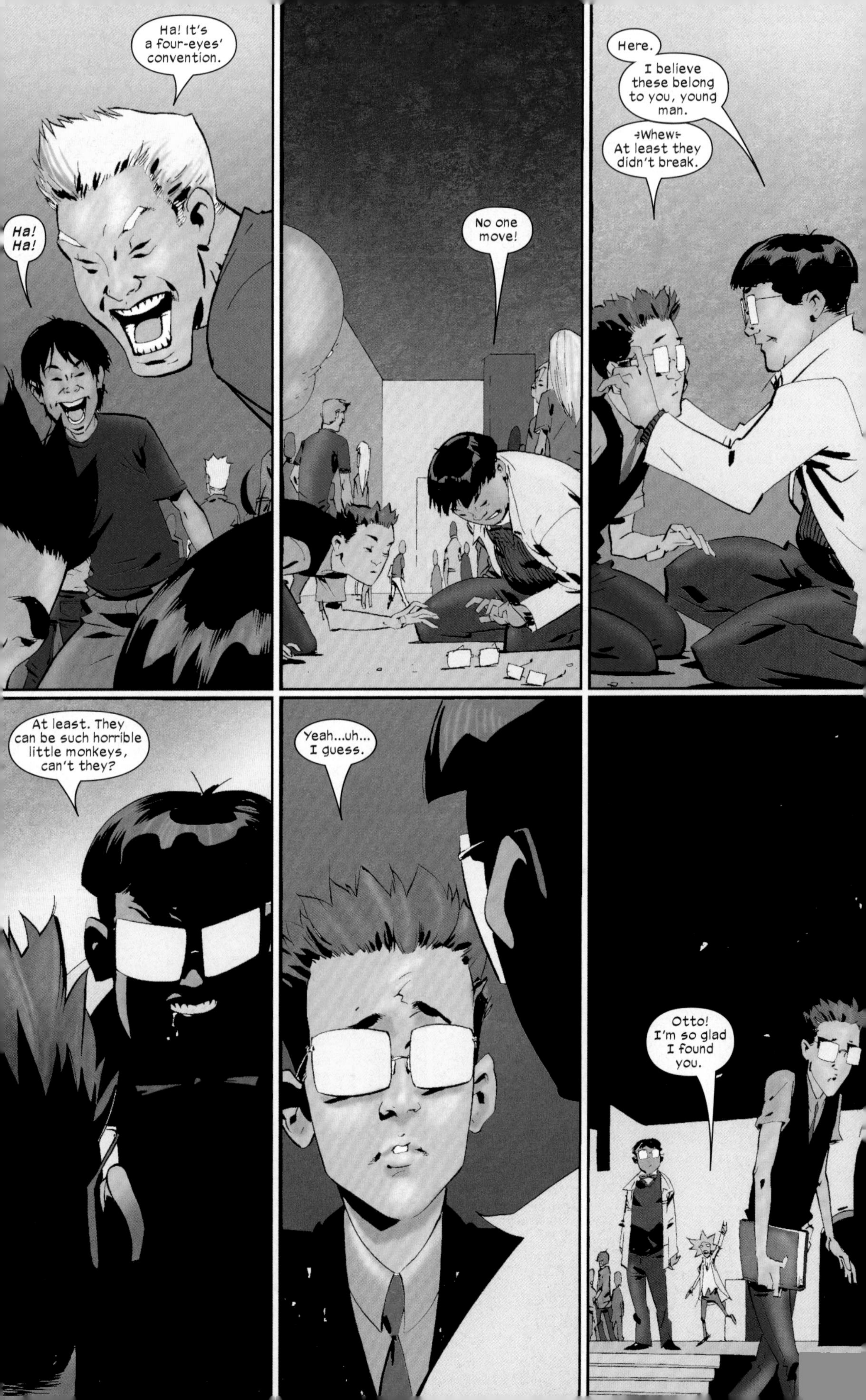
Ha! It's a four-eyes' convention.
Ha! Ha!
No one move!
Here.
I believe these belong to you, young man.
~Whew~ At least they didn't break.
At least. They can be such horrible little monkeys, can't they?
Yeah...uh... I guess.
Otto! I'm so glad I found you.

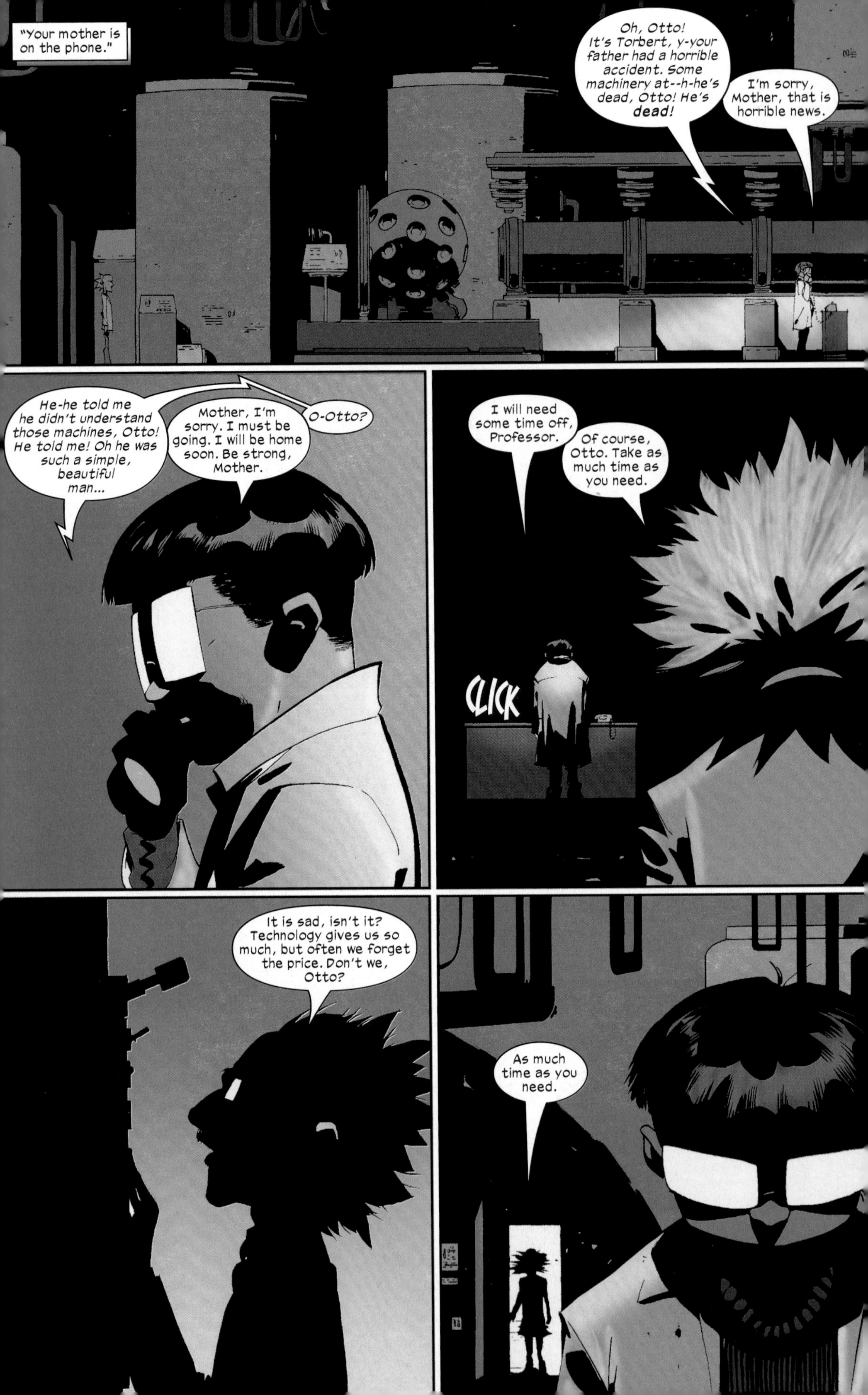

"Your mother is on the phone."
Oh, Otto! It's Torbert, y-your father had a horrible accident. Some machinery at--h-he's dead, Otto! He's **dead!**
I'm sorry, Mother, that is horrible news.
He-he told me he didn't understand those machines, Otto! He told me! Oh he was such a simple, beautiful man...
Mother, I'm sorry. I must be going. I will be home soon. Be strong, Mother.
O-Otto?
I will need some time off, Professor.
Of course, Otto. Take as much time as you need.
CLICK
It is sad, isn't it? Technology gives us so much, but often we forget the price. Don't we, Otto?
As much time as you need.

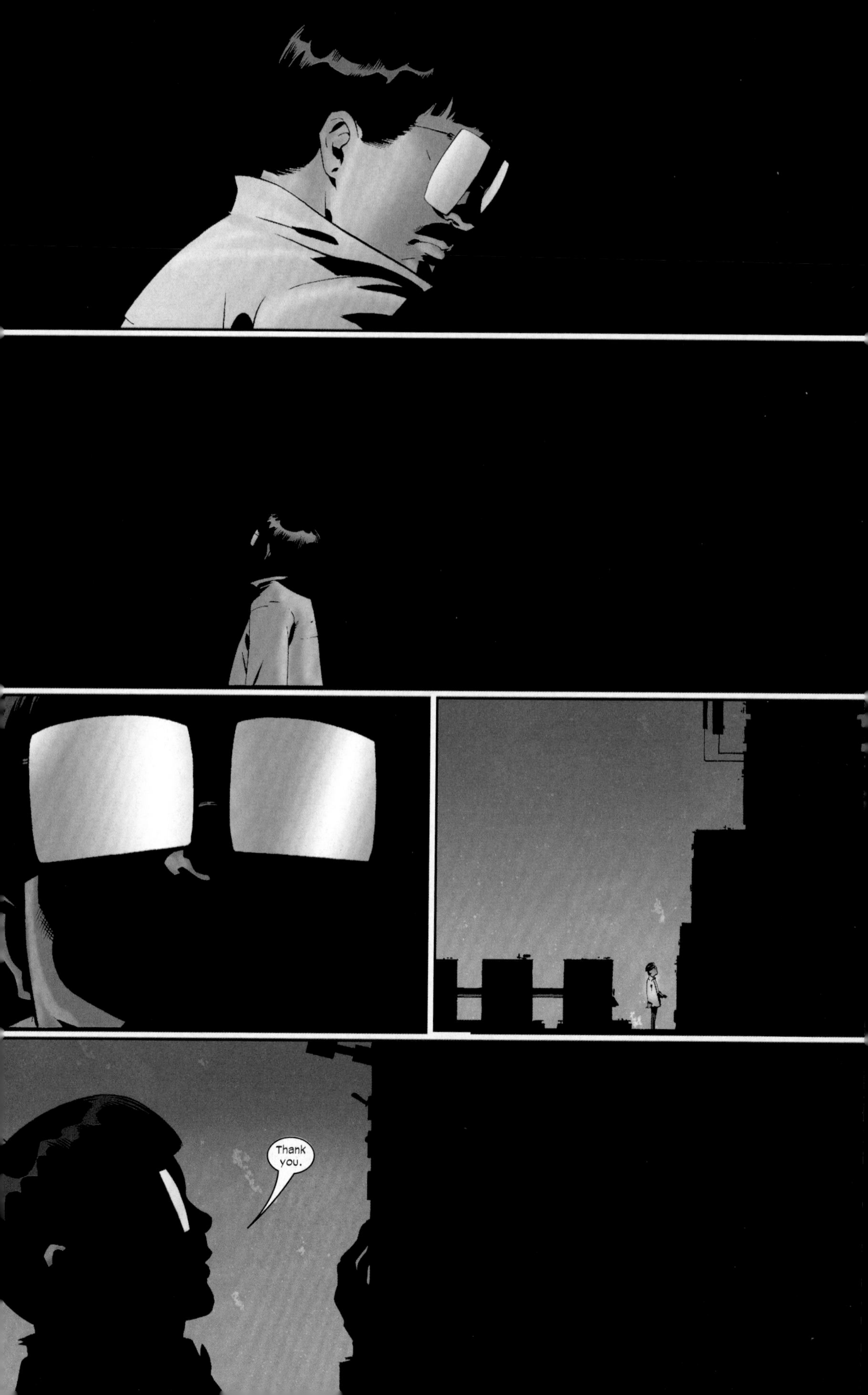
Thank you.

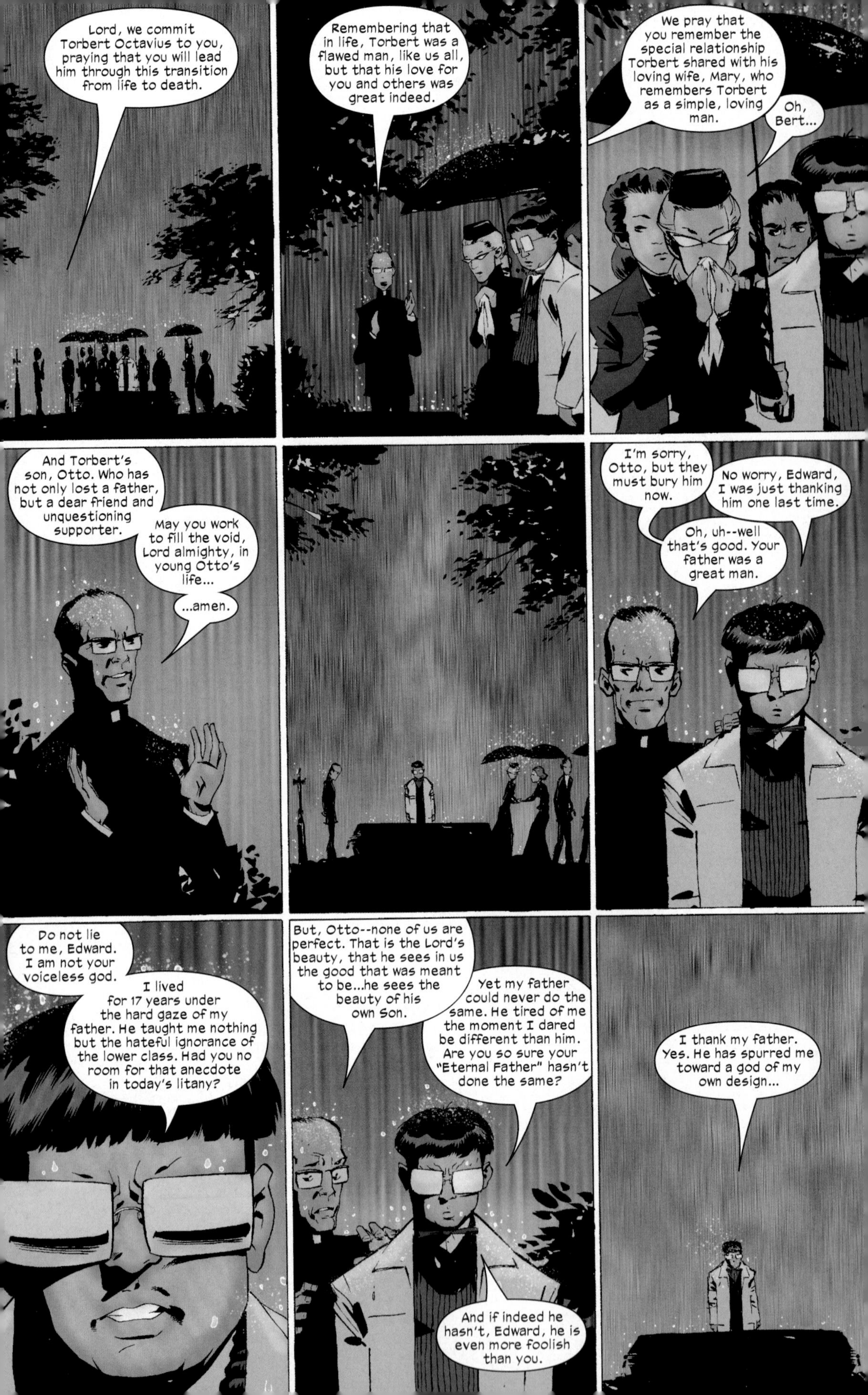
Lord, we commit Torbert Octavius to you, praying that you will lead him through this transition from life to death.
Remembering that in life, Torbert was a flawed man, like us all, but that his love for you and others was great indeed.
We pray that you remember the special relationship Torbert shared with his loving wife, Mary, who remembers Torbert as a simple, loving man.
Oh, Bert...
And Torbert's son, Otto. Who has not only lost a father, but a dear friend and unquestioning supporter.
May you work to fill the void, Lord almighty, in young Otto's life...
...amen.
I'm sorry, Otto, but they must bury him now.
No worry, Edward, I was just thanking him one last time.
Oh, uh--well that's good. Your father was a great man.
Do not lie to me, Edward. I am not your voiceless god.
I lived for 17 years under the hard gaze of my father. He taught me nothing but the hateful ignorance of the lower class. Had you no room for that anecdote in today's litany?
But, Otto--none of us are perfect. That is the Lord's beauty, that he sees in us the good that was meant to be...he sees the beauty of his own Son.
Yet my father could never do the same. He tired of me the moment I dared be different than him. Are you so sure your "Eternal Father" hasn't done the same?
And if indeed he hasn't, Edward, he is even more foolish than you.
I thank my father. Yes. He has spurred me toward a god of my own design...

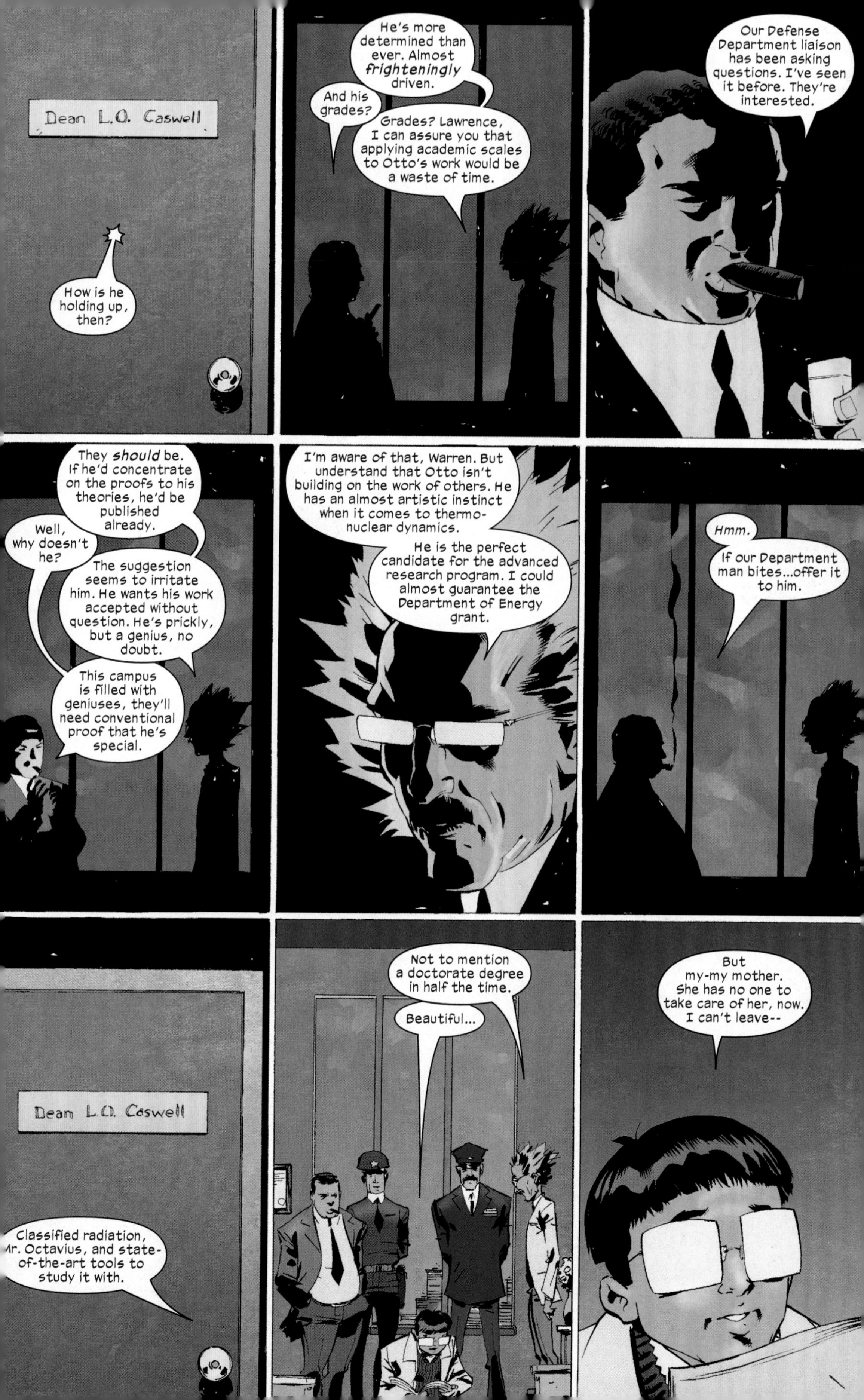
Dean L.O. Caswell
How is he holding up, then?
He's more determined than ever. Almost *frighteningly* driven.
And his grades?
Grades? Lawrence, I can assure you that applying academic scales to Otto's work would be a waste of time.
Our Defense Department liaison has been asking questions. I've seen it before. They're interested.
They *should* be. If he'd concentrate on the proofs to his theories, he'd be published already.
Well, why doesn't he?
The suggestion seems to irritate him. He wants his work accepted without question. He's prickly, but a genius, no doubt.
This campus is filled with geniuses, they'll need conventional proof that he's special.
I'm aware of that, Warren. But understand that Otto isn't building on the work of others. He has an almost artistic instinct when it comes to thermonuclear dynamics.
He is the perfect candidate for the advanced research program. I could almost guarantee the Department of Energy grant.
Hmm.
If our Department man bites...offer it to him.
Dean L.O. Caswell
Classified radiation, Mr. Octavius, and state-of-the-art tools to study it with.
Not to mention a doctorate degree in half the time.
Beautiful...
But my-my mother. She has no one to take care of her, now. I can't leave--

Bring her along, Otto! There is a generous stipend...

You'd be working for Uncle Sam, after all.

I'll take it. Of course.

Welcome to the good fight, young man.

Have the papers brought in immediately.

Yes, sir!

Enjoy your last minutes as a student, Otto. Your future is right around the corner.

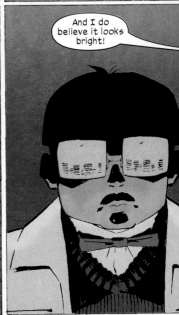

And I do believe it looks bright!

Yes...

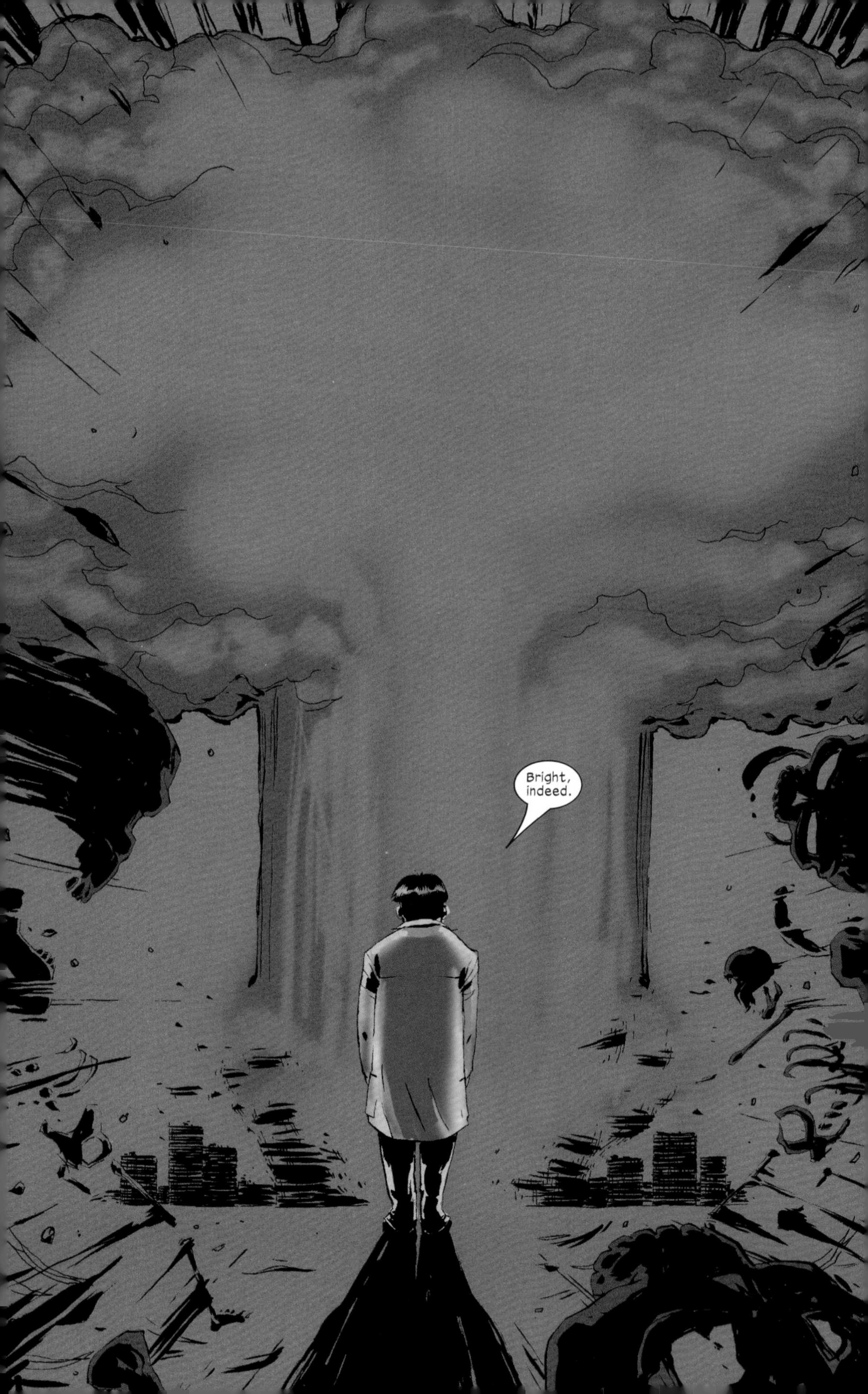
Bright, indeed.

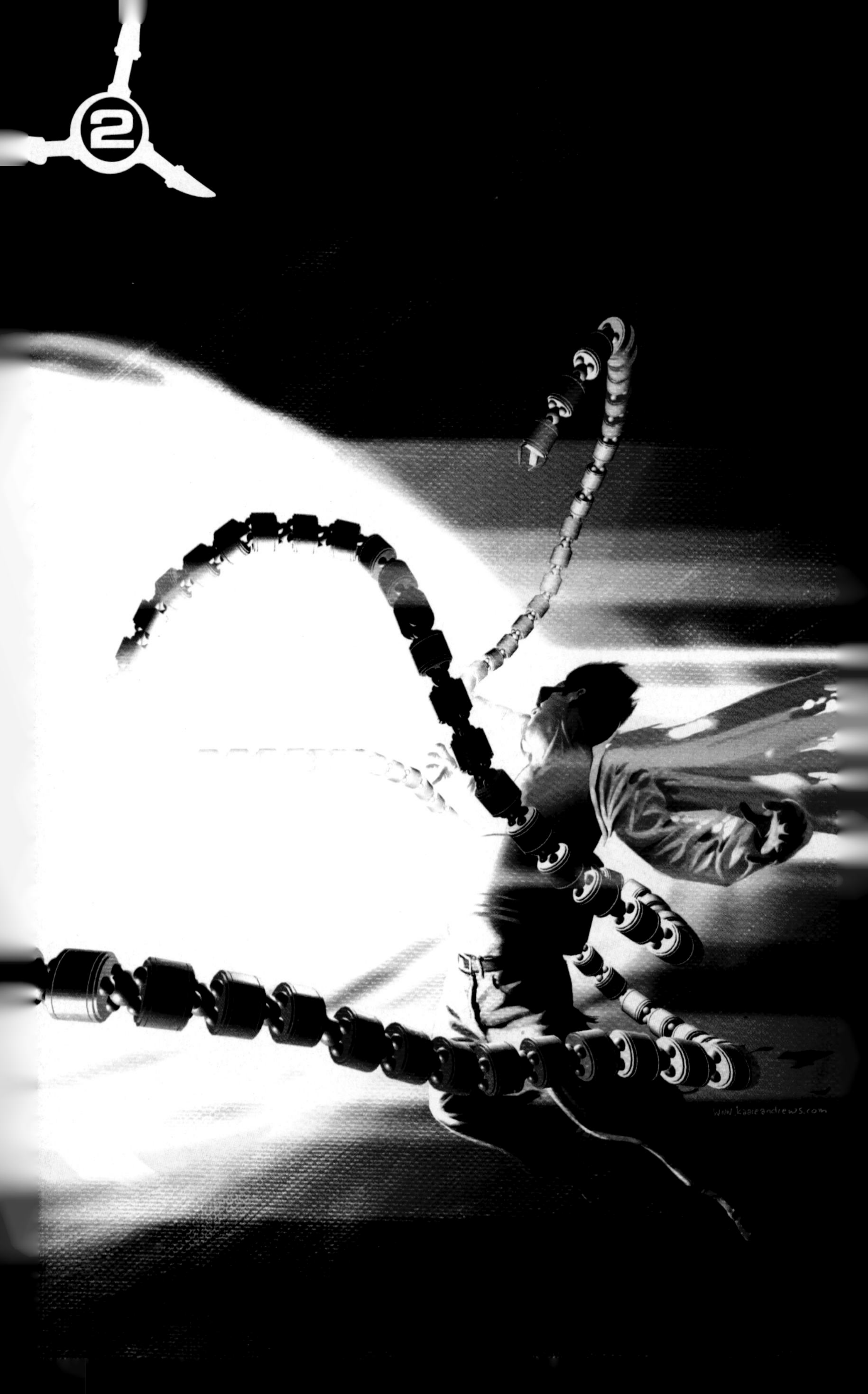
2
www.kaareandrews.com

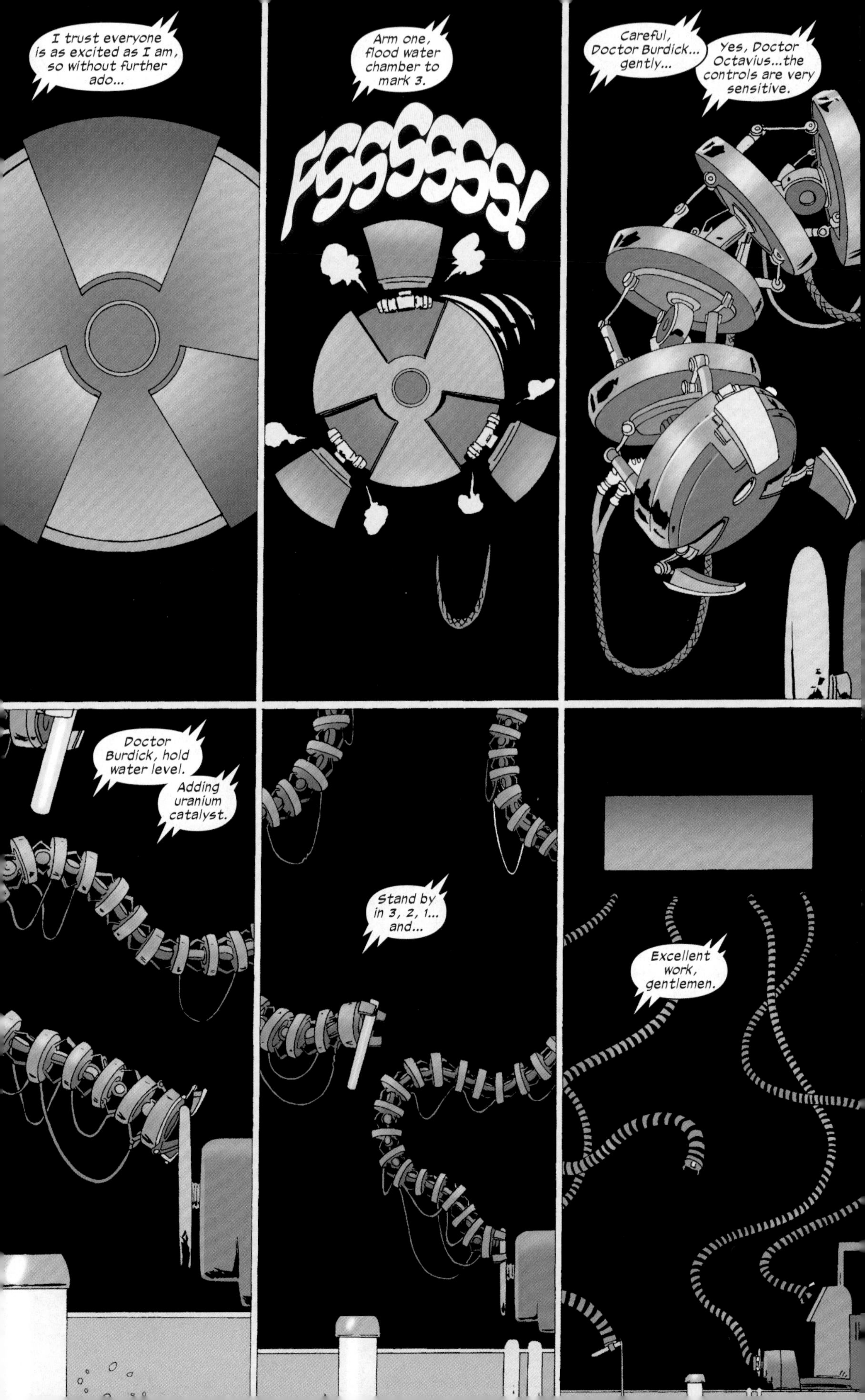
I trust everyone is as excited as I am, so without further ado...
Arm one, flood water chamber to mark 3.
FSSSSSS!
Careful, Doctor Burdick... gently...
Yes, Doctor Octavius...the controls are very sensitive.
Doctor Burdick, hold water level.
Adding uranium catalyst.
Stand by in 3, 2, 1... and...
Excellent work, gentlemen.

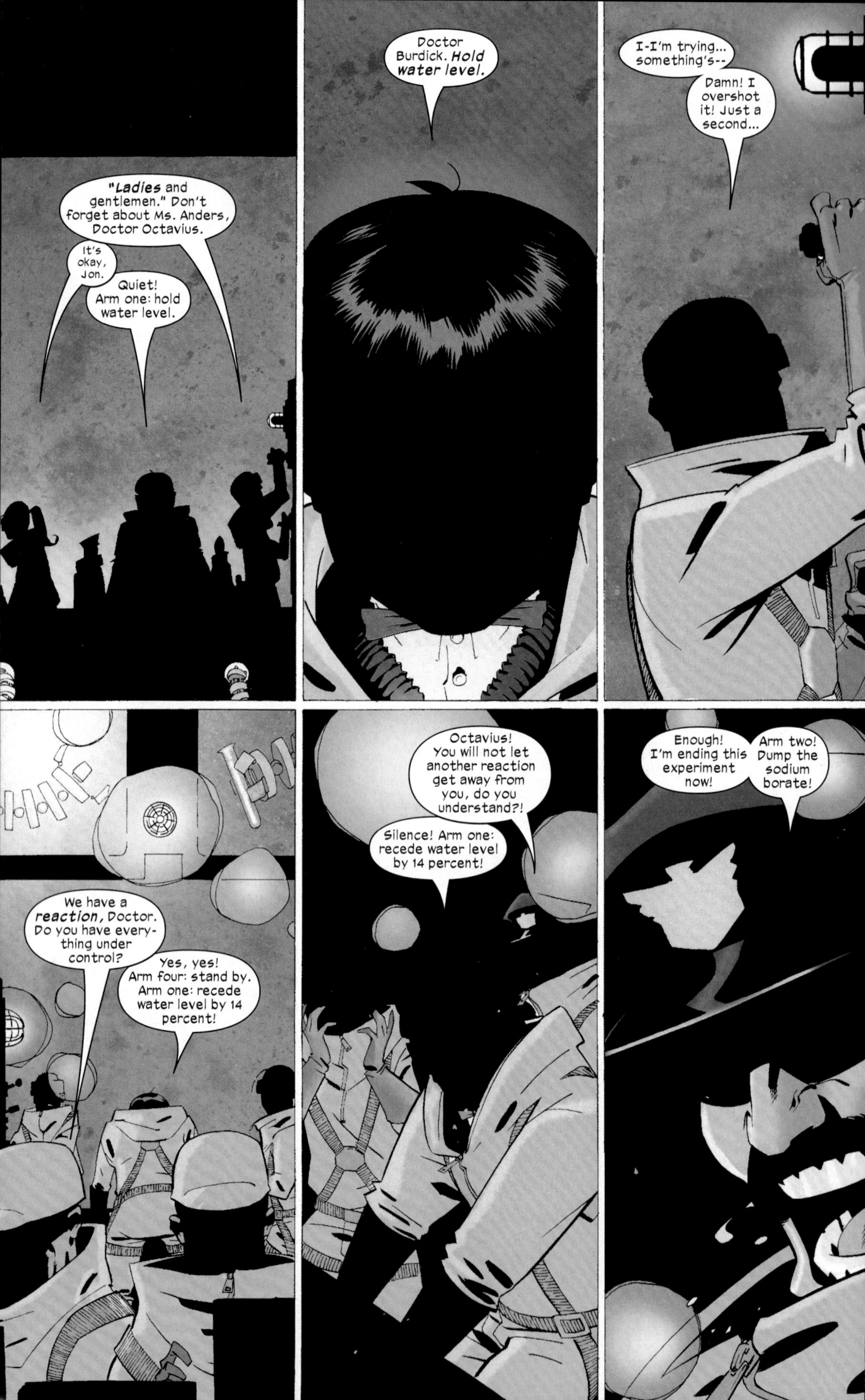
"Ladies and gentlemen." Don't forget about Ms. Anders, Doctor Octavius.
It's okay, Jon.
Quiet! Arm one: hold water level.
Doctor Burdick. Hold water level.
I-I'm trying... something's--
Damn! I overshot it! Just a second...
We have a reaction, Doctor. Do you have every-thing under control?
Yes, yes! Arm four: stand by. Arm one: recede water level by 14 percent!
Octavius! You will not let another reaction get away from you, do you understand?!
Silence! Arm one: recede water level by 14 percent!
Enough! I'm ending this experiment now!
Arm two! Dump the sodium borate!

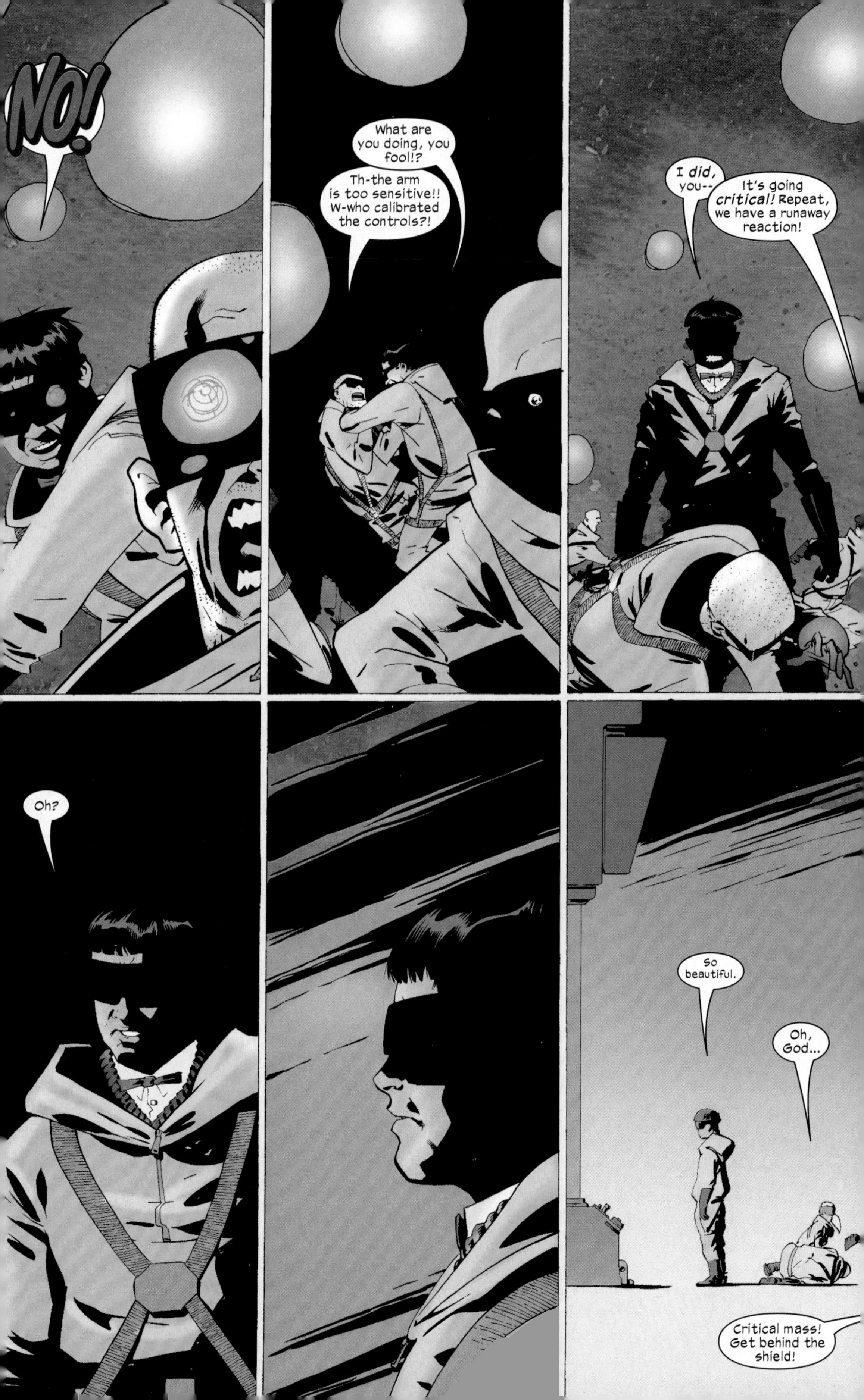
NO!
What are you doing, you fool!?
Th-the arm is too sensitive!! W-who calibrated the controls?!
I did, you--
It's going critical! Repeat, we have a runaway reaction!
Oh?
So beautiful.
Oh, God...
Critical mass! Get behind the shield!

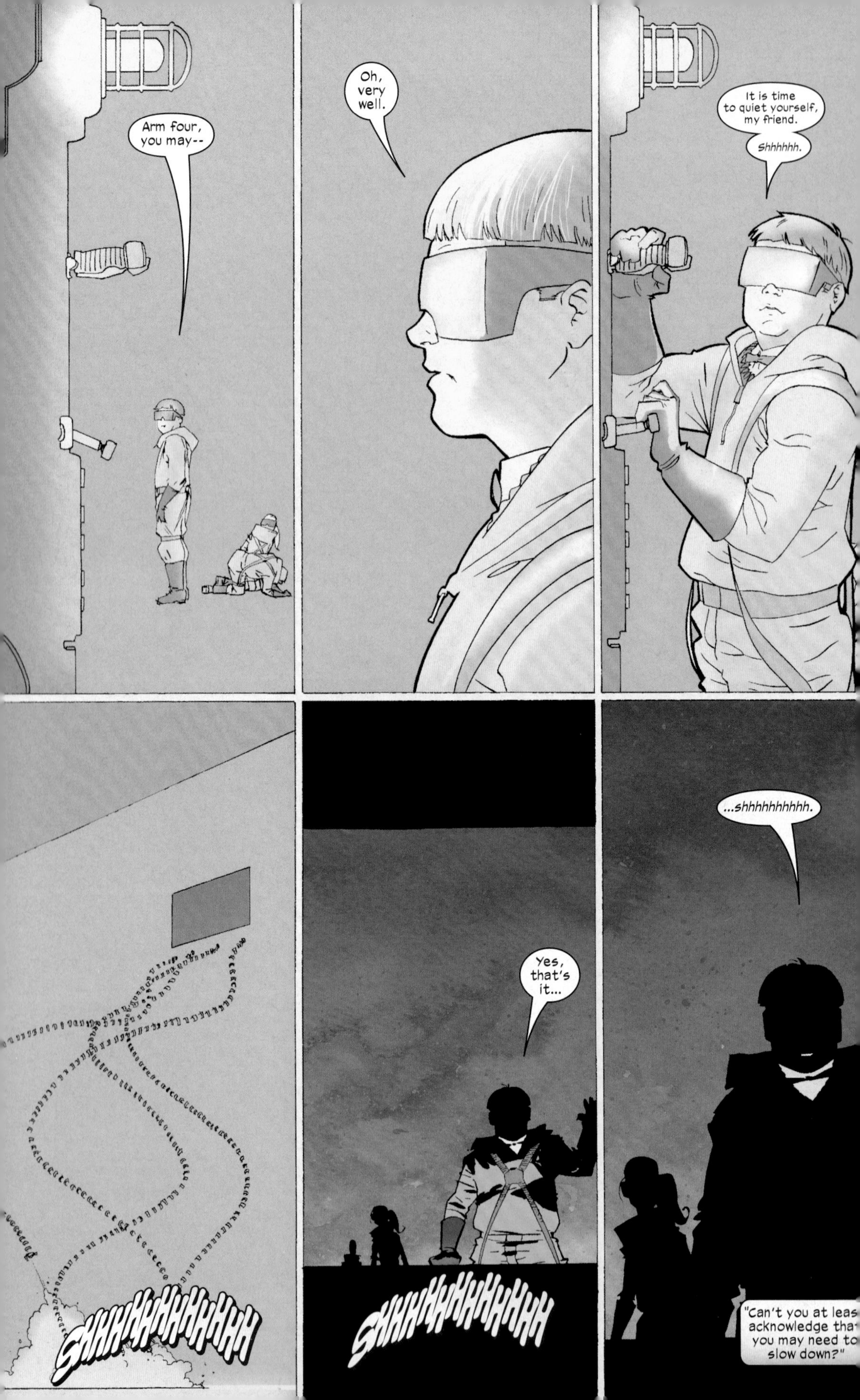
Arm four, you may--
Oh, very well.
It is time to quiet yourself, my friend.
Shhhhhh.
SHHHHHHHHHHHHH
Yes, that's it...
SHHHHHHHHHHHHHH
...shhhhhhhhhh.
"Can't you at leas acknowledge tha you may need to slow down?"

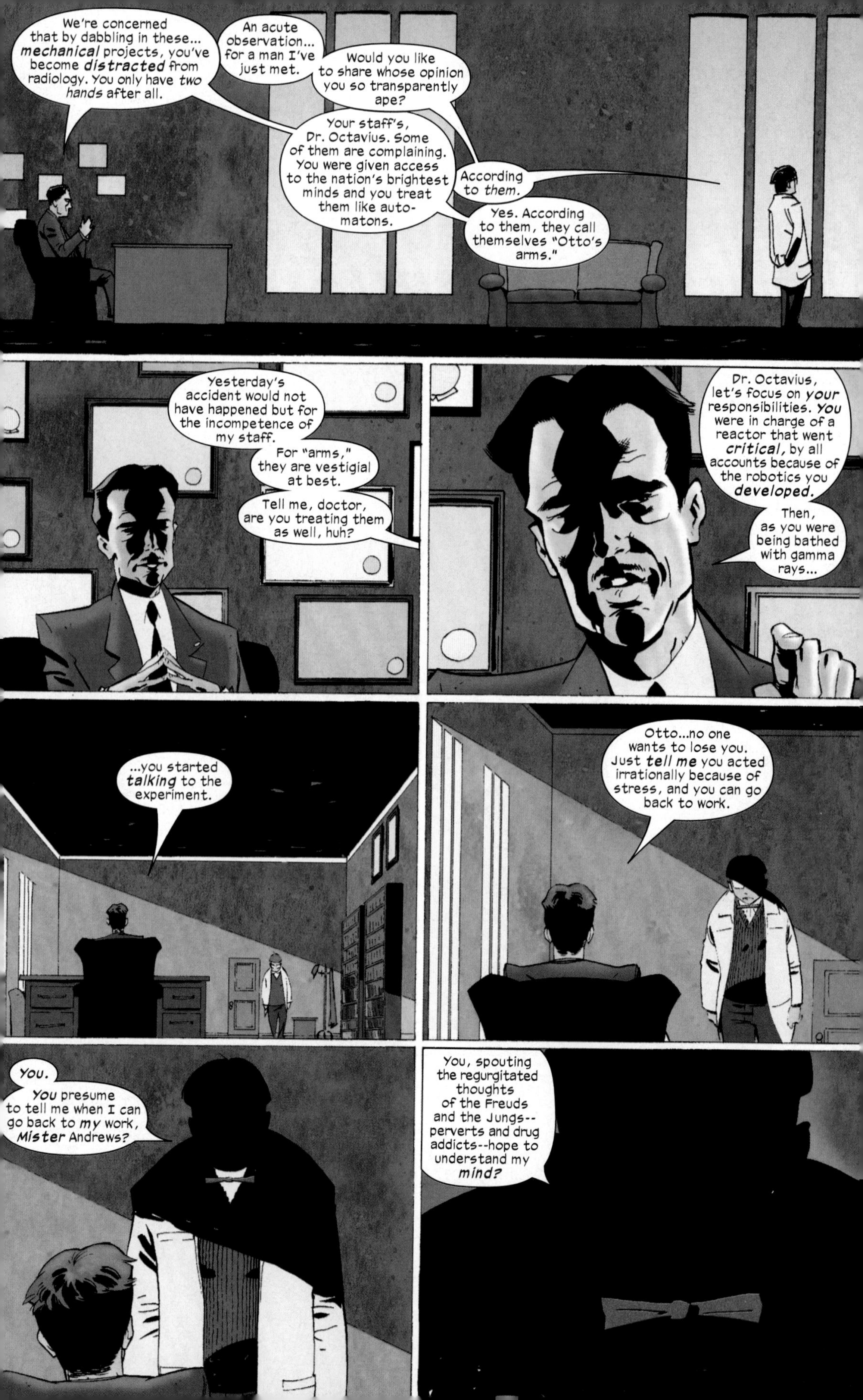
We're concerned that by dabbling in these... *mechanical* projects, you've become *distracted* from radiology. You only have *two hands* after all.
An acute observation... for a man I've just met.
Would you like to share whose opinion you so transparently ape?
Your staff's, Dr. Octavius. Some of them are complaining. You were given access to the nation's brightest minds and you treat them like automatons.
According to *them.*
Yes. According to them, they call themselves "Otto's arms."
Yesterday's accident would not have happened but for the incompetence of my staff.
For "arms," they are vestigial at best.
Tell me, doctor, are you treating them as well, huh?
Dr. Octavius, let's focus on *your* responsibilities. *You* were in charge of a reactor that went *critical,* by all accounts because of the robotics you *developed.*
Then, as you were being bathed with gamma rays...
...you started *talking* to the experiment.
Otto...no one wants to lose you. Just *tell me* you acted irrationally because of stress, and you can go back to work.
You.
You presume to tell me when I can go back to *my* work, *Mister* Andrews?
You, spouting the regurgitated thoughts of the Freuds and the Jungs--perverts and drug addicts--hope to understand my *mind?*

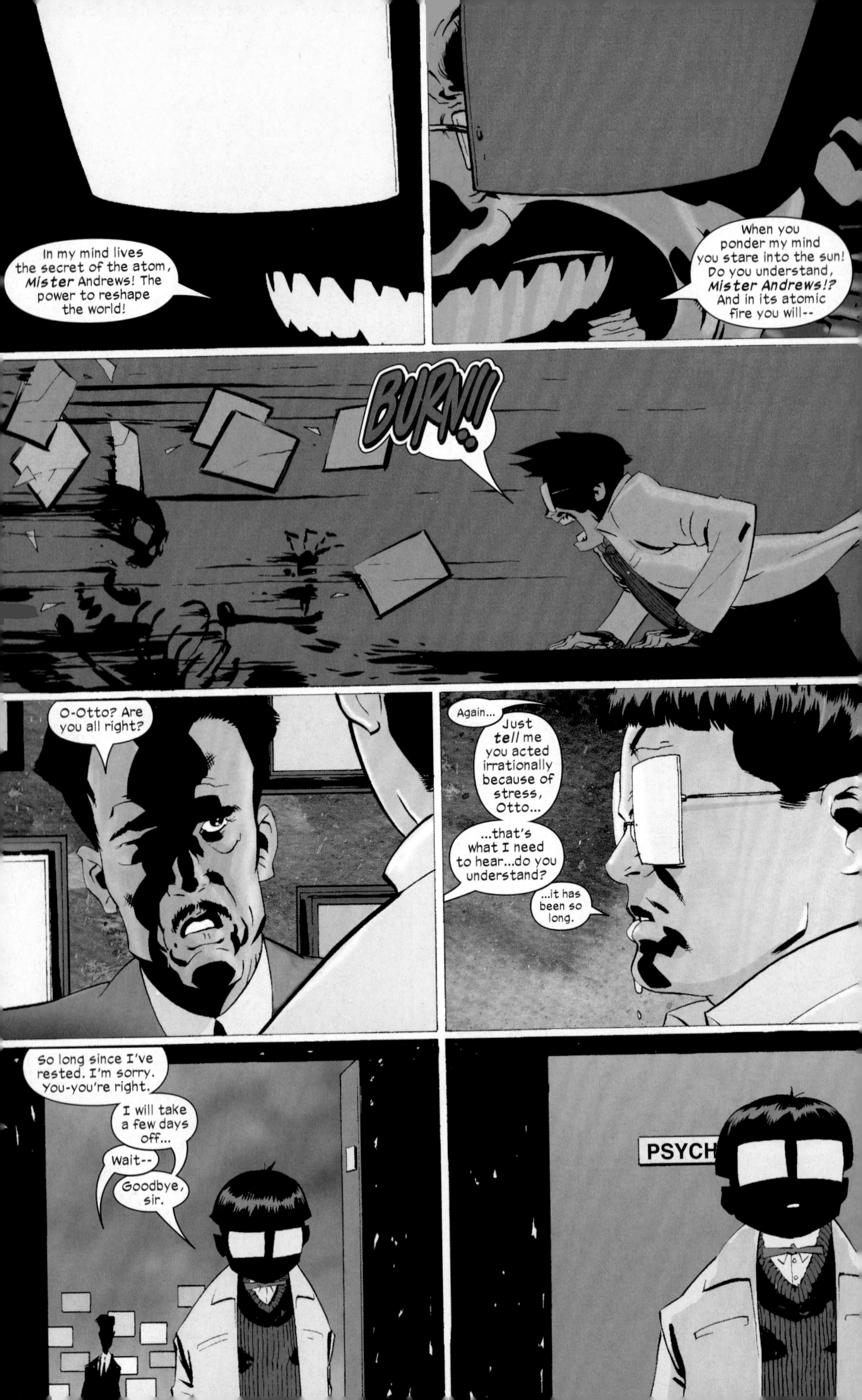
In my mind lives the secret of the atom, *Mister* Andrews! The power to reshape the world!
When you ponder my mind you stare into the sun! Do you understand, *Mister Andrews!?* And in its atomic fire you will--
BURN!!
O-Otto? Are you all right?
Again...
Just *tell* me you acted irrationally because of stress, Otto...
...that's what I need to hear...do you understand?
...it has been so long.
So long since I've rested. I'm sorry. You-you're right.
I will take a few days off...
Wait--
Goodbye, sir.
PSYCH

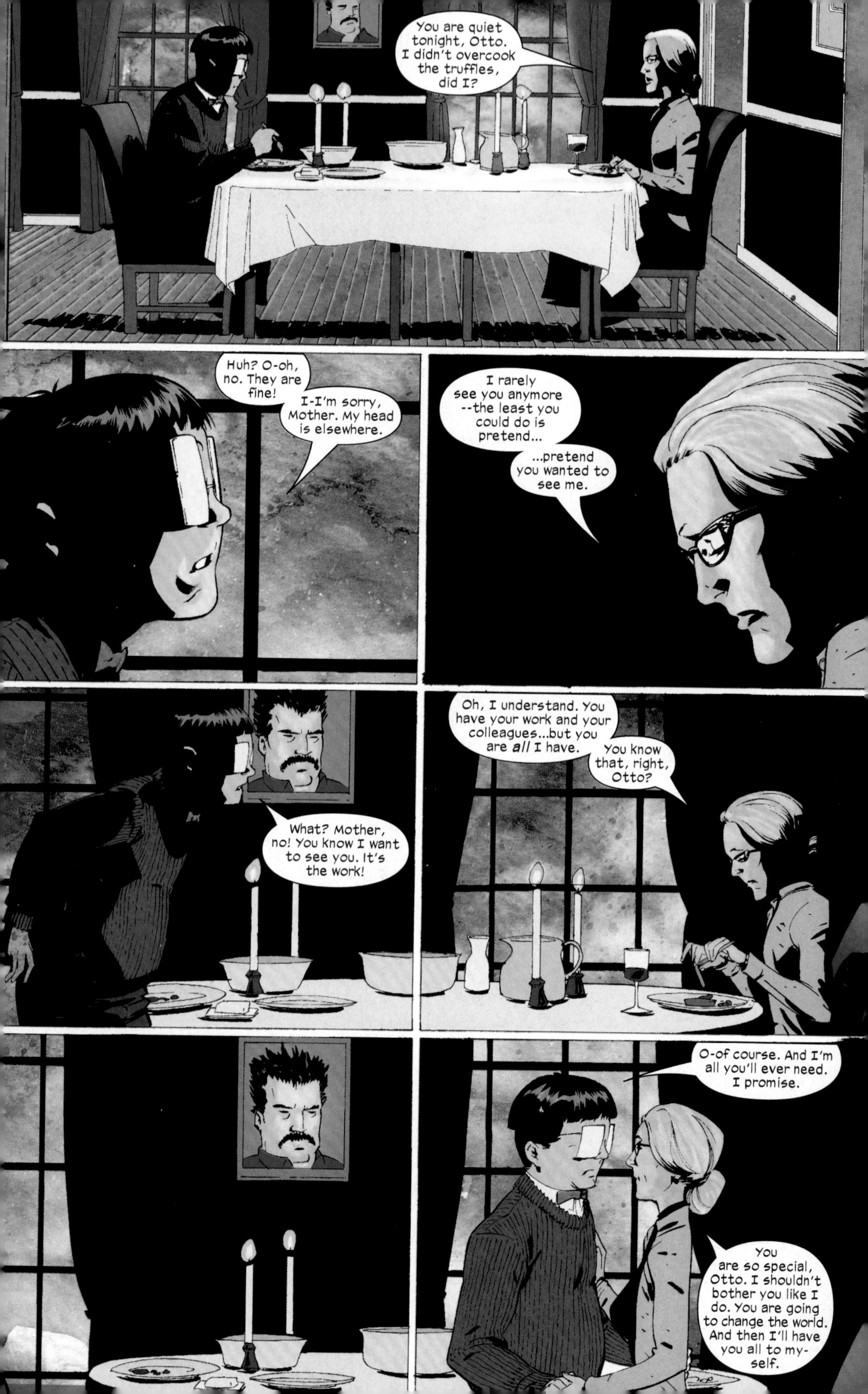
You are quiet tonight, Otto. I didn't overcook the truffles, did I?
Huh? O-oh, no. They are fine!
I-I'm sorry, Mother. My head is elsewhere.
I rarely see you anymore --the least you could do is pretend...
...pretend you wanted to see me.
What? Mother, no! You know I want to see you. It's the work!
Oh, I understand. You have your work and your colleagues...but you are *all* I have.
You know that, right, Otto?
O-of course. And I'm all you'll ever need. I promise.
You are so special, Otto. I shouldn't bother you like I do. You are going to change the world. And then I'll have you all to myself.

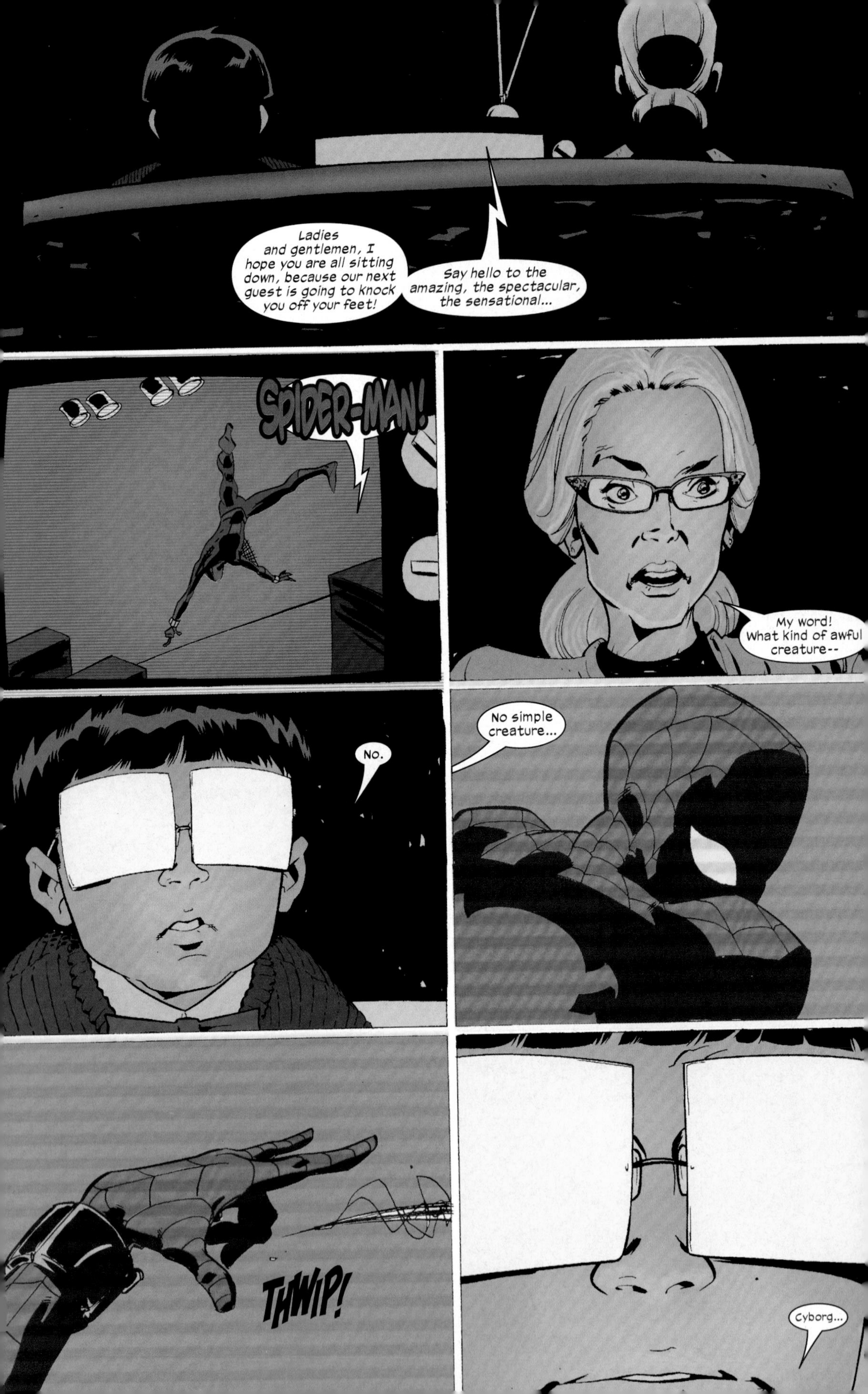
Ladies and gentlemen, I hope you are all sitting down, because our next guest is going to knock you off your feet!
Say hello to the amazing, the spectacular, the sensational...
SPIDER-MAN!
My word! What kind of awful creature--
No.
No simple creature...
THWIP!
Cyborg...

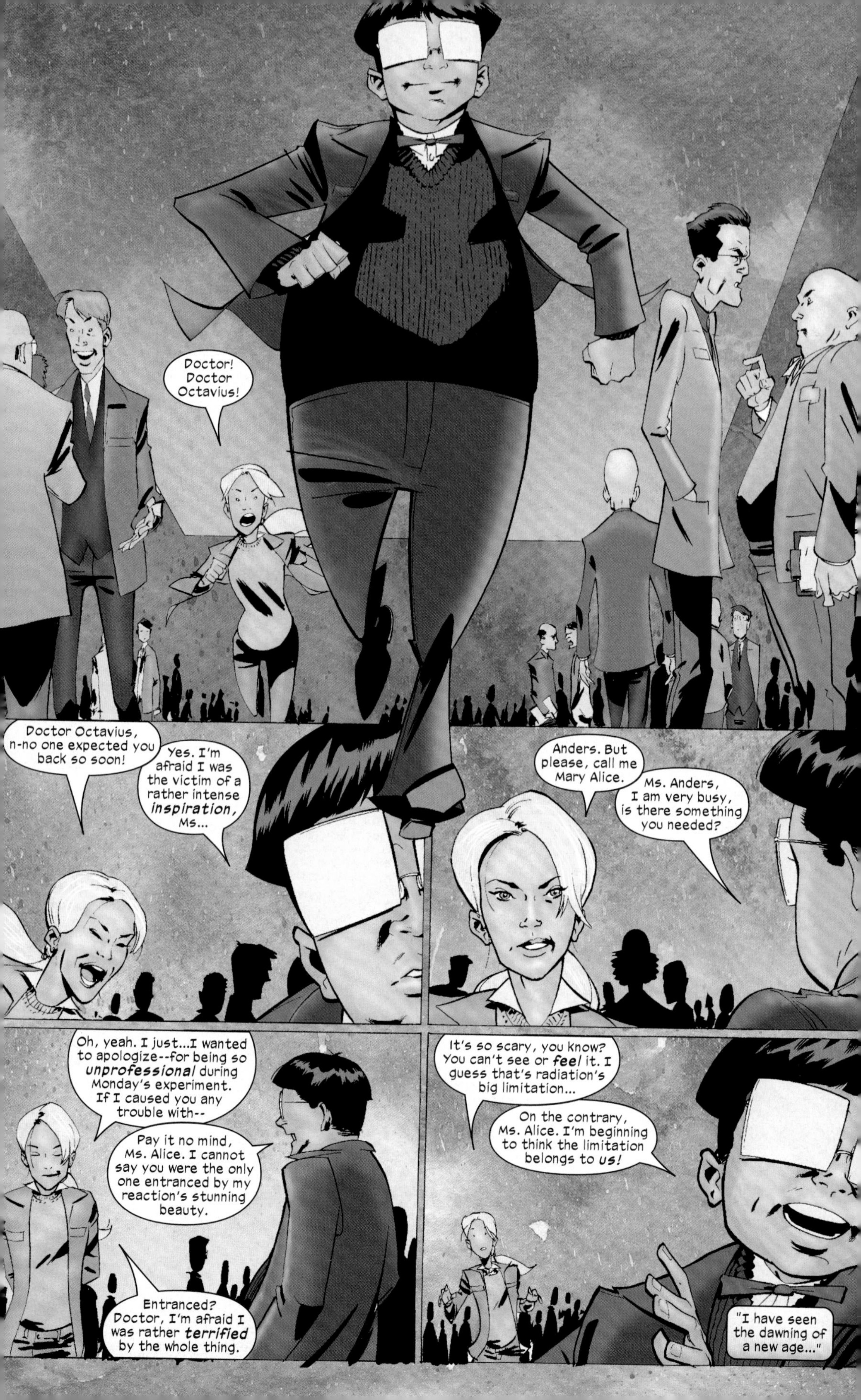
Doctor! Doctor Octavius!
Doctor Octavius, n-no one expected you back so soon!
Yes. I'm afraid I was the victim of a rather intense *inspiration,* Ms...
Anders. But please, call me Mary Alice.
Ms. Anders, I am very busy, is there something you needed?
Oh, yeah. I just...I wanted to apologize--for being so *unprofessional* during Monday's experiment. If I caused you any trouble with--
Pay it no mind, Ms. Alice. I cannot say you were the only one entranced by my reaction's stunning beauty.
Entranced? Doctor, I'm afraid I was rather *terrified* by the whole thing.
It's so scary, you know? You can't see or *feel* it. I guess that's radiation's big limitation...
On the contrary, Ms. Alice. I'm beginning to think the limitation belongs to *us!*
"I have seen the dawning of a new age..."

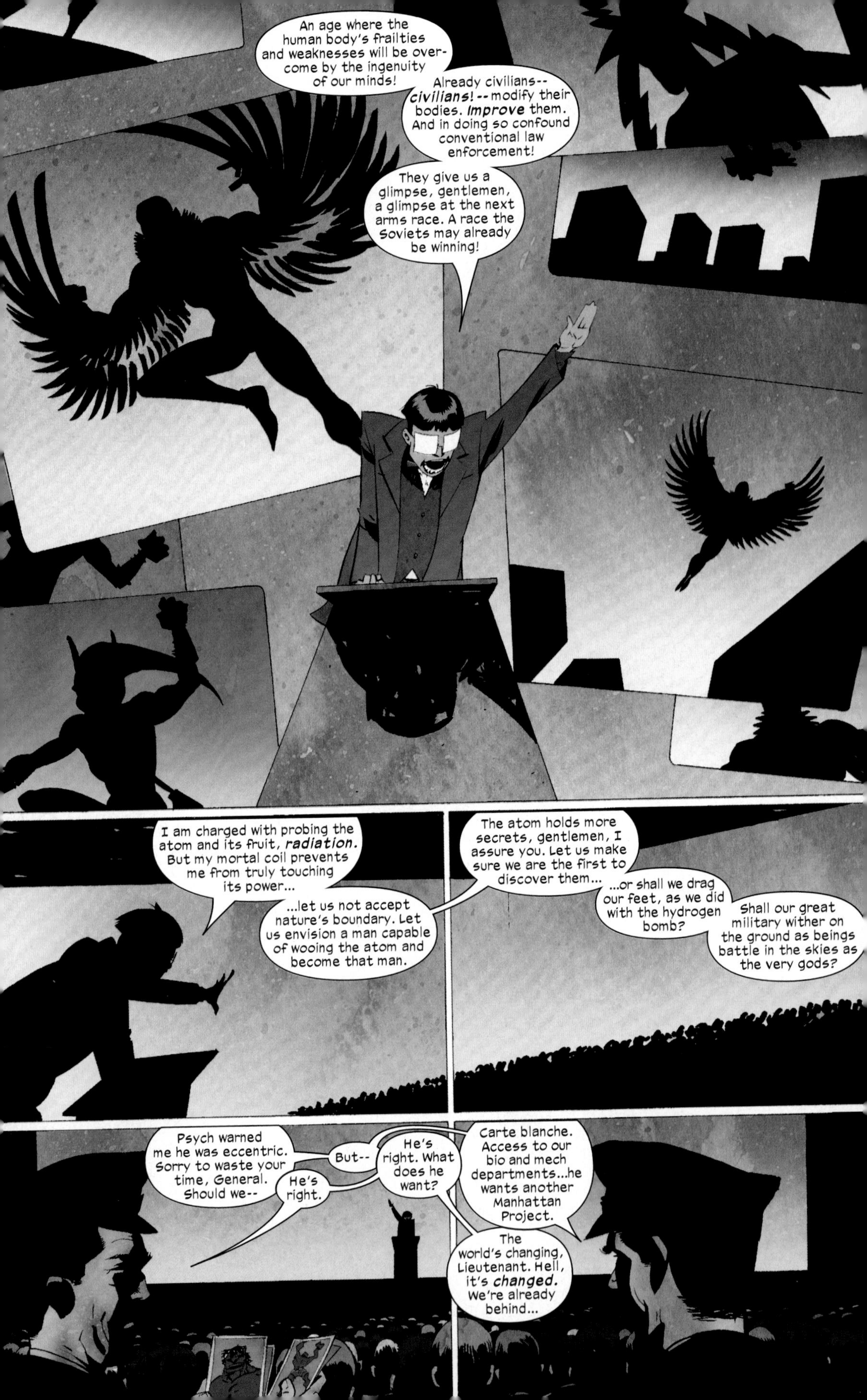
An age where the human body's frailties and weaknesses will be overcome by the ingenuity of our minds!
Already civilians-- civilians! --modify their bodies. Improve them. And in doing so confound conventional law enforcement!
They give us a glimpse, gentlemen, a glimpse at the next arms race. A race the Soviets may already be winning!
I am charged with probing the atom and its fruit, radiation. But my mortal coil prevents me from truly touching its power...
...let us not accept nature's boundary. Let us envision a man capable of wooing the atom and become that man.
The atom holds more secrets, gentlemen, I assure you. Let us make sure we are the first to discover them...
...or shall we drag our feet, as we did with the hydrogen bomb?
Shall our great military wither on the ground as beings battle in the skies as the very gods?
Psych warned me he was eccentric. Sorry to waste your time, General. Should we--
But--
He's right.
He's right. What does he want?
Carte blanche. Access to our bio and mech departments...he wants another Manhattan Project.
The world's changing, Lieutenant. Hell, it's changed. We're already behind...

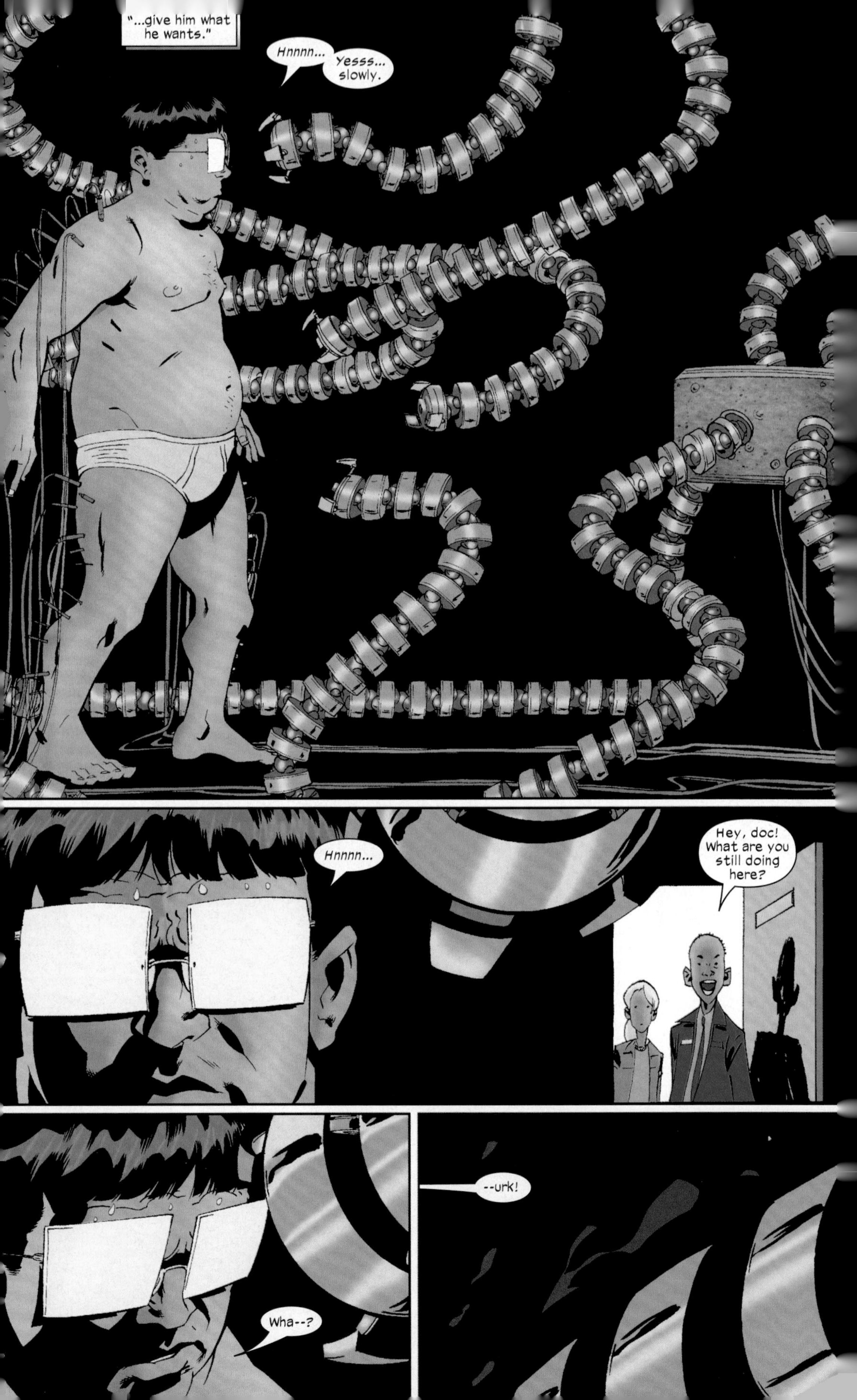
"...give him what he wants."
Hnnnn...
Yesss... slowly.
Hnnnn...
Hey, doc! What are you still doing here?
Wha--?
--urk!

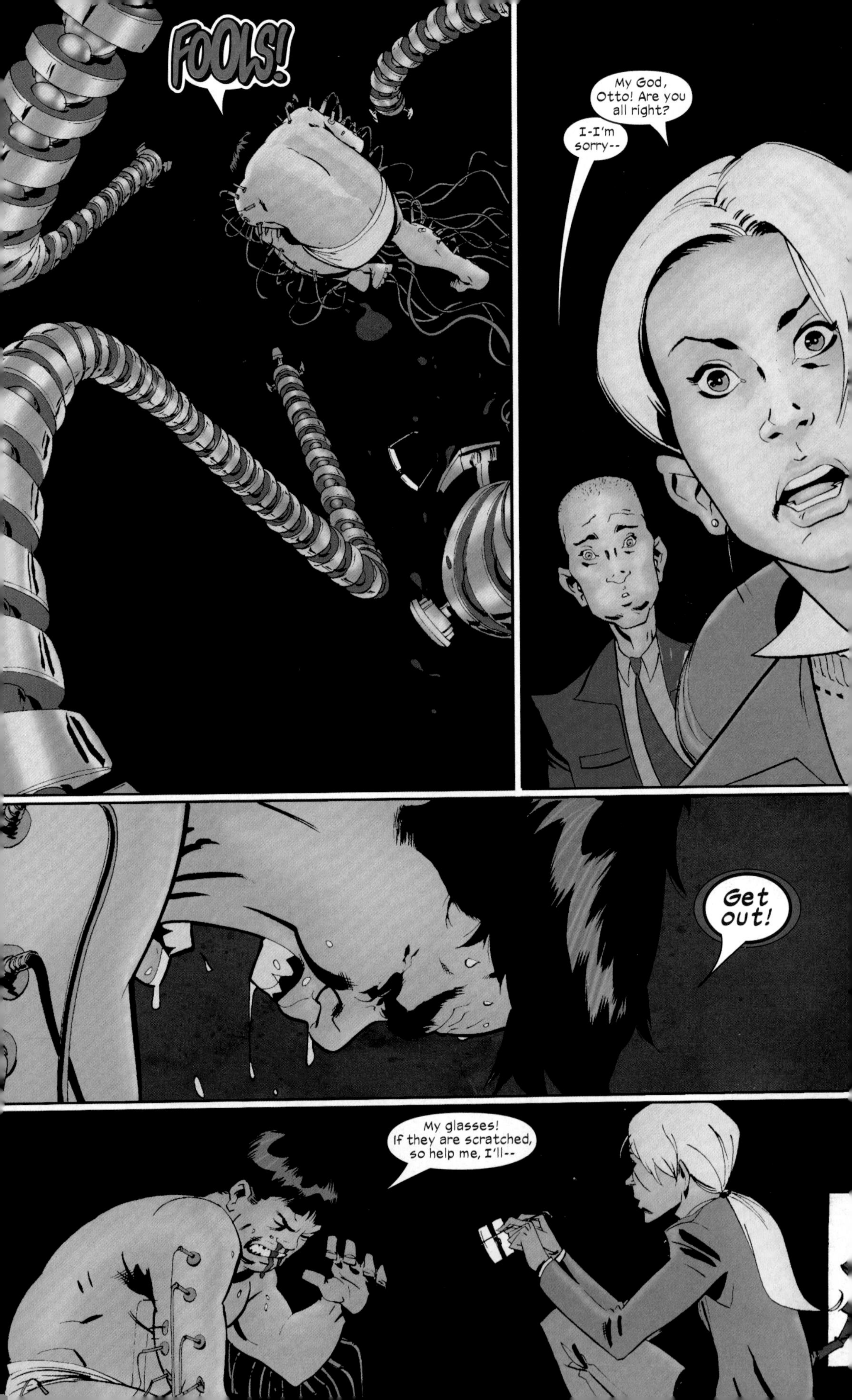
FOOLS!
My God, Otto! Are you all right?
I-I'm sorry--
Get out!
My glasses! If they are scratched, so help me, I'll--

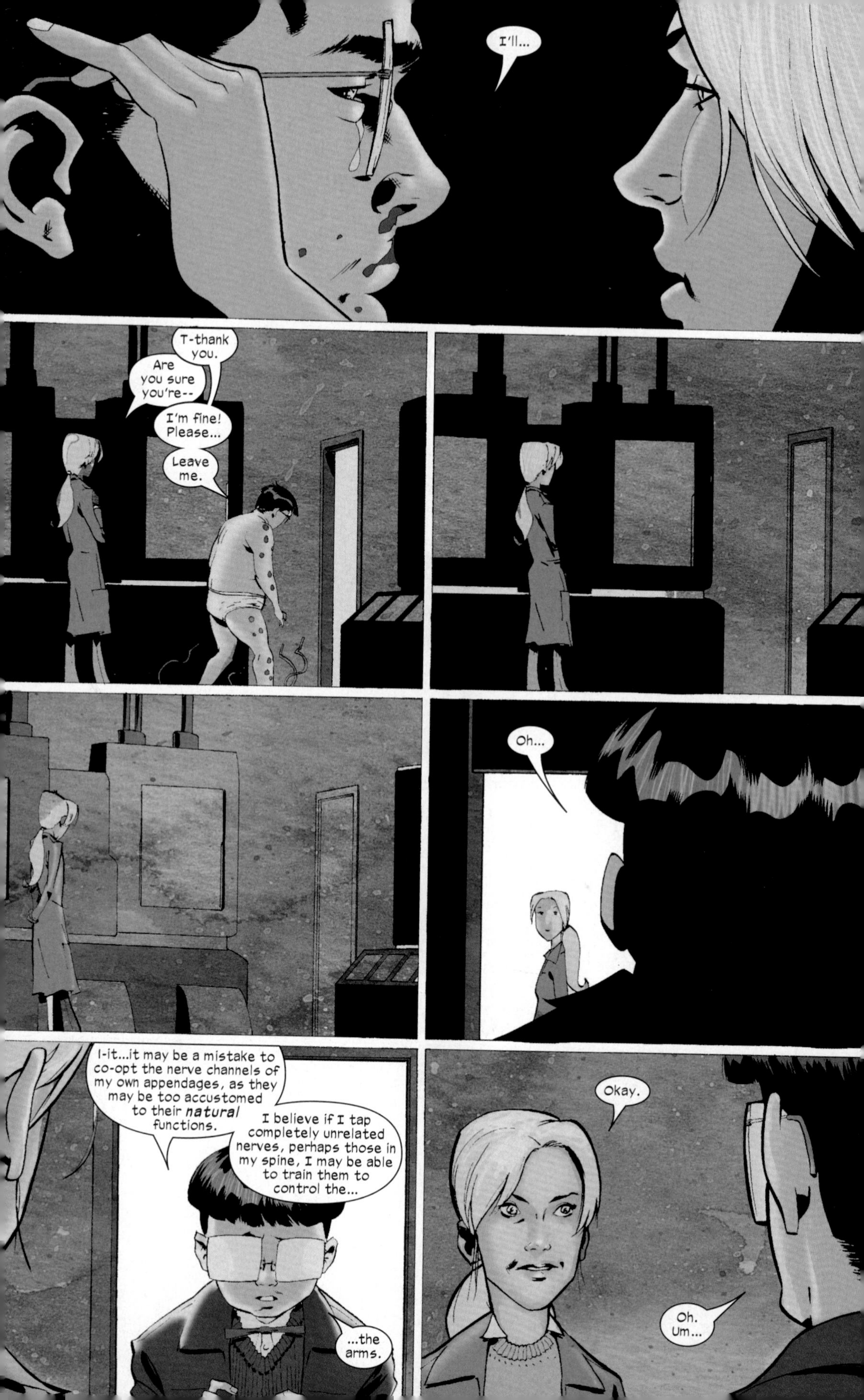
I'll...
Are you sure you're--
T-thank you.
I'm fine! Please...
Leave me.
Oh...
I-it...it may be a mistake to co-opt the nerve channels of my own appendages, as they may be too accustomed to their *natural* functions.
I believe if I tap completely unrelated nerves, perhaps those in my spine, I may be able to train them to control the...
...the arms.
Okay.
Oh. Um...

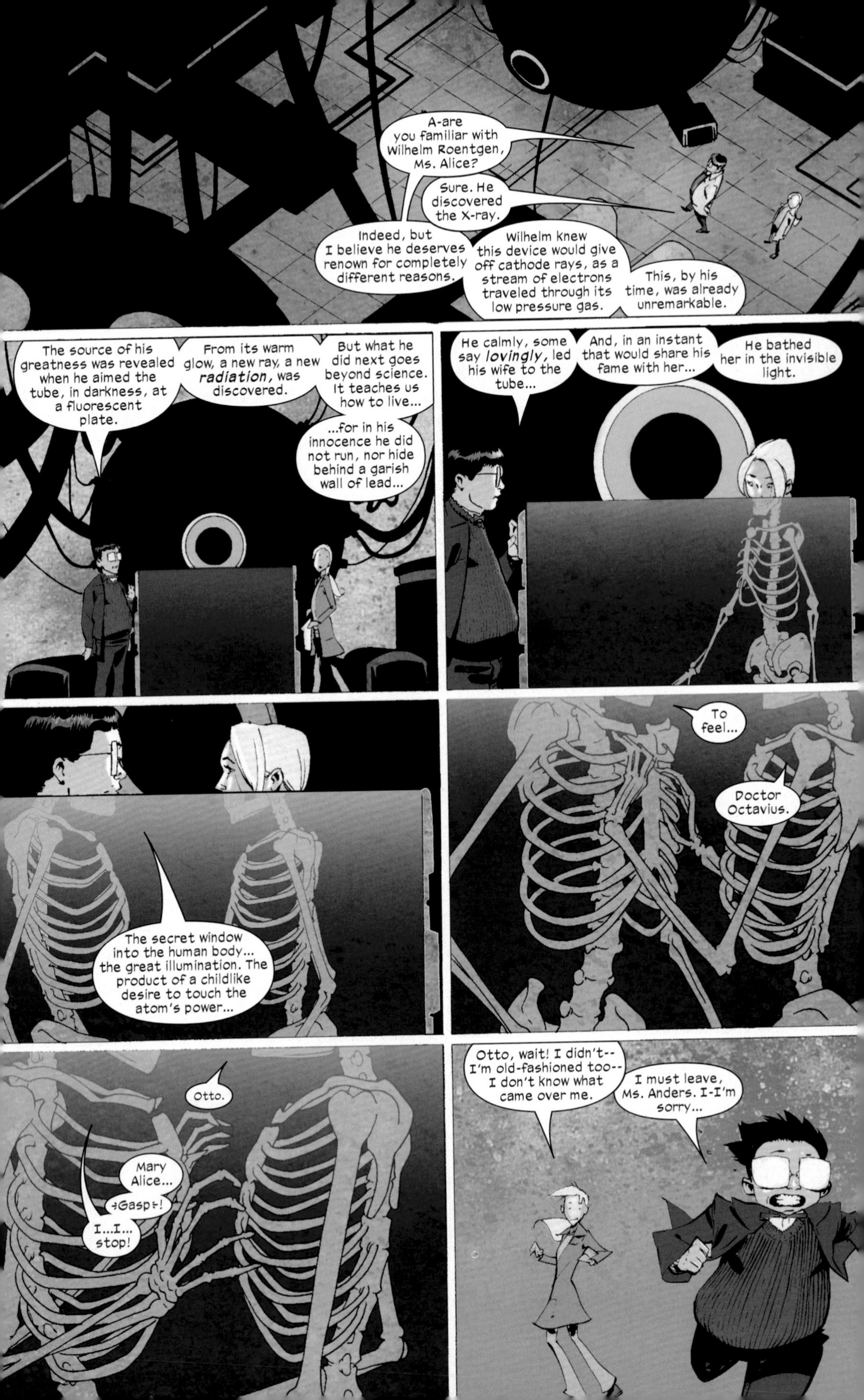
A-are you familiar with Wilhelm Roentgen, Ms. Alice?
Sure. He discovered the X-ray.
Indeed, but I believe he deserves renown for completely different reasons.
Wilhelm knew this device would give off cathode rays, as a stream of electrons traveled through its low pressure gas.
This, by his time, was already unremarkable.
The source of his greatness was revealed when he aimed the tube, in darkness, at a fluorescent plate.
From its warm glow, a new ray, a new *radiation*, was discovered.
But what he did next goes beyond science. It teaches us how to live...
...for in his innocence he did not run, nor hide behind a garish wall of lead...
He calmly, some say *lovingly*, led his wife to the tube...
And, in an instant that would share his fame with her...
He bathed her in the invisible light.
The secret window into the human body... the great illumination. The product of a childlike desire to touch the atom's power...
To feel...
Doctor Octavius.
Otto.
Mary Alice...
÷Gasp÷!
I...I... stop!
Otto, wait! I didn't-- I'm old-fashioned too-- I don't know what came over me.
I must leave, Ms. Anders. I-I'm sorry...

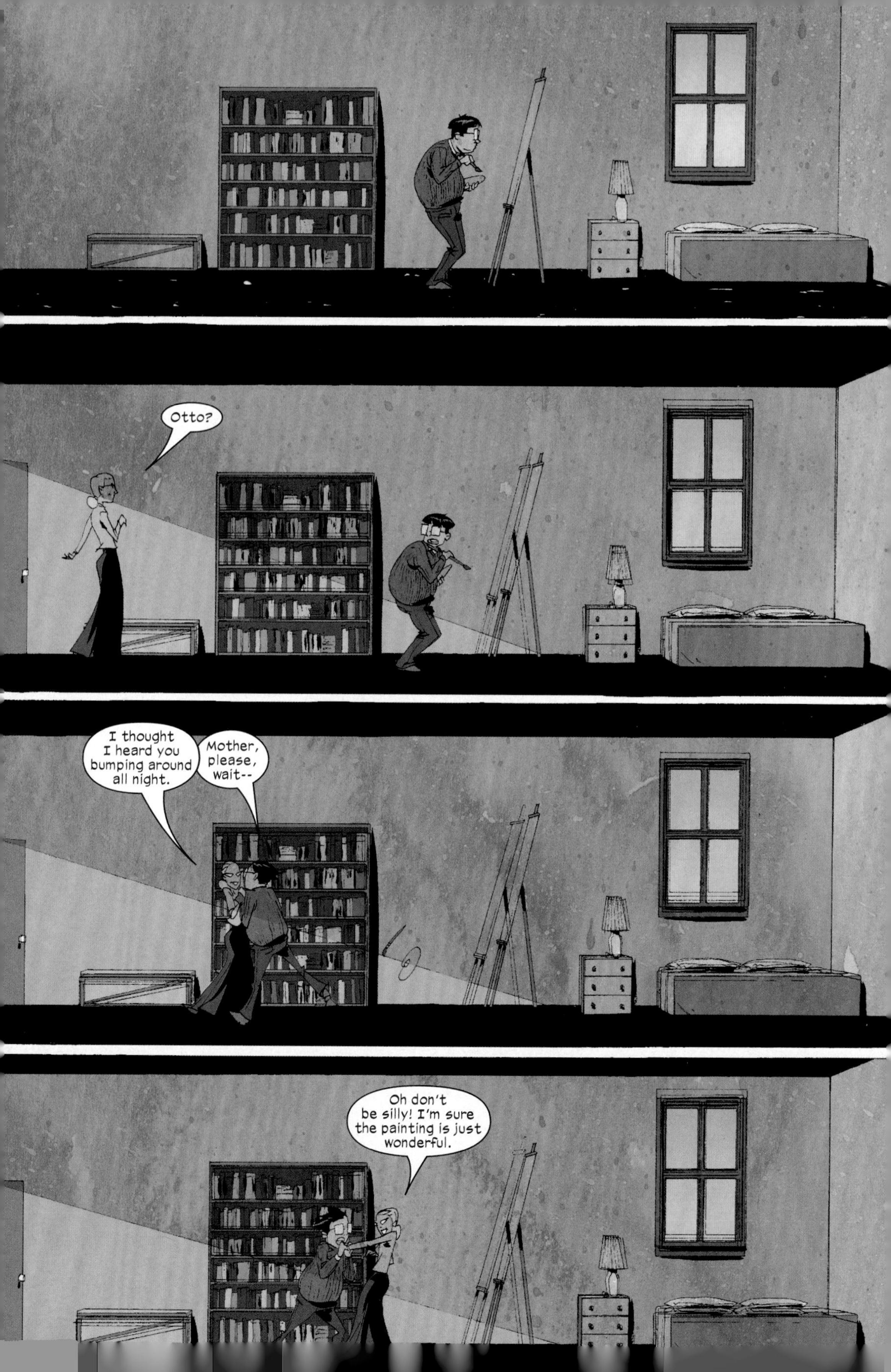

Otto?
I thought I heard you bumping around all night.
Mother, please, wait--
Oh don't be silly! I'm sure the painting is just wonderful.

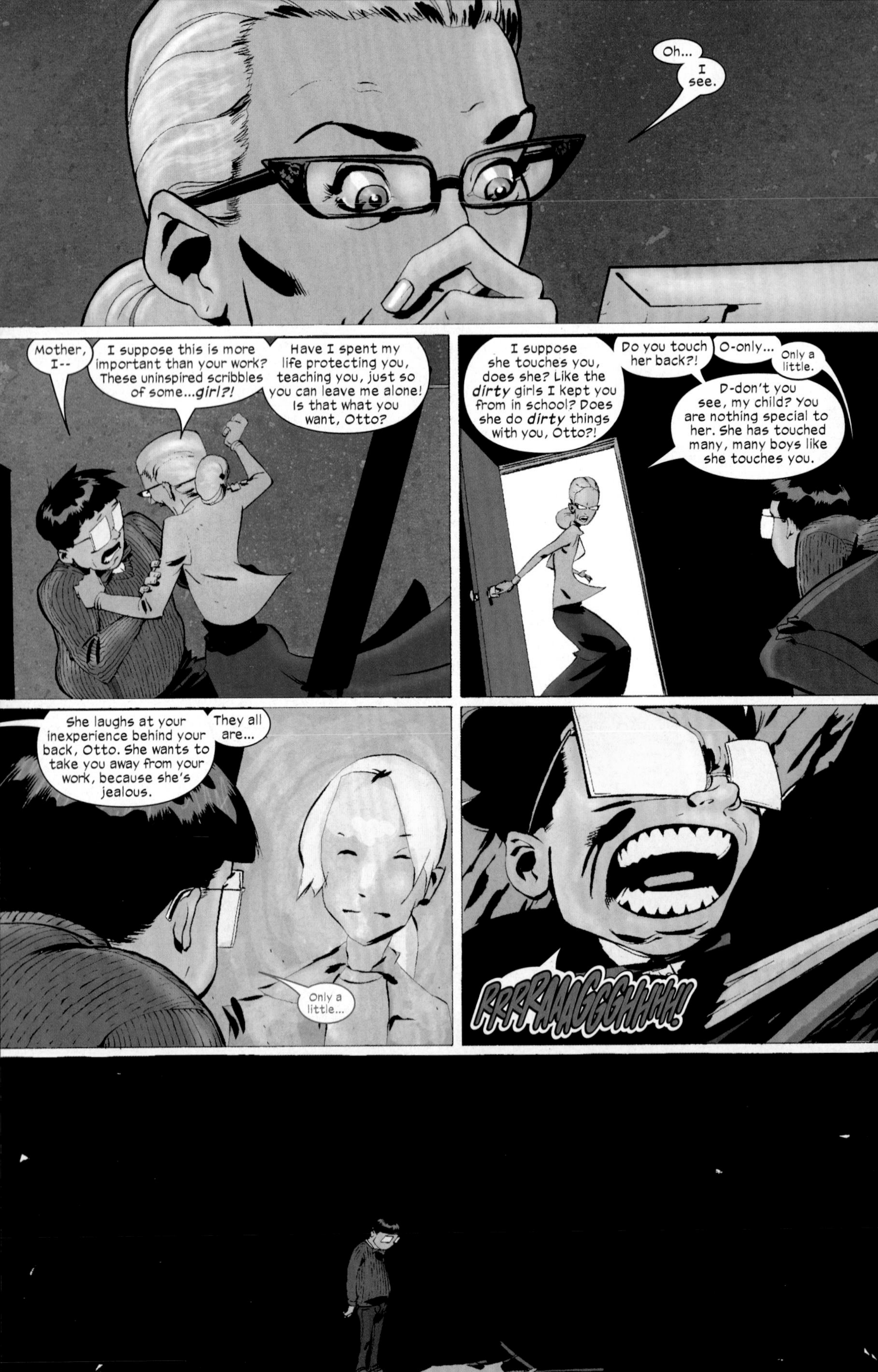
Oh... I see.
Mother, I--
I suppose this is more important than your work? These uninspired scribbles of some...*girl?!*
Have I spent my life protecting you, teaching you, just so you can leave me alone! Is that what you want, Otto?
I suppose she touches you, does she? Like the *dirty* girls I kept you from in school? Does she do *dirty* things with you, Otto?!
Do you touch her back?!
O-only...
Only a little.
D-don't you see, my child? You are nothing special to her. She has touched many, many boys like she touches you.
She laughs at your inexperience behind your back, Otto. She wants to take you away from your work, because she's jealous.
They all are...
Only a little...
RRRRAAAGGGHHHH!

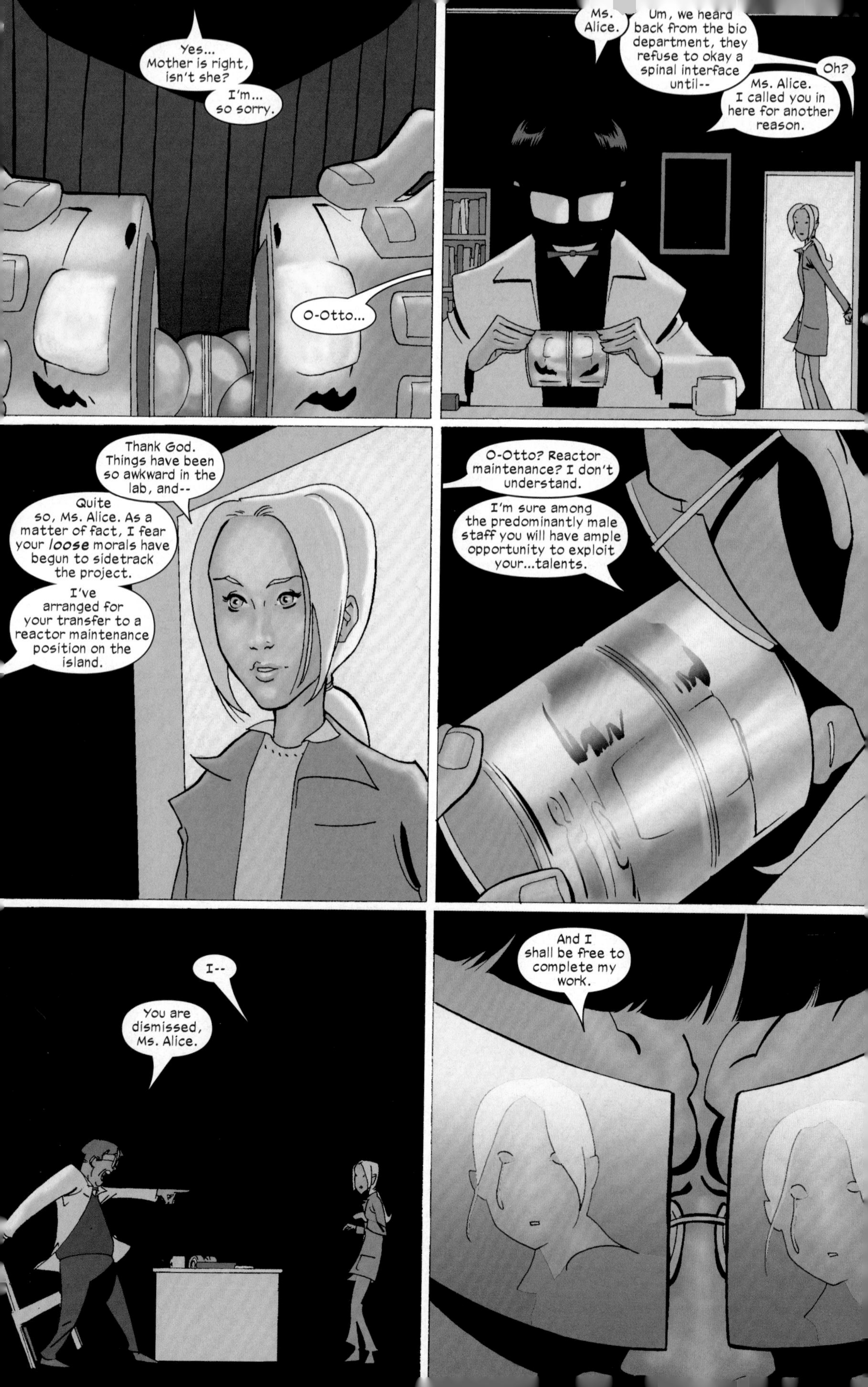
Yes... Mother is right, isn't she?
I'm... so sorry.
O-Otto...
Ms. Alice.
Um, we heard back from the bio department, they refuse to okay a spinal interface until--
Oh?
Ms. Alice. I called you in here for another reason.
Thank God. Things have been so awkward in the lab, and--
Quite so, Ms. Alice. As a matter of fact, I fear your *loose* morals have begun to sidetrack the project.
I've arranged for your transfer to a reactor maintenance position on the island.
O-Otto? Reactor maintenance? I don't understand.
I'm sure among the predominantly male staff you will have ample opportunity to exploit your...talents.
I--
You are dismissed, Ms. Alice.
And I shall be free to complete my work.

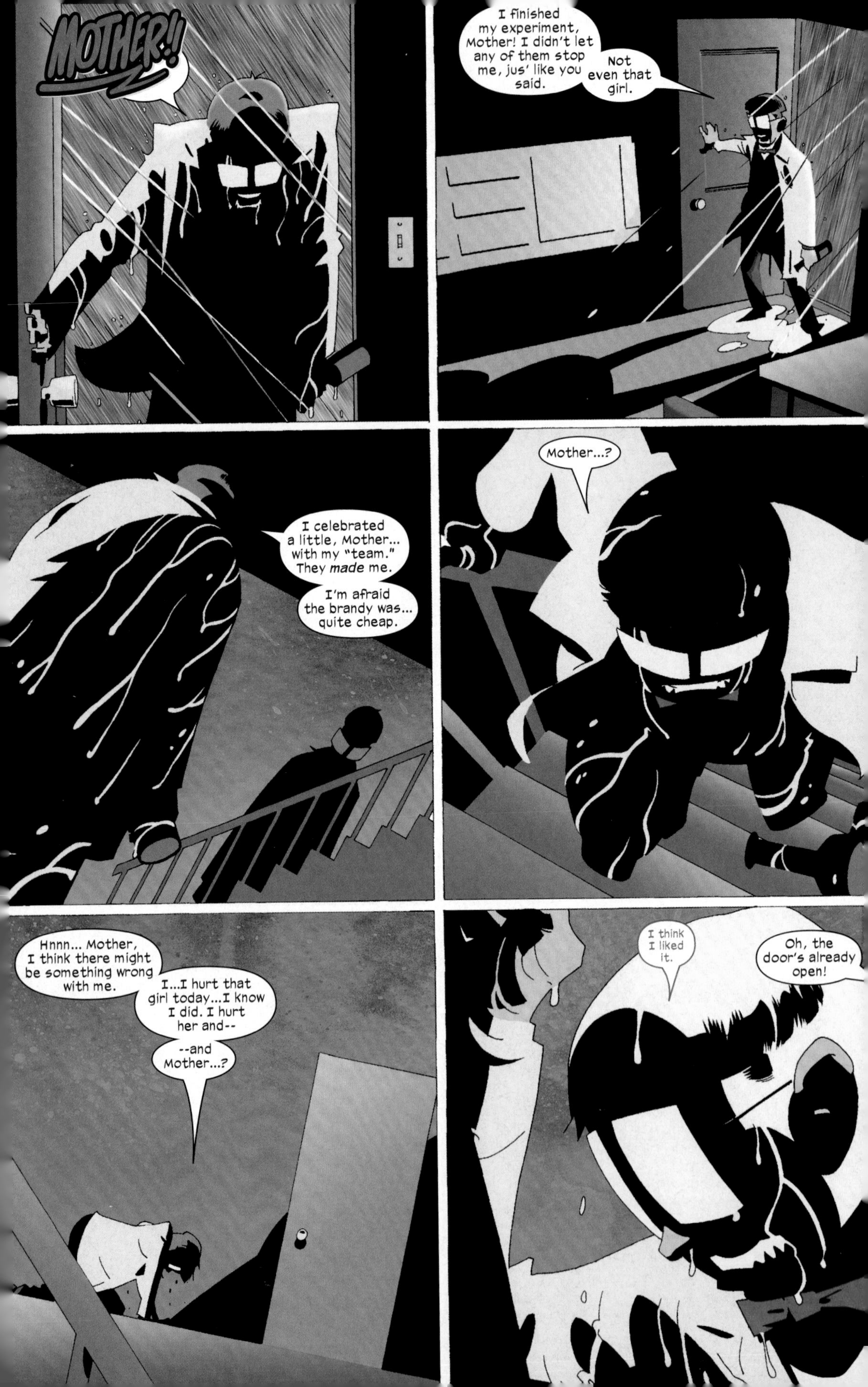
MOTHER!!
I finished my experiment, Mother! I didn't let any of them stop me, jus' like you said.
Not even that girl.
I celebrated a little, Mother... with my "team." They *made* me.
I'm afraid the brandy was... quite cheap.
Mother...?
Hnnn... Mother, I think there might be something wrong with me.
I...I hurt that girl today...I know I did. I hurt her and--
--and Mother...?
I think I liked it.
Oh, the door's already open!

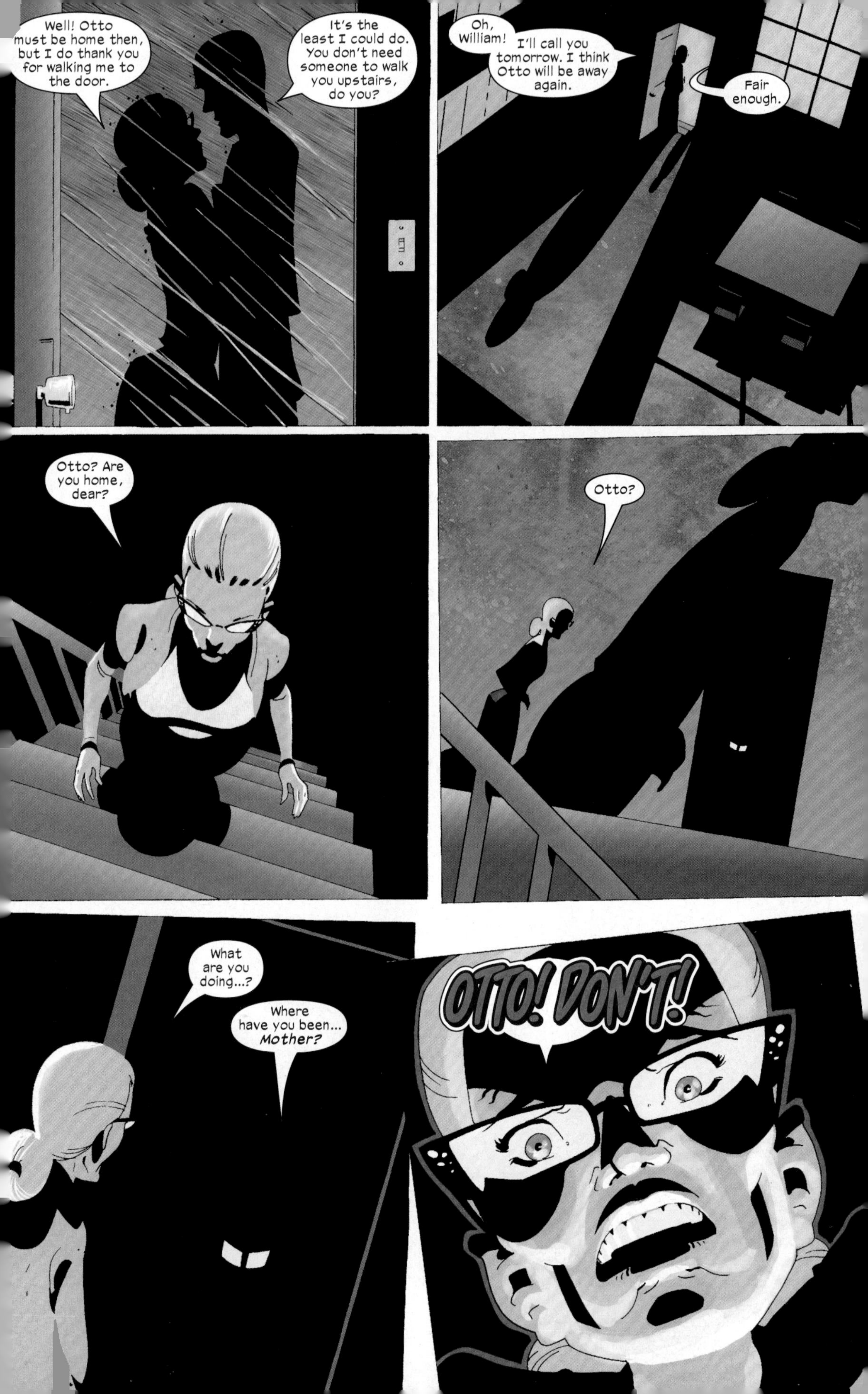
Well! Otto must be home then, but I do thank you for walking me to the door.
It's the least I could do. You don't need someone to walk you upstairs, do you?
Oh, William!
I'll call you tomorrow. I think Otto will be away again.
Fair enough.
Otto? Are you home, dear?
Otto?
What are you doing...?
Where have you been... *Mother?*
OTTO! DON'T!

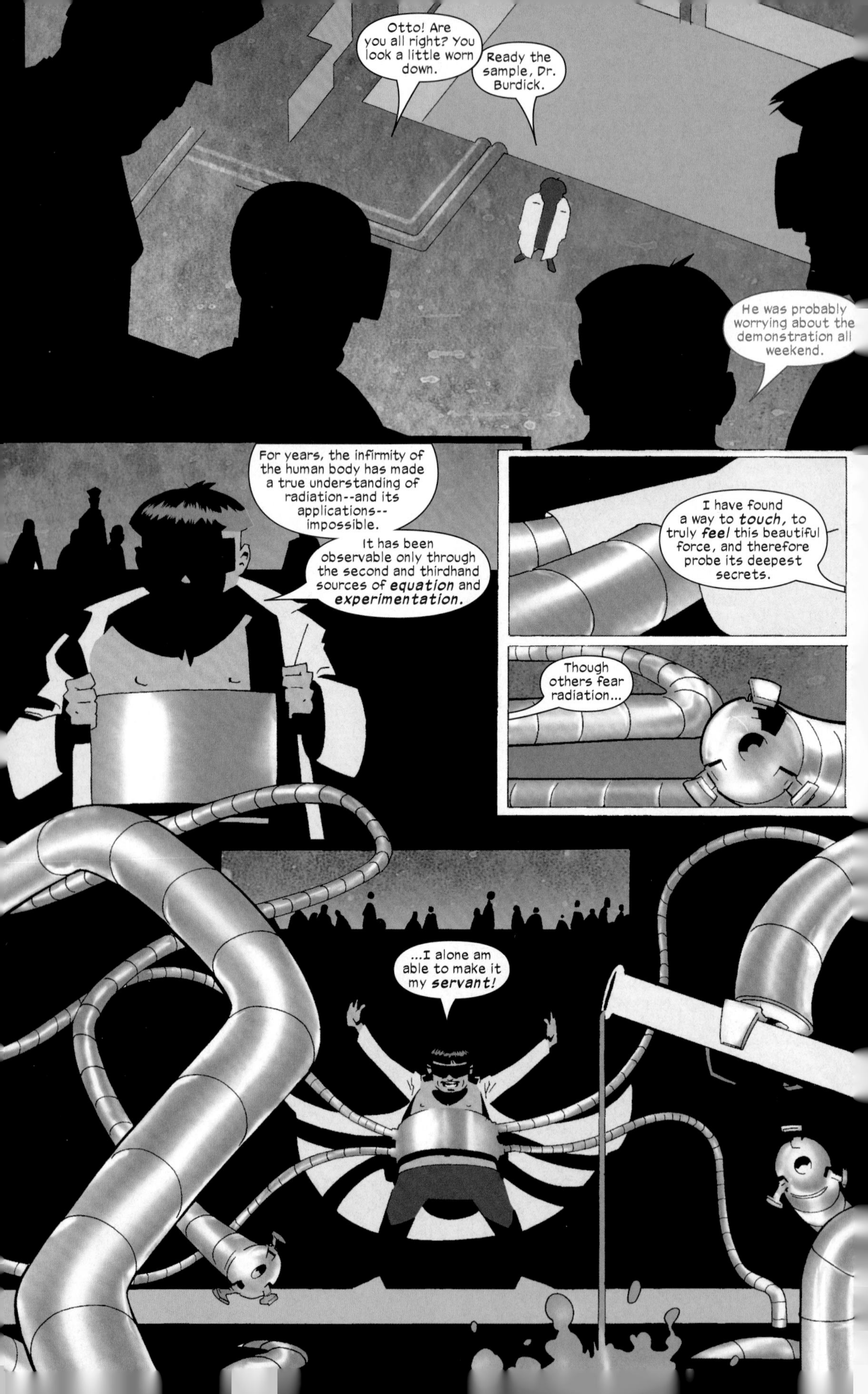
Otto! Are you all right? You look a little worn down.
Ready the sample, Dr. Burdick.
He was probably worrying about the demonstration all weekend.
For years, the infirmity of the human body has made a true understanding of radiation--and its applications--impossible.
It has been observable only through the second and thirdhand sources of *equation* and *experimentation.*
I have found a way to *touch,* to truly *feel* this beautiful force, and therefore probe its deepest secrets.
Though others fear radiation...
...I alone am able to make it my *servant!*

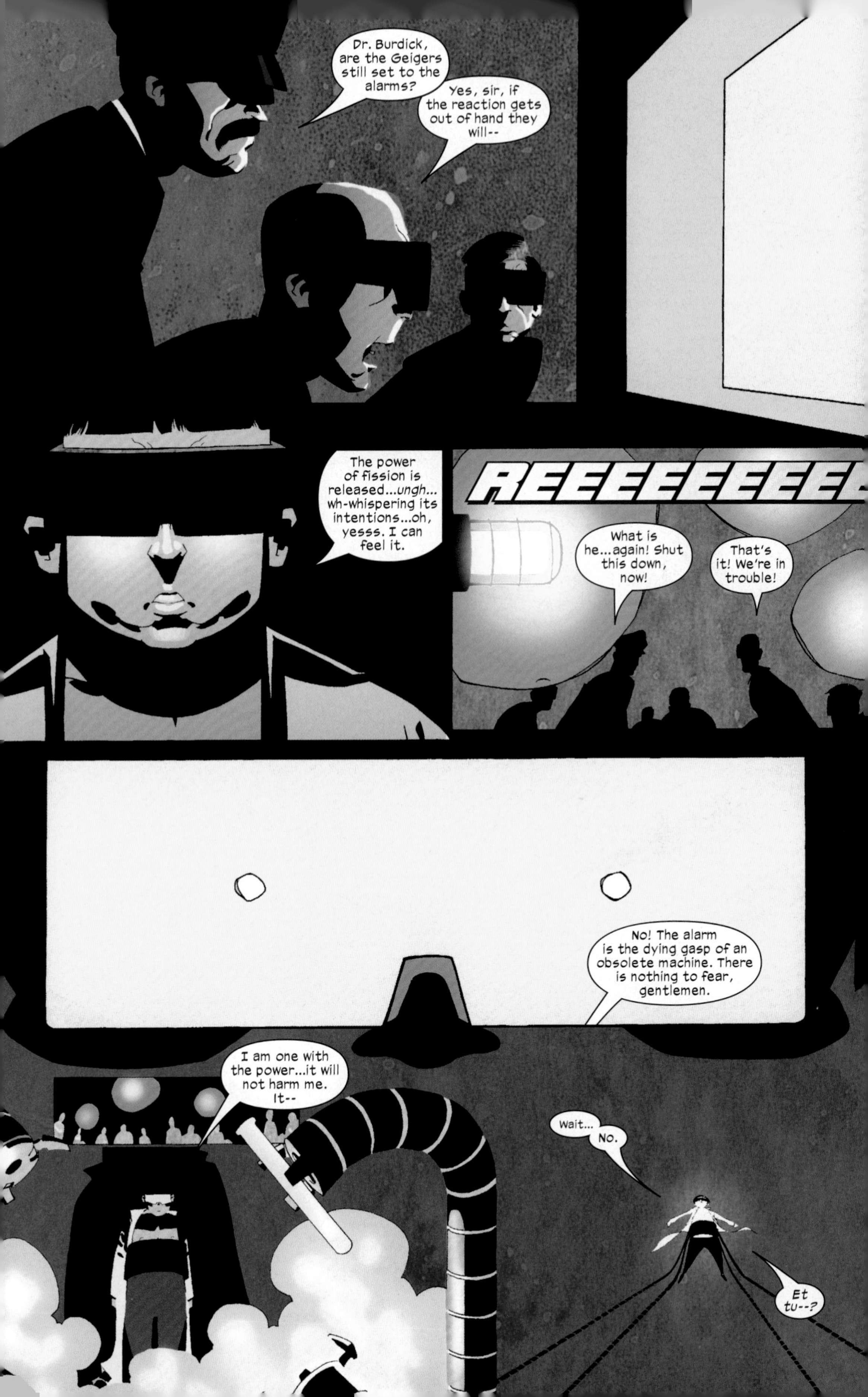

Dr. Burdick, are the Geigers still set to the alarms?
Yes, sir, if the reaction gets out of hand they will--
The power of fission is released...*ungh*... wh-whispering its intentions...oh, yesss. I can feel it.
REEEEEEEEEE
What is he...again! Shut this down, now!
That's it! We're in trouble!
No! The alarm is the dying gasp of an obsolete machine. There is nothing to fear, gentlemen.
I am one with the power...it will not harm me. It--
Wait...
No.
Et tu--?

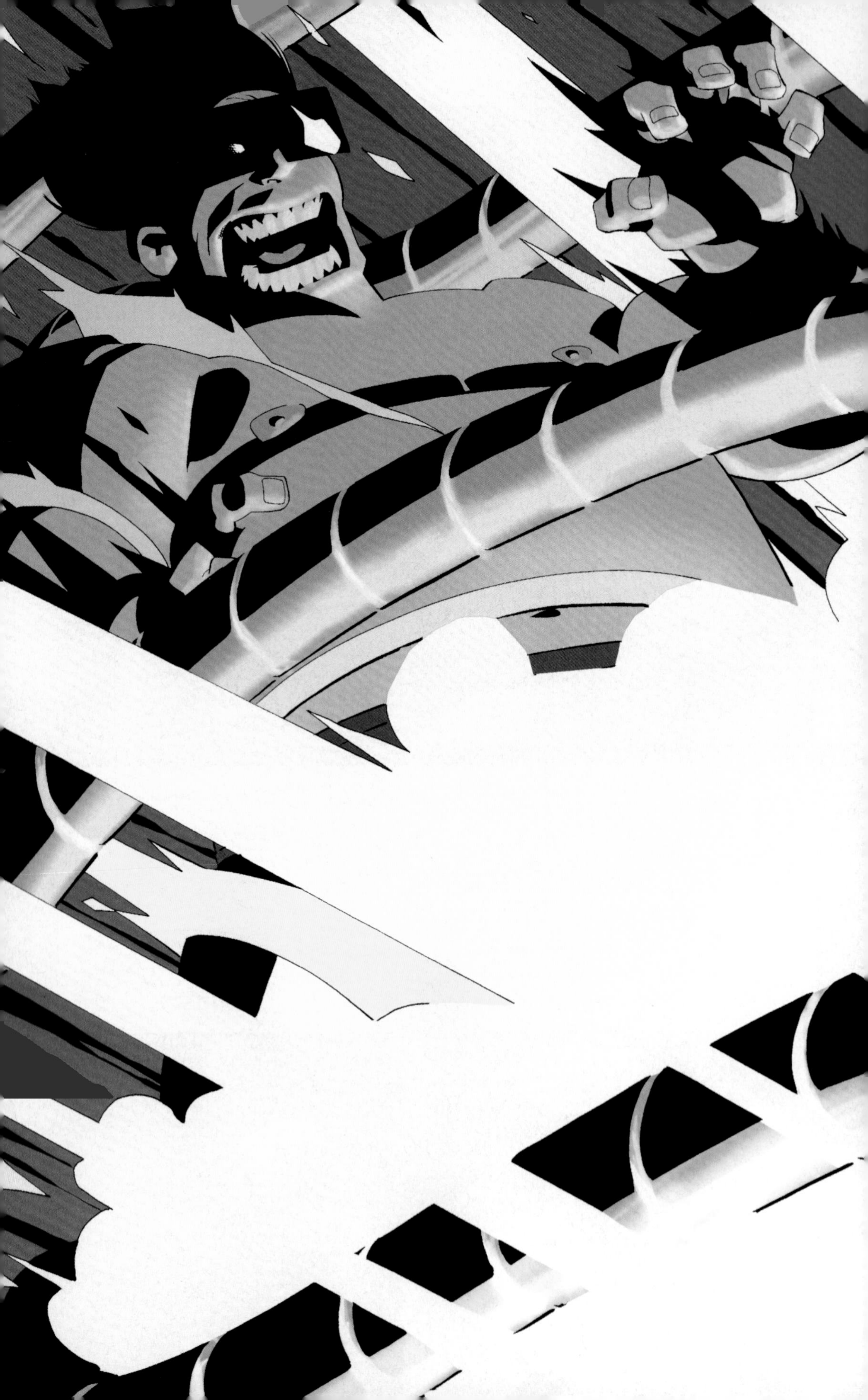

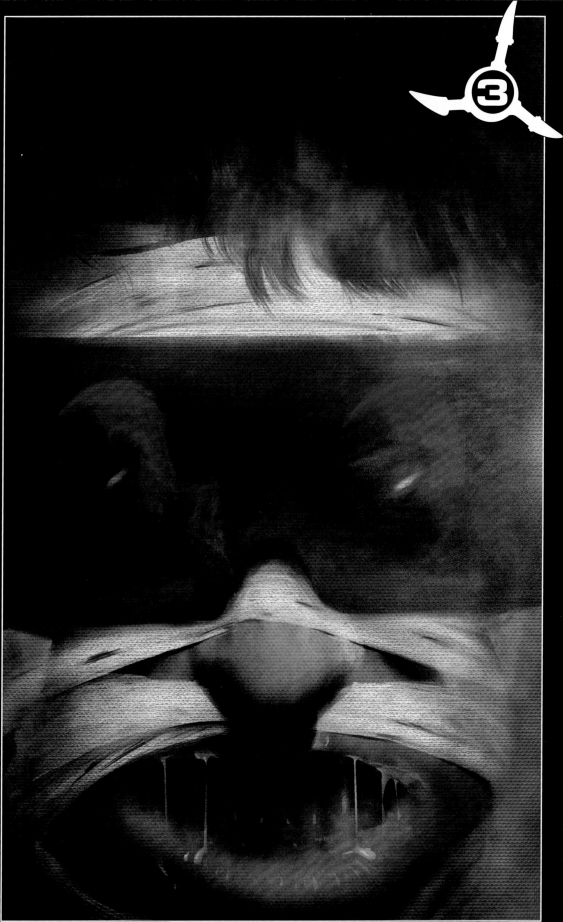

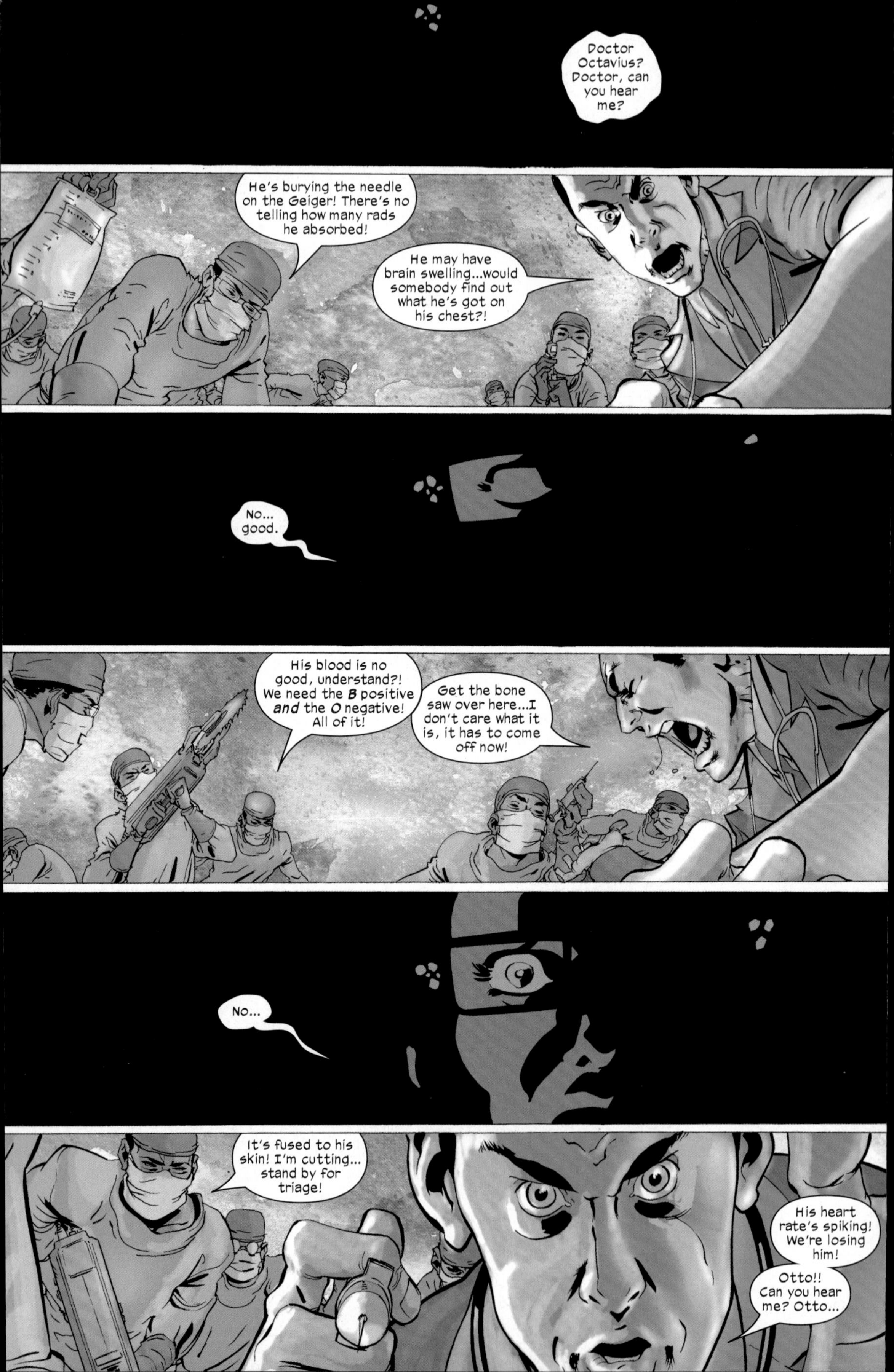
Doctor Octavius? Doctor, can you hear me?
He's burying the needle on the Geiger! There's no telling how many rads he absorbed!
He may have brain swelling...would somebody find out what he's got on his chest?!
No... good.
His blood is no good, understand?! We need the B positive and the O negative! All of it!
Get the bone saw over here...I don't care what it is, it has to come off now!
No...
It's fused to his skin! I'm cutting... stand by for triage!
His heart rate's spiking! We're losing him!
Otto!! Can you hear me? Otto...

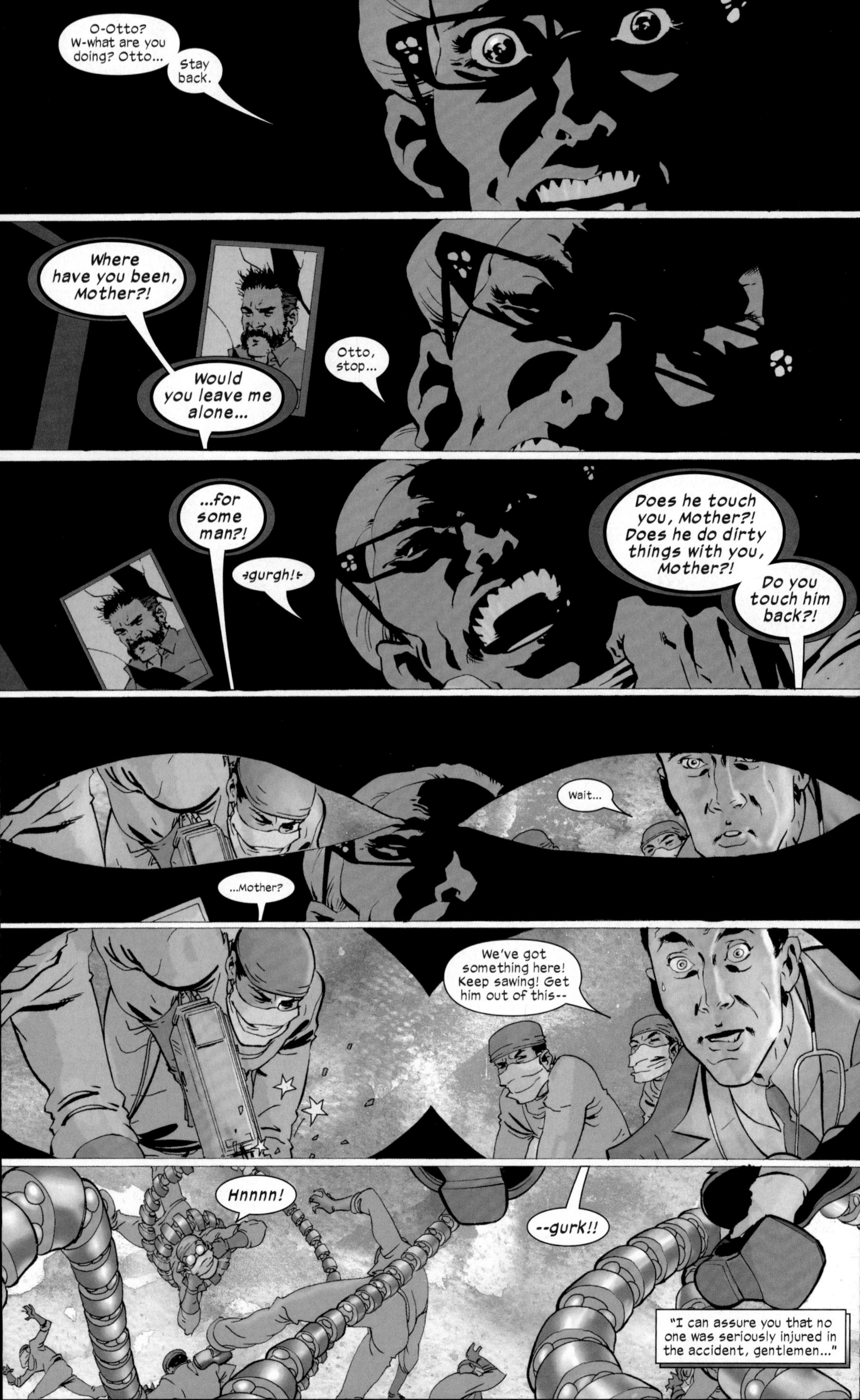
O-Otto? W-what are you doing? Otto...
Stay back.
Where have you been, Mother?!
Would you leave me alone...
Otto, stop...
...for some man?!
gurgh!
Does he touch you, Mother?! Does he do dirty things with you, Mother?!
Do you touch him back?!
Wait...
...Mother?
We've got something here! Keep sawing! Get him out of this--
Hnnnn!
--gurk!!
"I can assure you that no one was seriously injured in the accident, gentlemen..."

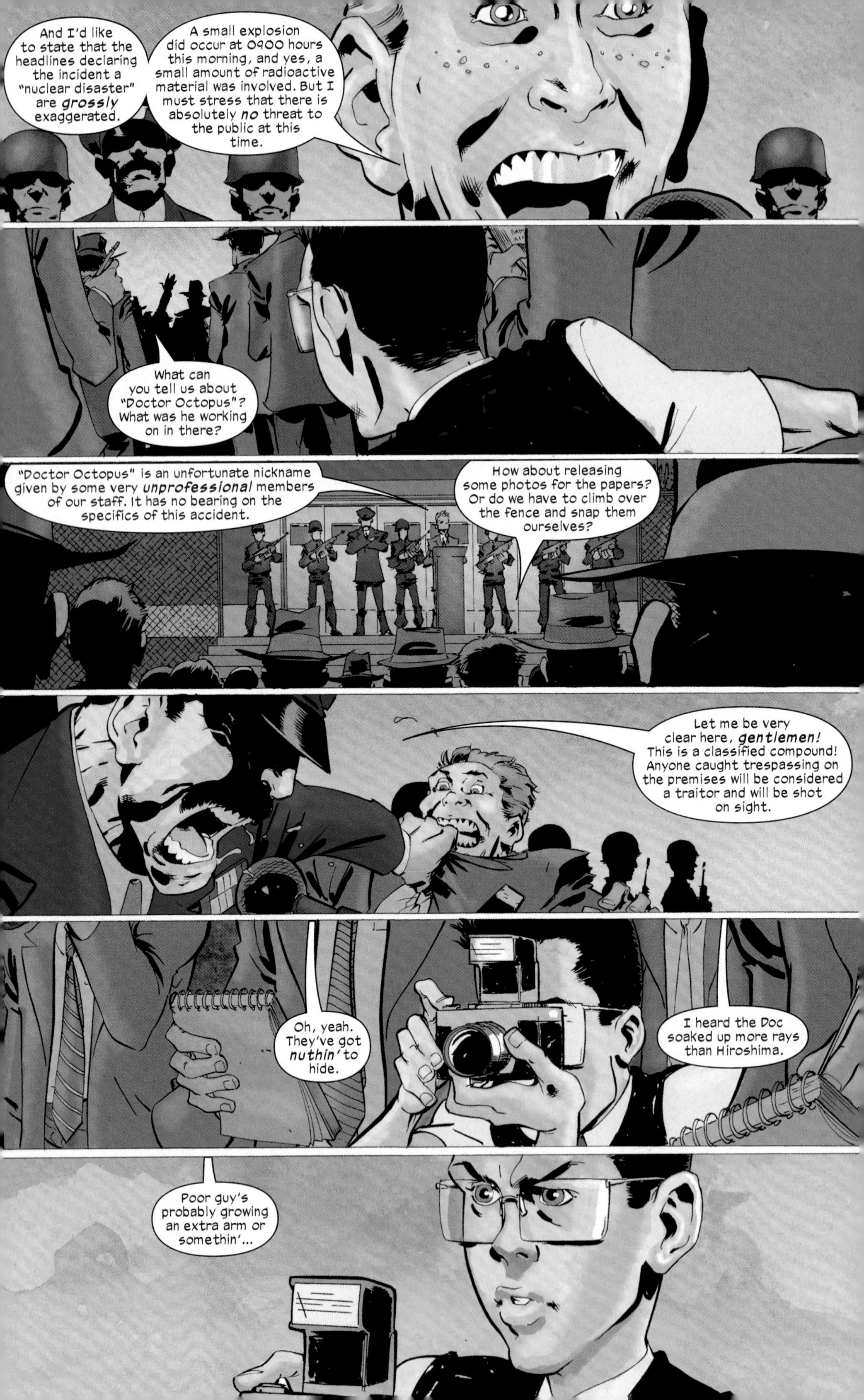
And I'd like to state that the headlines declaring the incident a "nuclear disaster" are *grossly* exaggerated.
A small explosion did occur at 0900 hours this morning, and yes, a small amount of radioactive material was involved. But I must stress that there is absolutely *no* threat to the public at this time.
What can you tell us about "Doctor Octopus"? What was he working on in there?
"Doctor Octopus" is an unfortunate nickname given by some very *unprofessional* members of our staff. It has no bearing on the specifics of this accident.
How about releasing some photos for the papers? Or do we have to climb over the fence and snap them ourselves?
Let me be very clear here, *gentlemen!* This is a classified compound! Anyone caught trespassing on the premises will be considered a traitor and will be shot on sight.
Oh, yeah. They've got *nuthin'* to hide.
I heard the Doc soaked up more rays than Hiroshima.
Poor guy's probably growing an extra arm or somethin'...

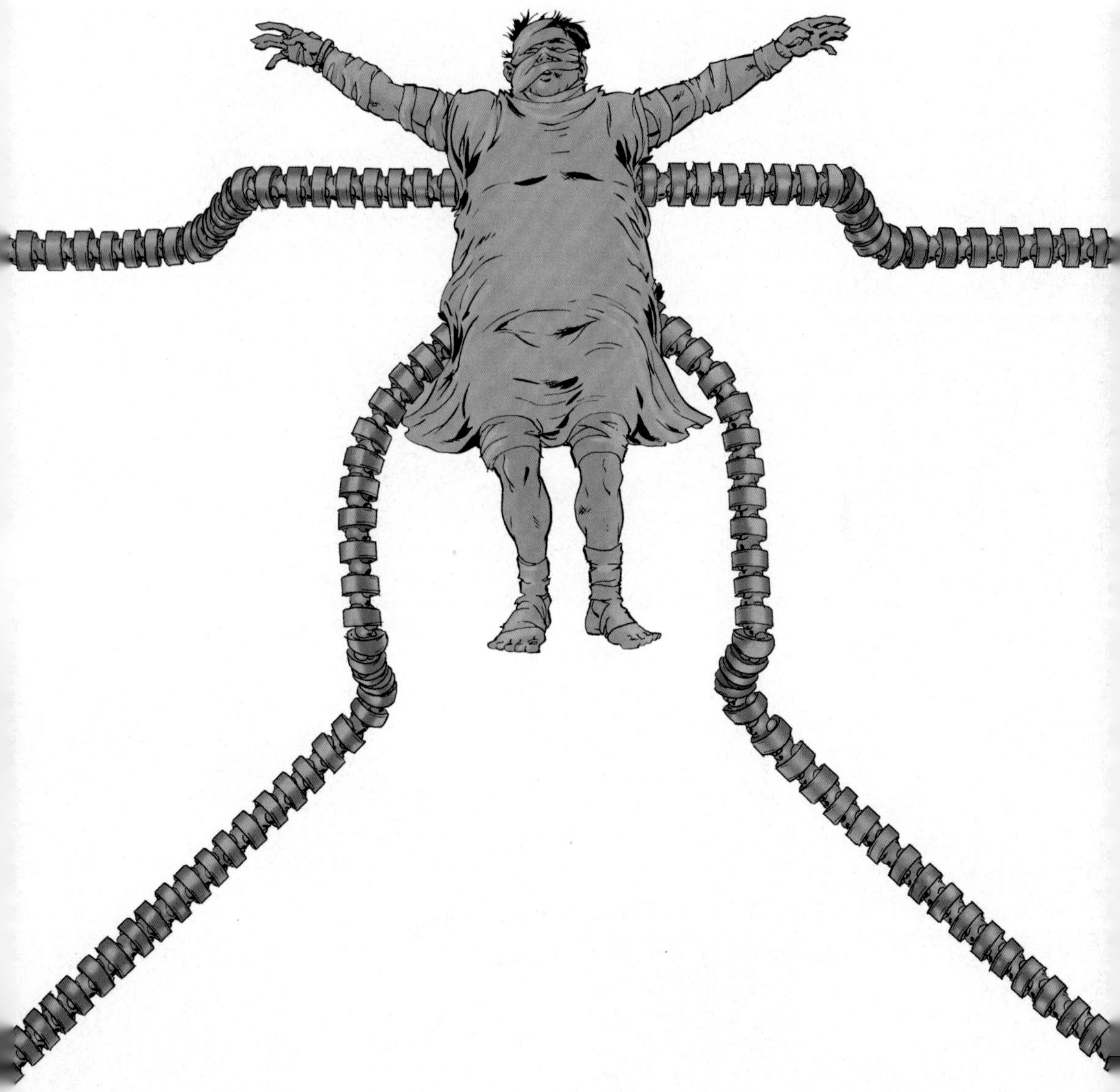

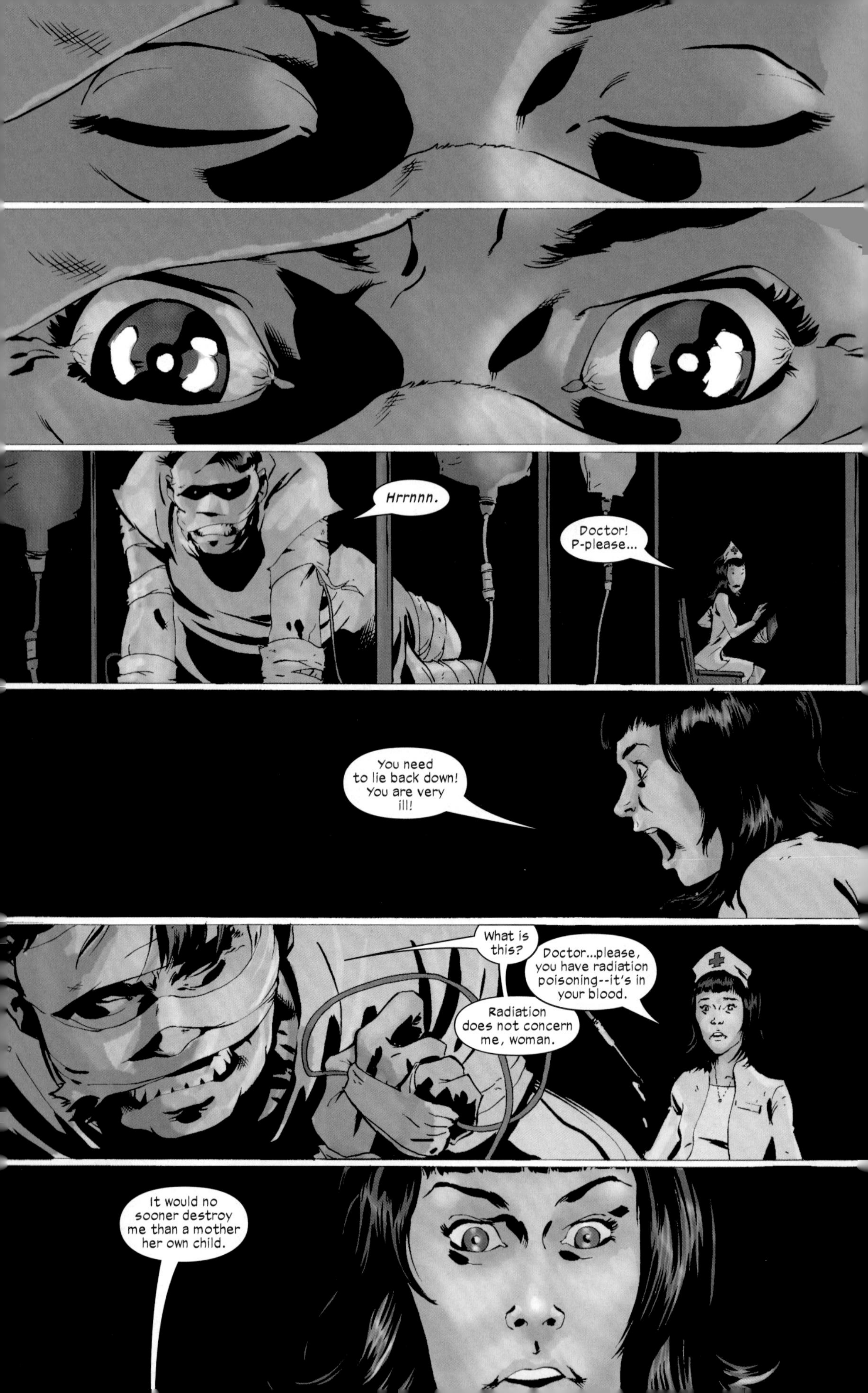
Hrrnnn.
Doctor! P-please...
You need to lie back down! You are very ill!
What is this?
Doctor...please, you have radiation poisoning--it's in your blood.
Radiation does not concern me, woman.
It would no sooner destroy me than a mother her own child.

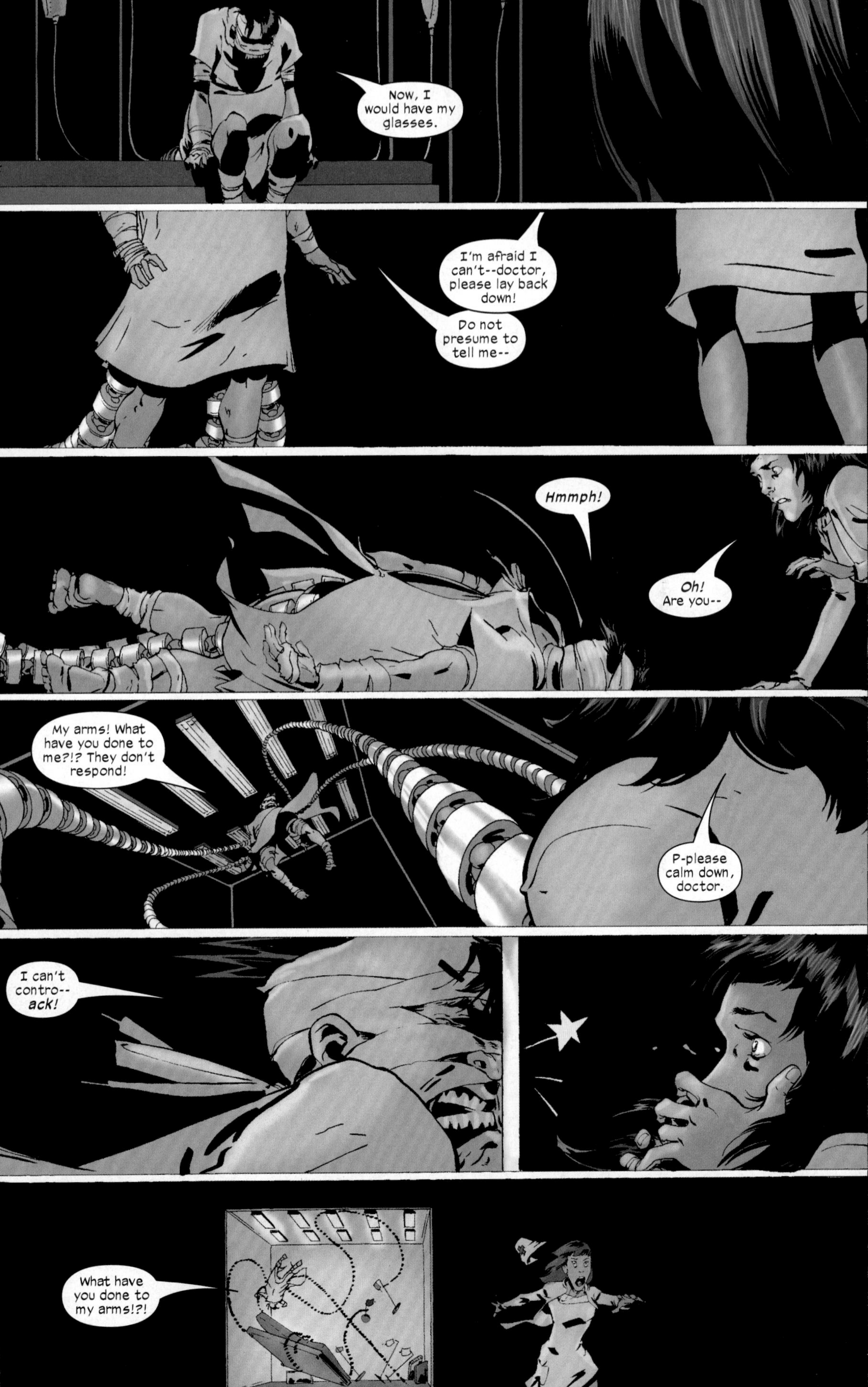
Now, I would have my glasses.
I'm afraid I can't--doctor, please lay back down!
Do not presume to tell me--
Hmmph!
Oh! Are you--
My arms! What have you done to me?!? They don't respond!
P-please calm down, doctor.
I can't contro-- *ack!*
What have you done to my arms!?!

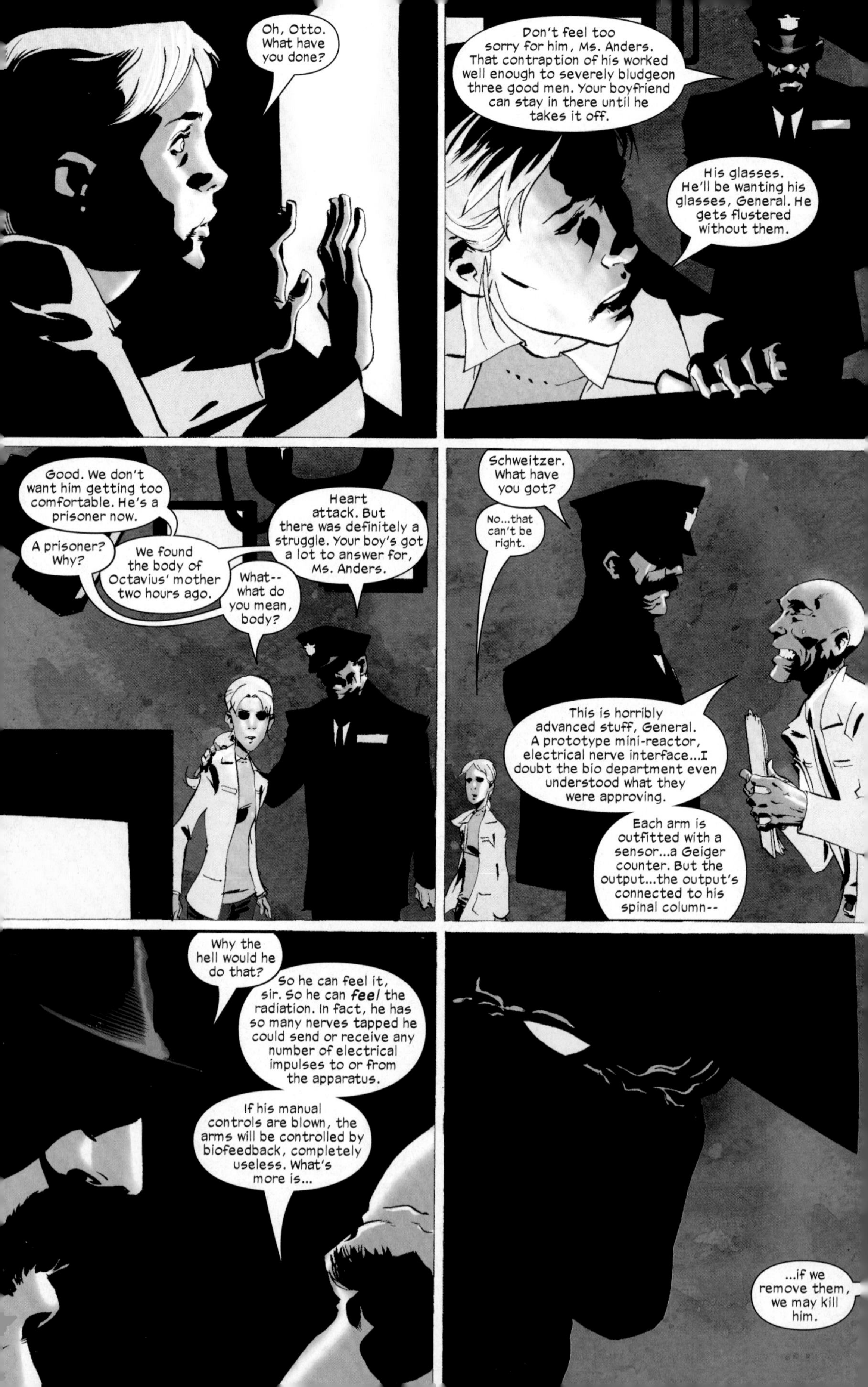

Oh, Otto. What have you done?
Don't feel too sorry for him, Ms. Anders. That contraption of his worked well enough to severely bludgeon three good men. Your boyfriend can stay in there until he takes it off.
His glasses. He'll be wanting his glasses, General. He gets flustered without them.
Good. We don't want him getting too comfortable. He's a prisoner now.
A prisoner? Why?
We found the body of Octavius' mother two hours ago.
What--what do you mean, body?
Heart attack. But there was definitely a struggle. Your boy's got a lot to answer for, Ms. Anders.
Schweitzer. What have you got?
No...that can't be right.
This is horribly advanced stuff, General. A prototype mini-reactor, electrical nerve interface...I doubt the bio department even understood what they were approving.
Each arm is outfitted with a sensor...a Geiger counter. But the output...the output's connected to his spinal column--
Why the hell would he do that?
So he can feel it, sir. So he can *feel* the radiation. In fact, he has so many nerves tapped he could send or receive any number of electrical impulses to or from the apparatus.
If his manual controls are blown, the arms will be controlled by biofeedback, completely useless. What's more is...
...if we remove them, we may kill him.

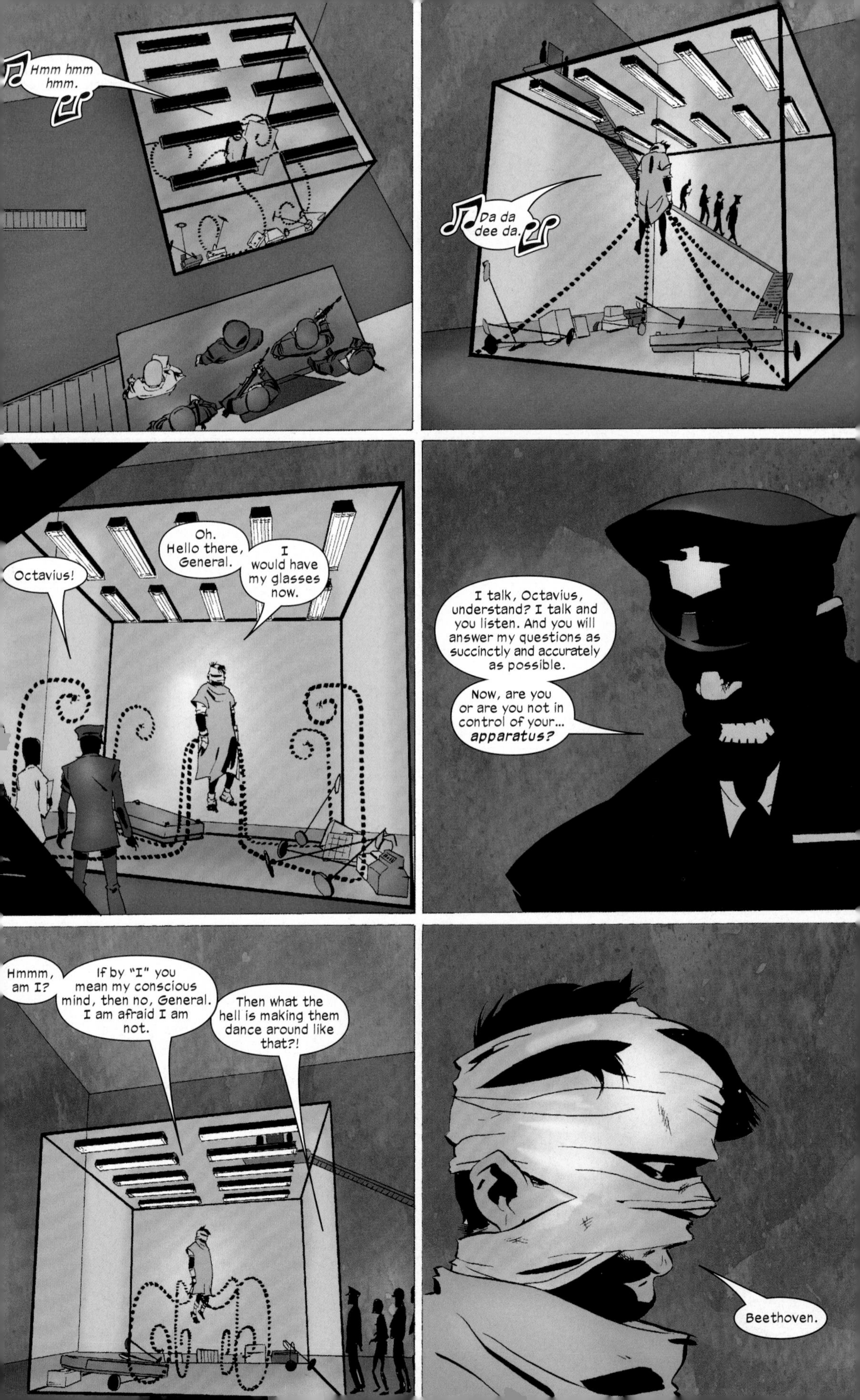
Hmm hmm hmm.
Da da dee da.
Octavius!
Oh. Hello there, General.
I would have my glasses now.
I talk, Octavius, understand? I talk and you listen. And you will answer my questions as succinctly and accurately as possible.
Now, are you or are you not in control of your... *apparatus?*
Hmmm, am I?
If by "I" you mean my conscious mind, then no, General. I am afraid I am not.
Then what the hell is making them dance around like that?!
Beethoven.

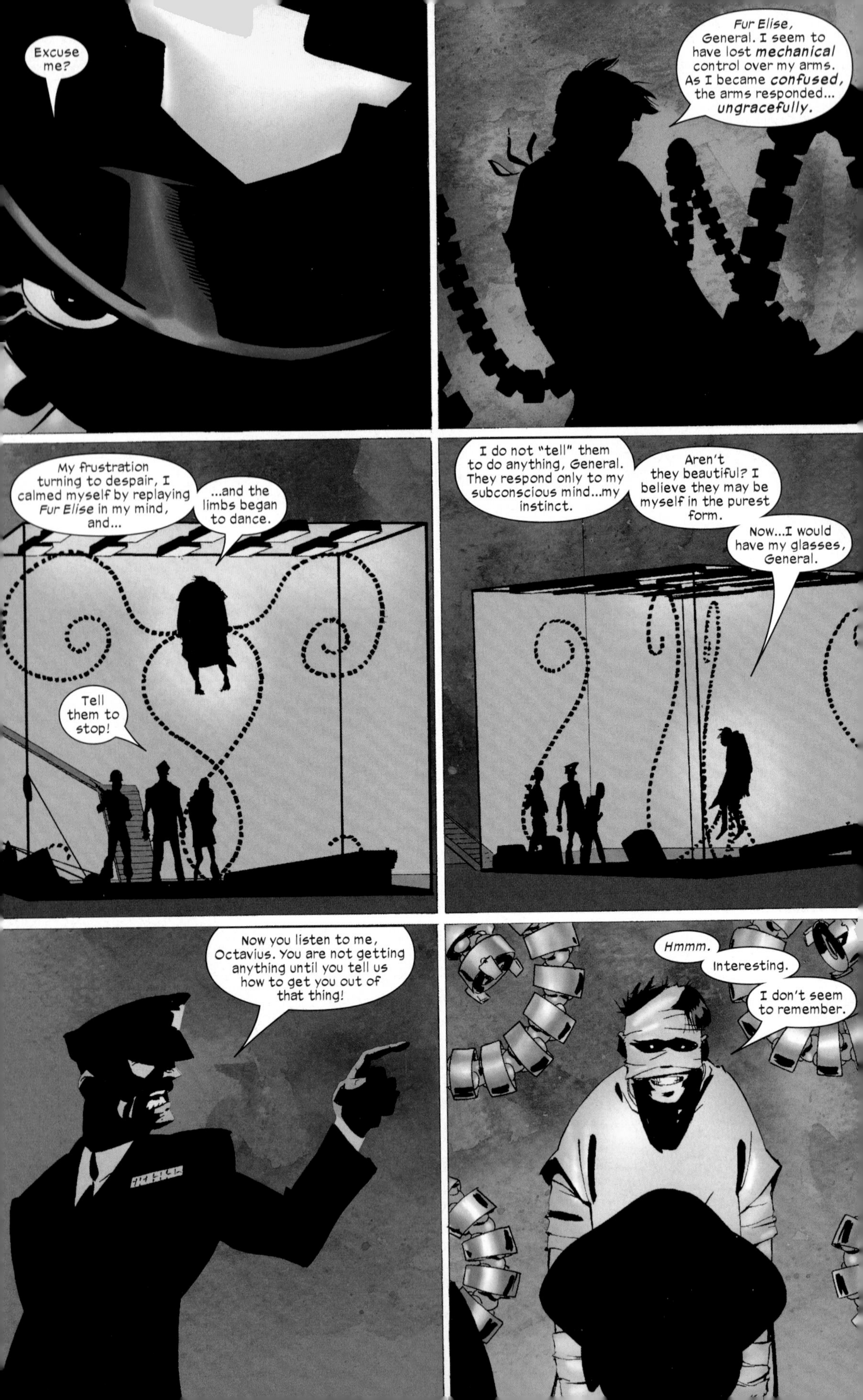
Excuse me?
Fur Elise, General. I seem to have lost mechanical control over my arms. As I became confused, the arms responded... ungracefully.
My frustration turning to despair, I calmed myself by replaying Fur Elise in my mind, and...
...and the limbs began to dance.
Tell them to stop!
I do not "tell" them to do anything, General. They respond only to my subconscious mind...my instinct.
Aren't they beautiful? I believe they may be myself in the purest form.
Now...I would have my glasses, General.
Now you listen to me, Octavius. You are not getting anything until you tell us how to get you out of that thing!
Hmmm.
Interesting.
I don't seem to remember.

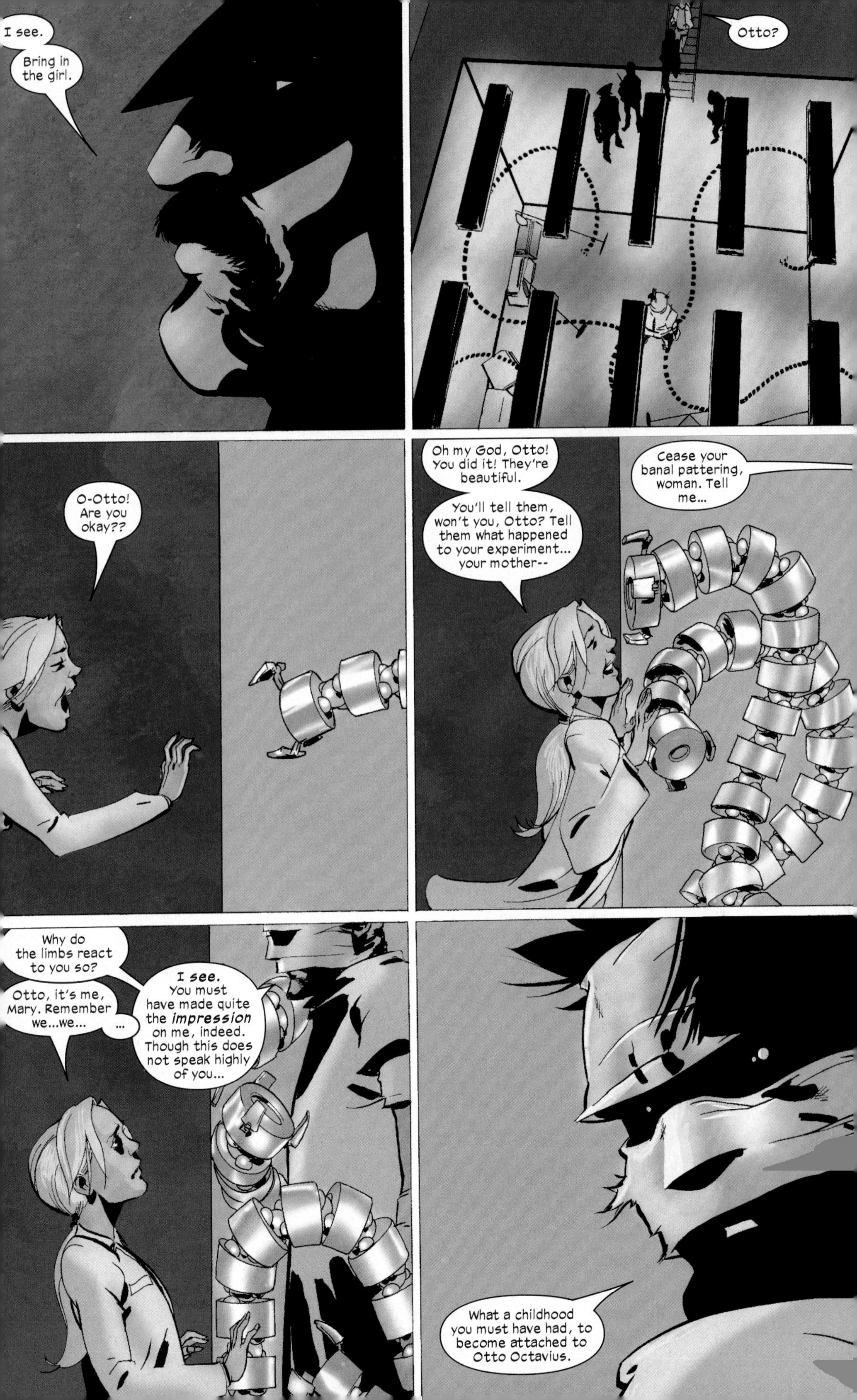
I see.
Bring in the girl.
Otto?
O-Otto! Are you okay??
Oh my God, Otto! You did it! They're beautiful.
You'll tell them, won't you, Otto? Tell them what happened to your experiment... your mother--
Cease your banal pattering, woman. Tell me...
Why do the limbs react to you so?
Otto, it's me, Mary. Remember we...we...
...
I *see.* You must have made quite the *impression* on me, indeed. Though this does not speak highly of you...
What a childhood you must have had, to become attached to Otto Octavius.

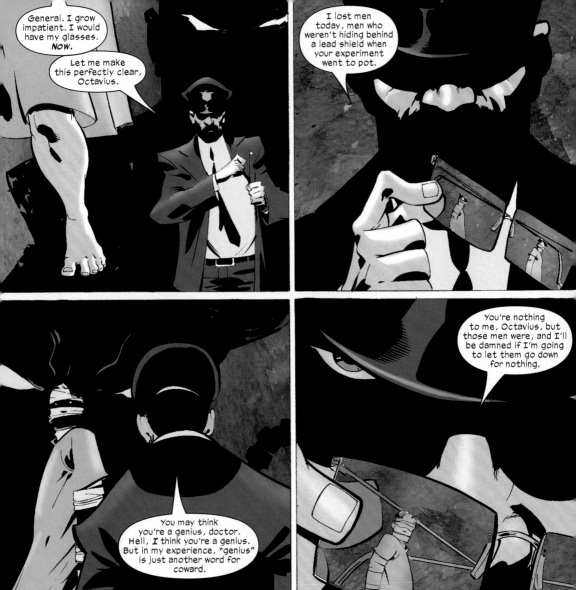

General. I grow impatient. I would have my glasses. NOW.

Let me make this perfectly clear, Octavius.

I lost men today, men who weren't hiding behind a lead shield when your experiment went to pot.

You may think you're a genius, doctor. Hell, I think you're a genius. But in my experience, "genius" is just another word for coward.

You're nothing to me, Octavius, but those men were, and I'll be damned if I'm going to let them go down for nothing.

So if I have to yank those arms off you one by one, I will!! You are going to tell me the intimate details of your project, starting now!

And then you're going to tell me what you did to your mother, you sick little freak!!

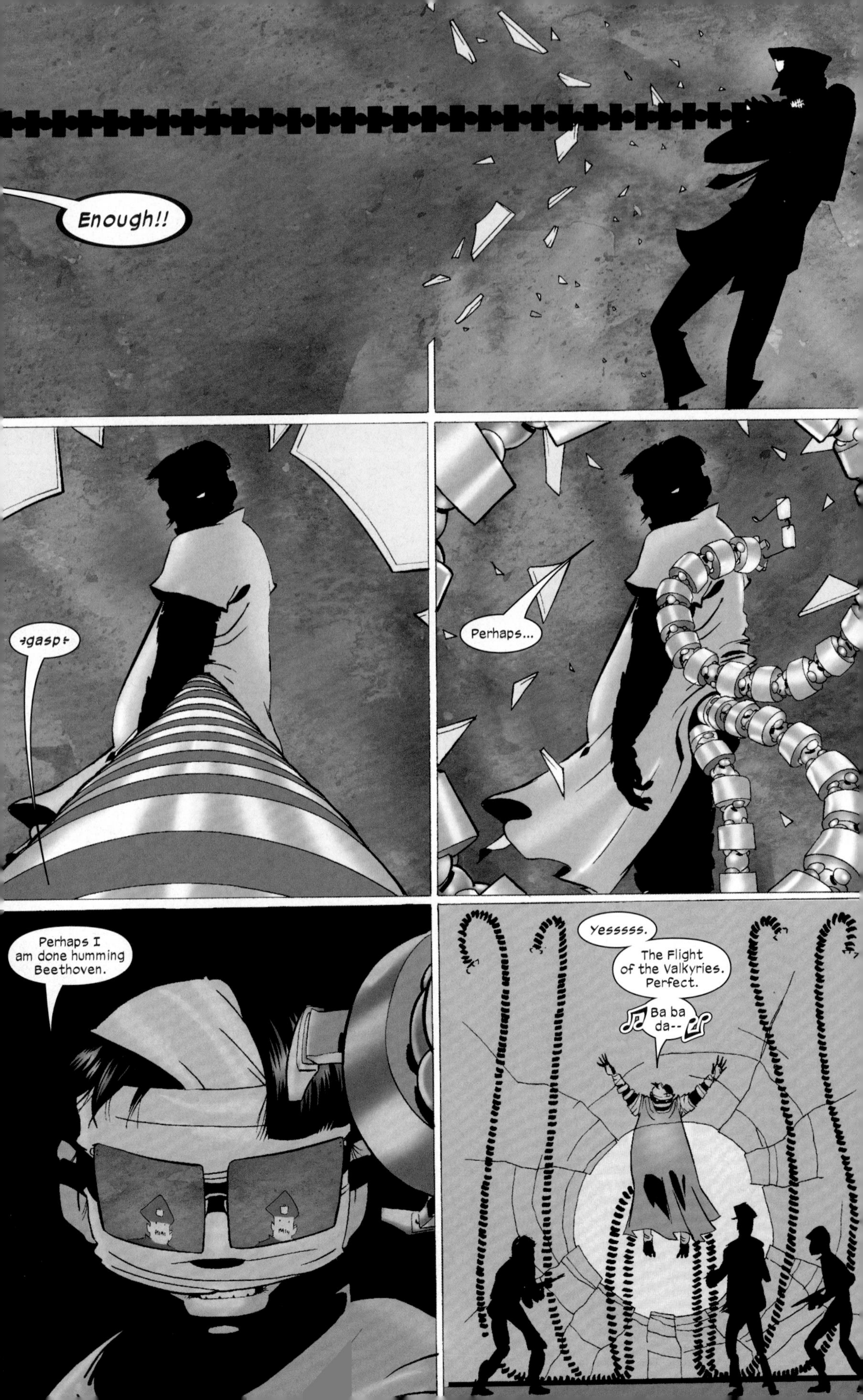
Enough!!
-gasp-
Perhaps...
Perhaps I am done humming Beethoven.
Yessssss.
The Flight of the Valkyries. Perfect.
Ba ba da--

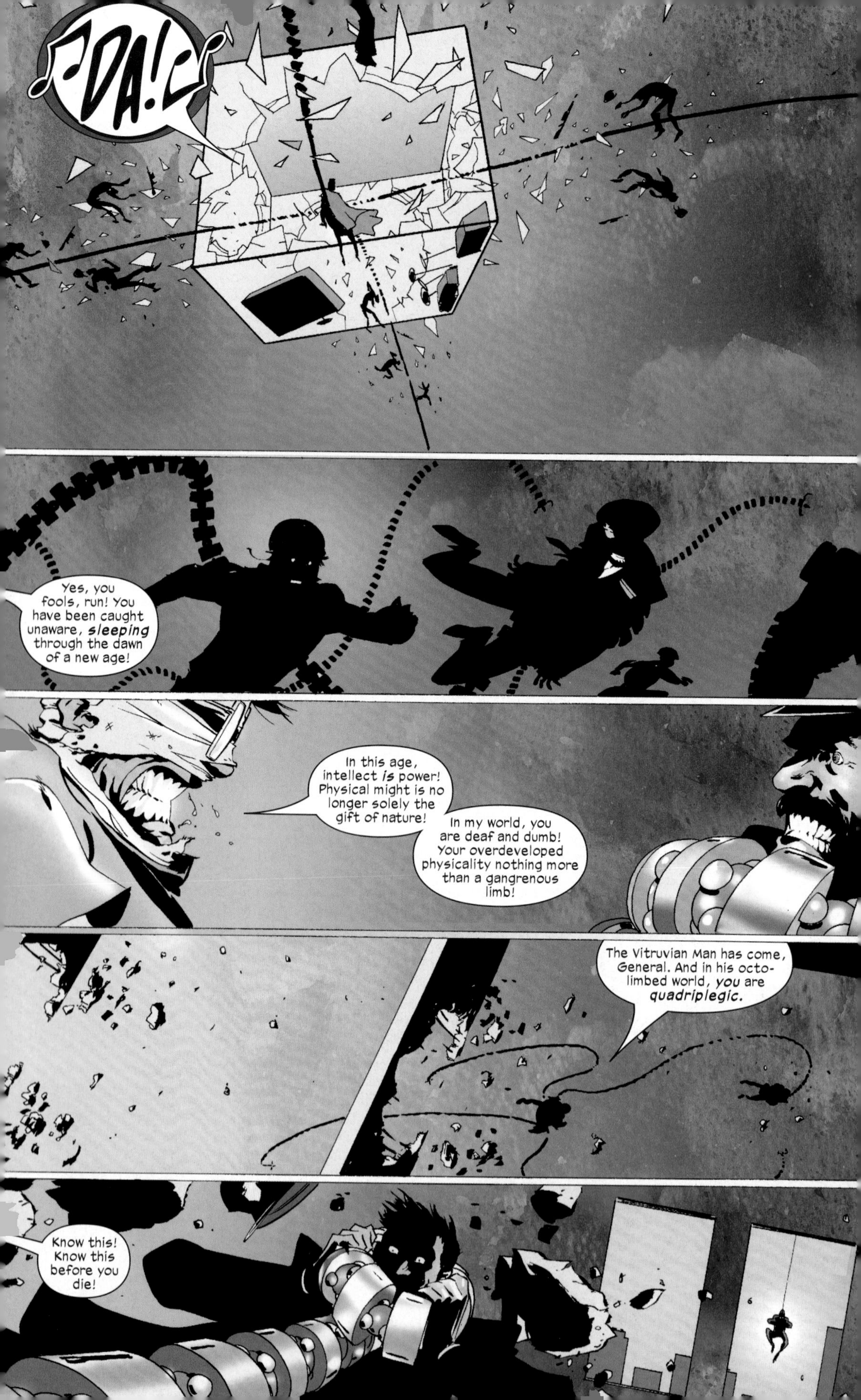

DA!
Yes, you fools, run! You have been caught unaware, *sleeping* through the dawn of a new age!
In this age, intellect *is* power! Physical might is no longer solely the gift of nature!
In my world, you are deaf and dumb! Your overdeveloped physicality nothing more than a gangrenous limb!
The Vitruvian Man has come, General. And in his octo-limbed world, *you* are ***quadriplegic.***
Know this! Know this before you die!

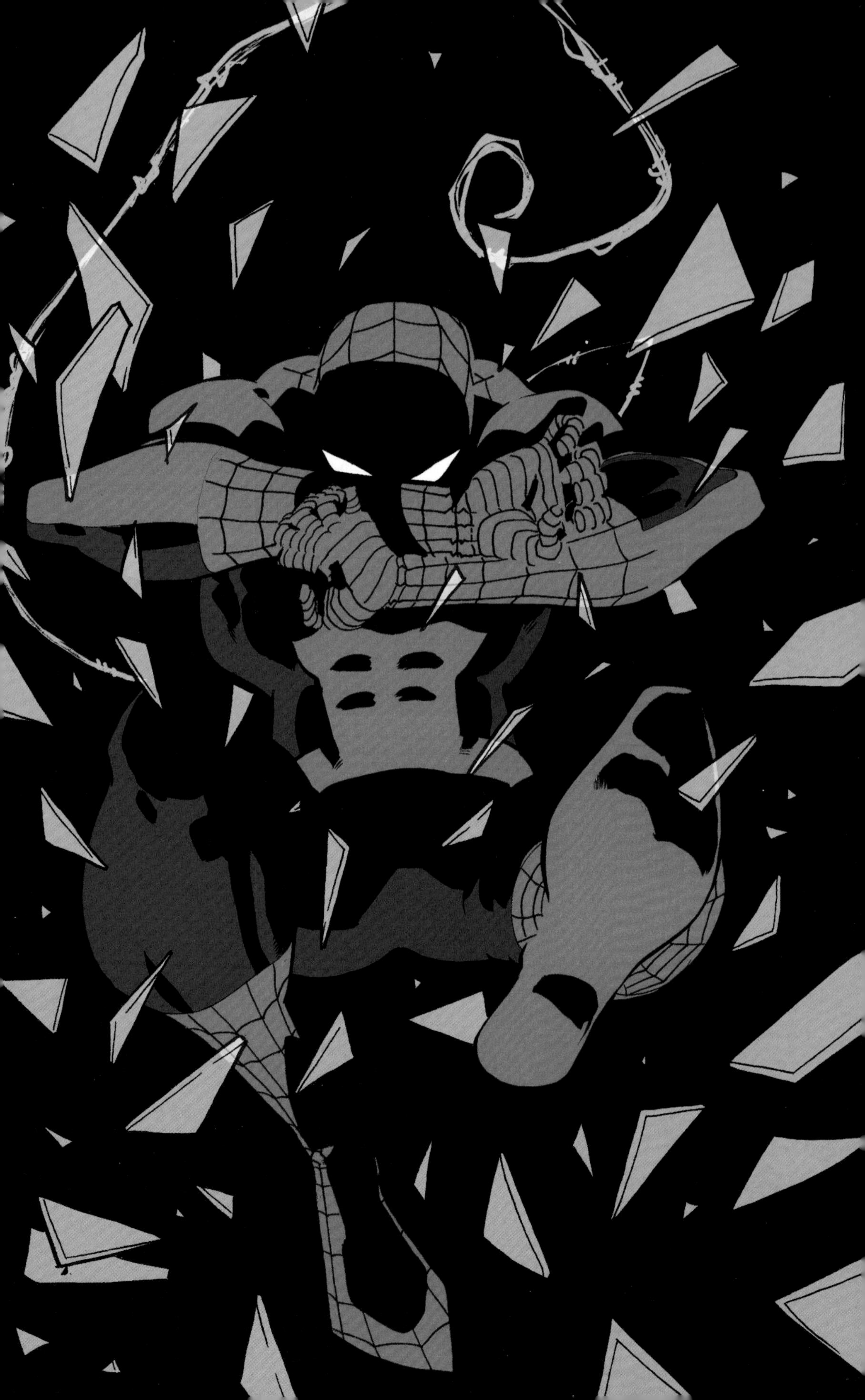

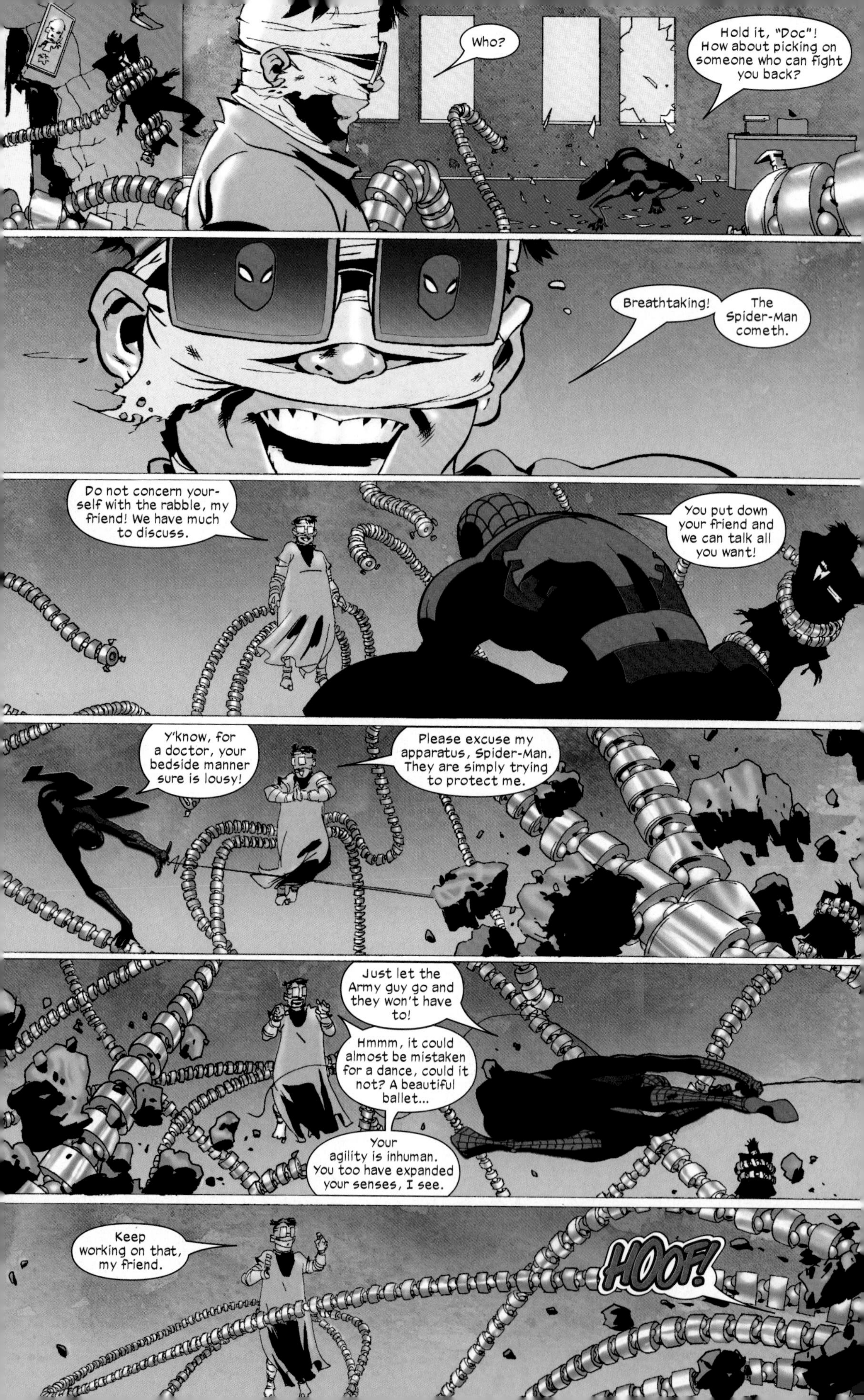
Who?
Hold it, "Doc"! How about picking on someone who can fight you back?
Breathtaking! The Spider-Man cometh.
Do not concern yourself with the rabble, my friend! We have much to discuss.
You put down your friend and we can talk all you want!
Y'know, for a doctor, your bedside manner sure is lousy!
Please excuse my apparatus, Spider-Man. They are simply trying to protect me.
Just let the Army guy go and they won't have to!
Hmmm, it could almost be mistaken for a dance, could it not? A beautiful ballet...
Your agility is inhuman. You too have expanded your senses, I see.
Keep working on that, my friend.
HOOF!

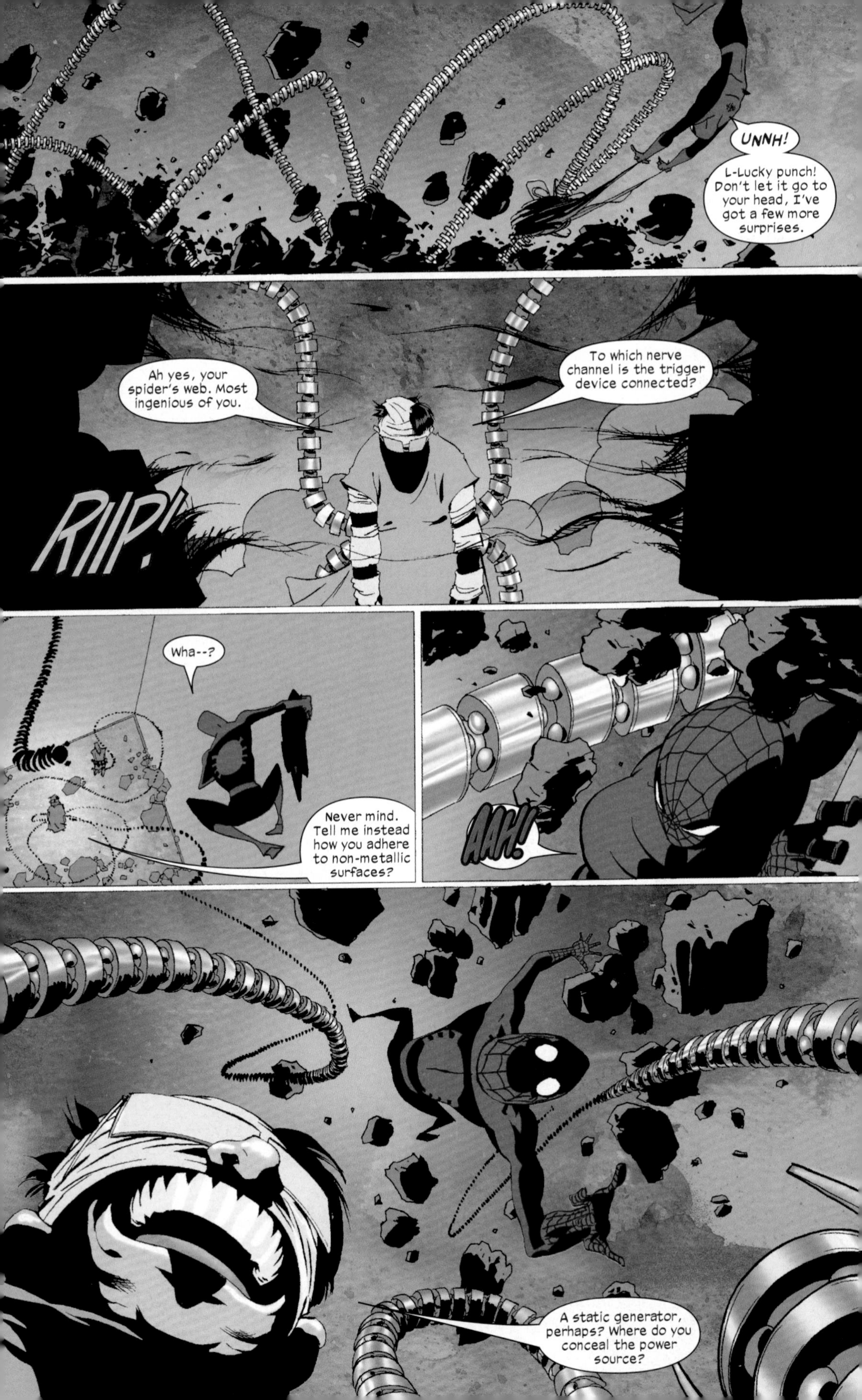
UNNH!
L-Lucky punch! Don't let it go to your head, I've got a few more surprises.
Ah yes, your spider's web. Most ingenious of you.
To which nerve channel is the trigger device connected?
RIIP!
Wha--?
Never mind. Tell me instead how you adhere to non-metallic surfaces?
AAH!
A static generator, perhaps? Where do you conceal the power source?

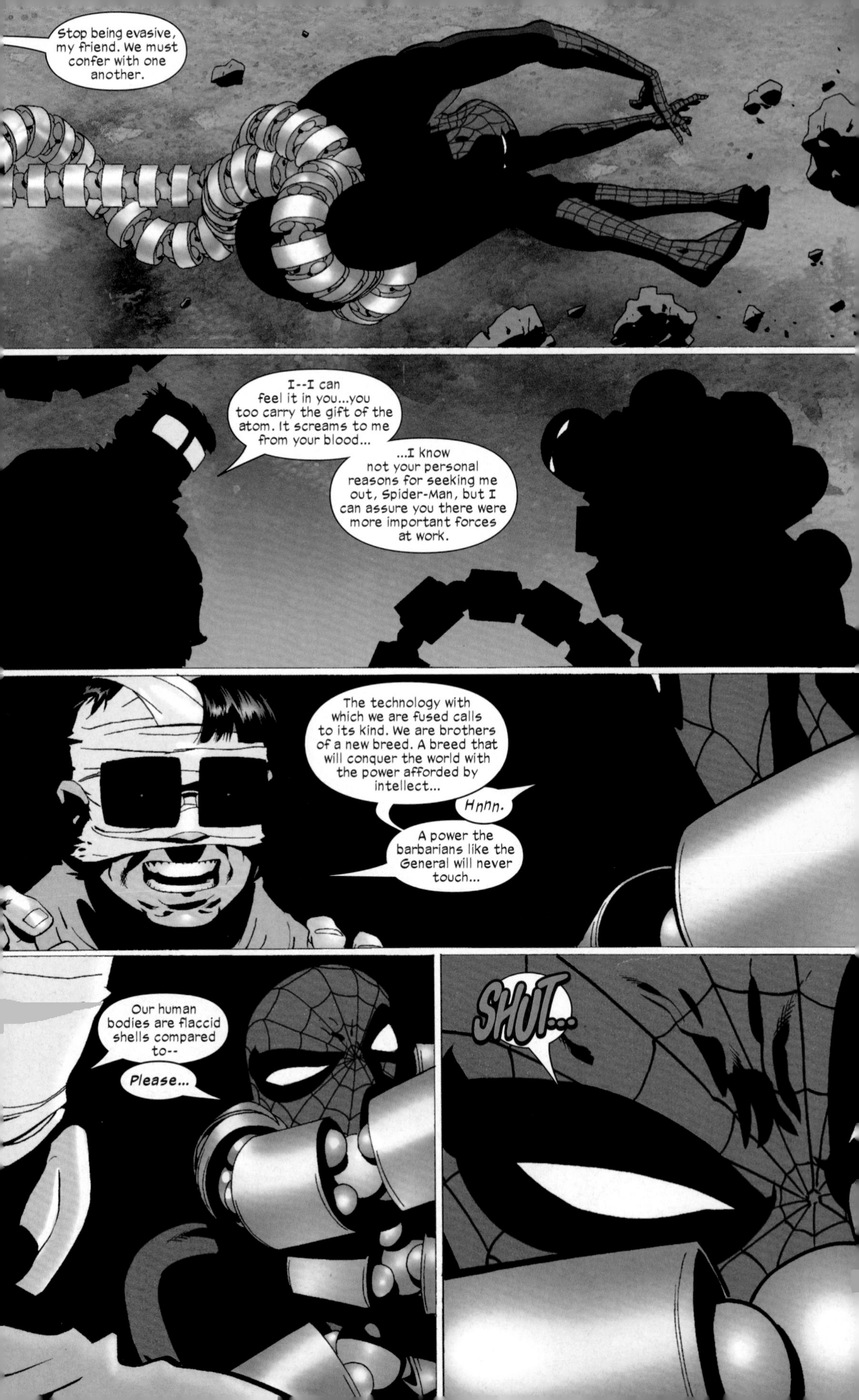
Stop being evasive, my friend. We must confer with one another.
I--I can feel it in you...you too carry the gift of the atom. It screams to me from your blood...
...I know not your personal reasons for seeking me out, Spider-Man, but I can assure you there were more important forces at work.
The technology with which we are fused calls to its kind. We are brothers of a new breed. A breed that will conquer the world with the power afforded by intellect...
Hnnn.
A power the barbarians like the General will never touch...
Our human bodies are flaccid shells compared to--
Please...
SHUT...

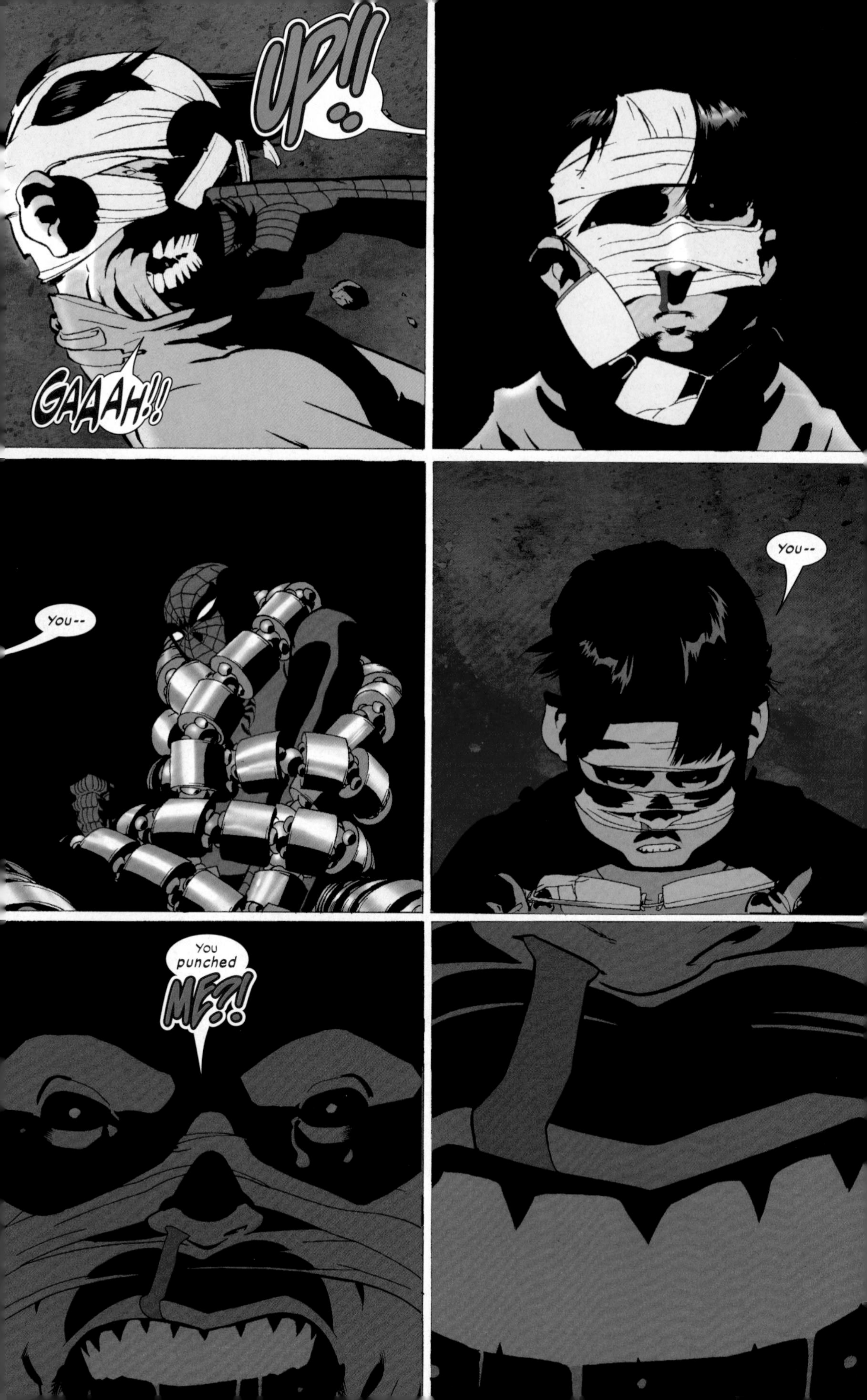
UP!!
GAAAH!!
YOU--
YOU--
You punched ME?!

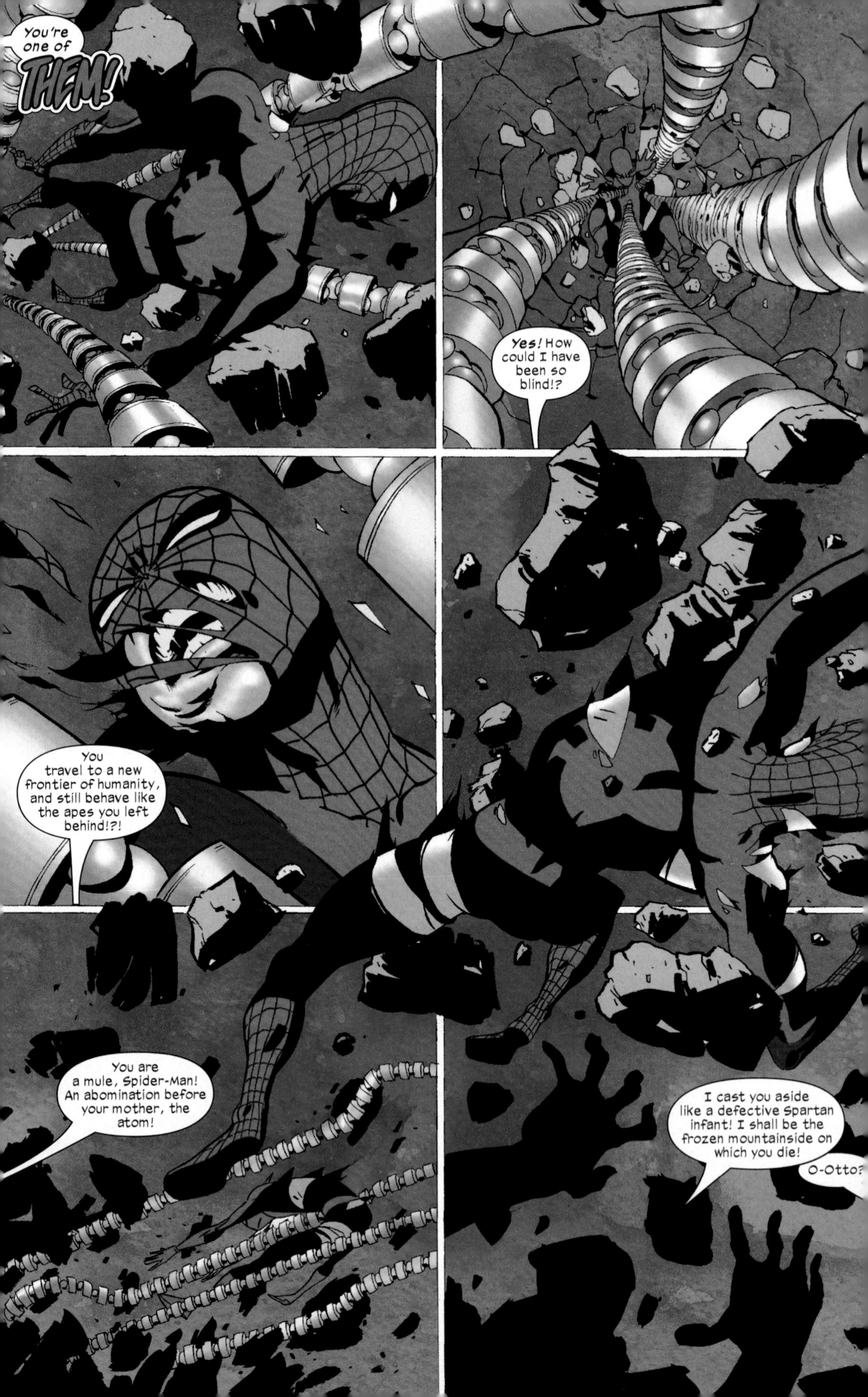
You're one of THEM!
Yes! How could I have been so blind!?
You travel to a new frontier of humanity, and still behave like the apes you left behind!?!
You are a mule, Spider-Man! An abomination before your mother, the atom!
I cast you aside like a defective Spartan infant! I shall be the frozen mountainside on which you die!
O-Otto?

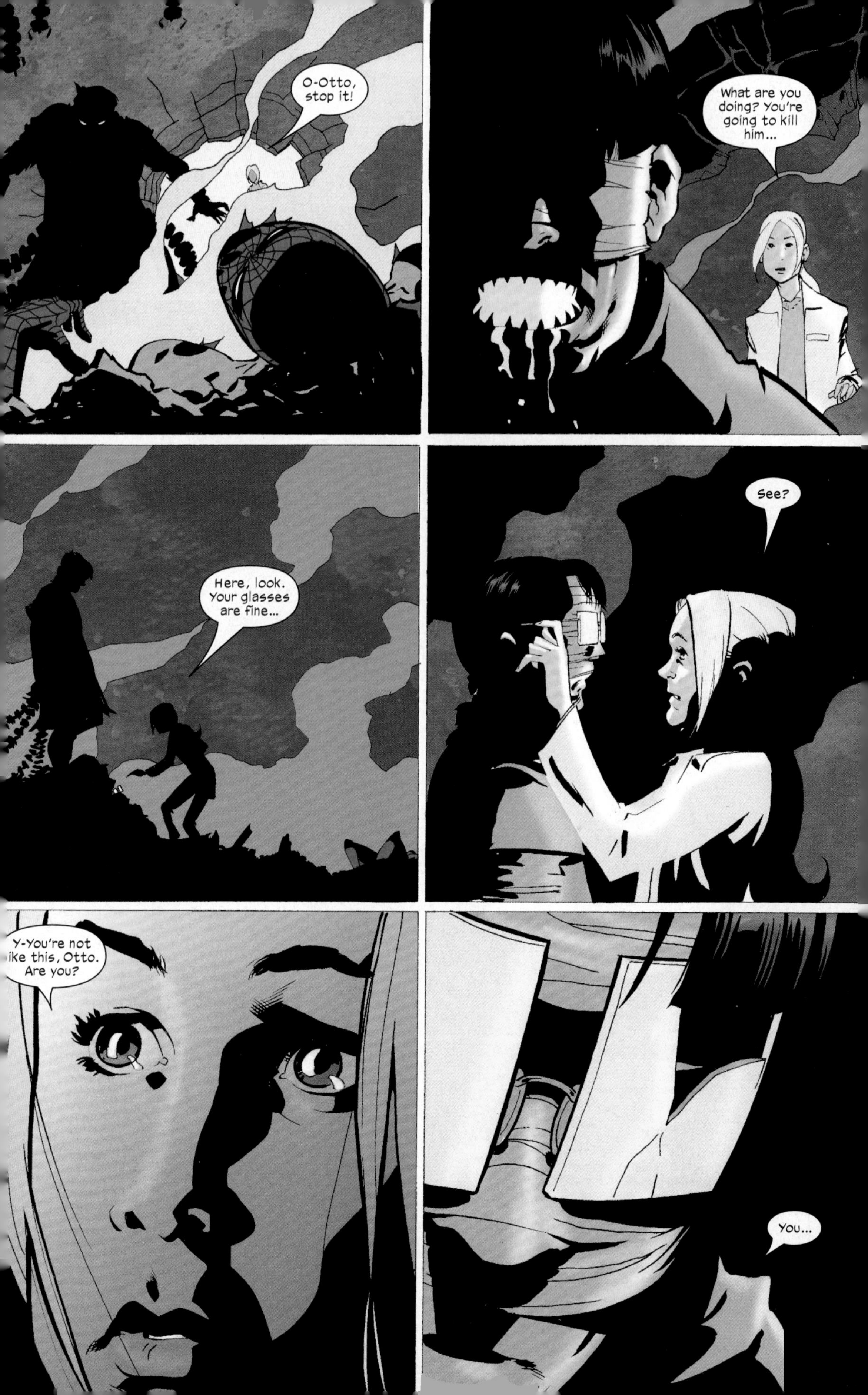
O-Otto, stop it!
What are you doing? You're going to kill him...
Here, look. Your glasses are fine...
See?
Y-You're not ike this, Otto. Are you?
You...

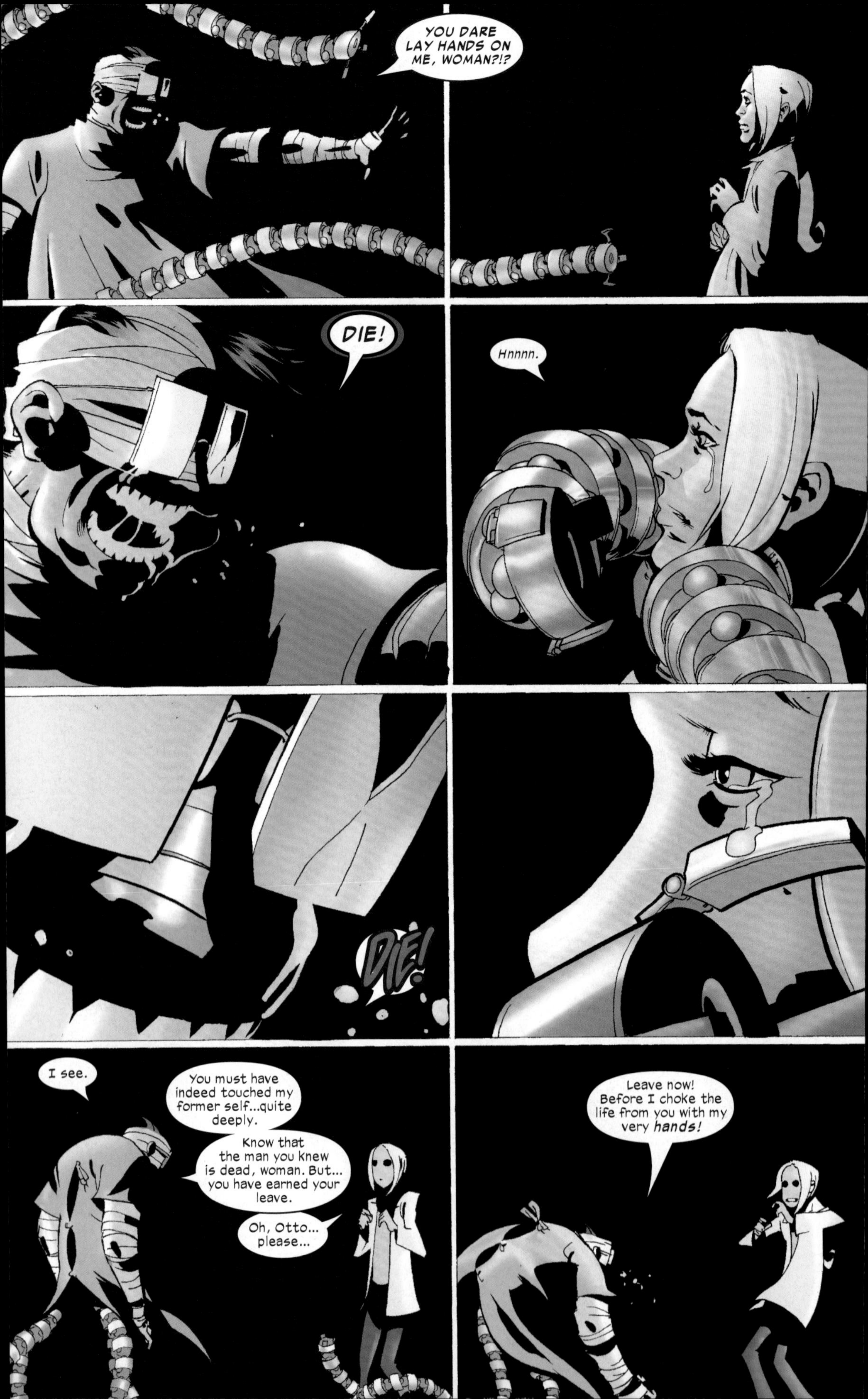
YOU DARE LAY HANDS ON ME, WOMAN?!?
DIE!
Hnnnn.
DIE!
I see.
You must have indeed touched my former self...quite deeply.
Know that the man you knew is dead, woman. But... you have earned your leave.
Oh, Otto... please...
Leave now! Before I choke the life from you with my very *hands!*

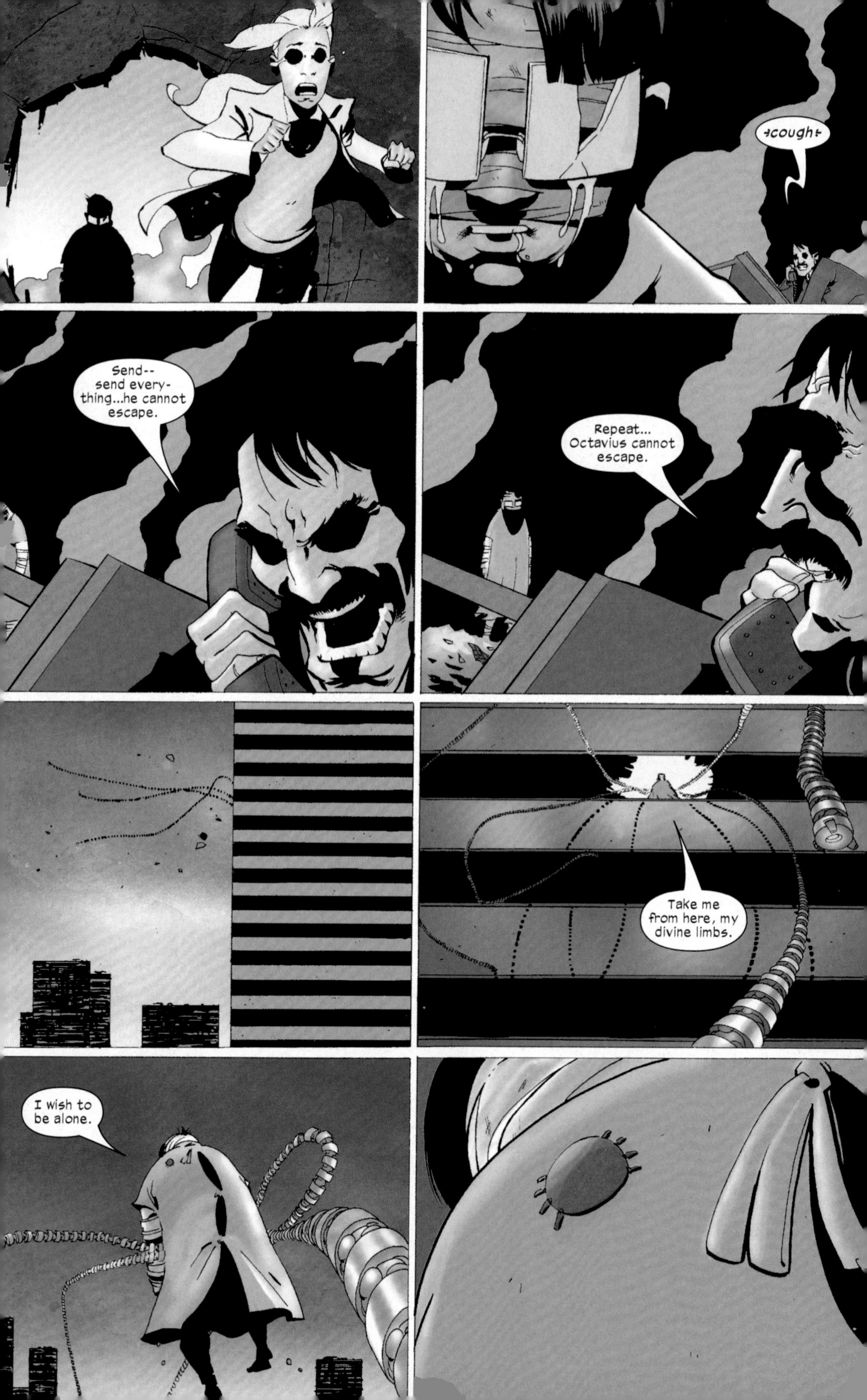

cough
Send--
send every-
thing...he cannot
escape.
Repeat...
Octavius cannot
escape.
Take me
from here, my
divine limbs.
I wish to
be alone.

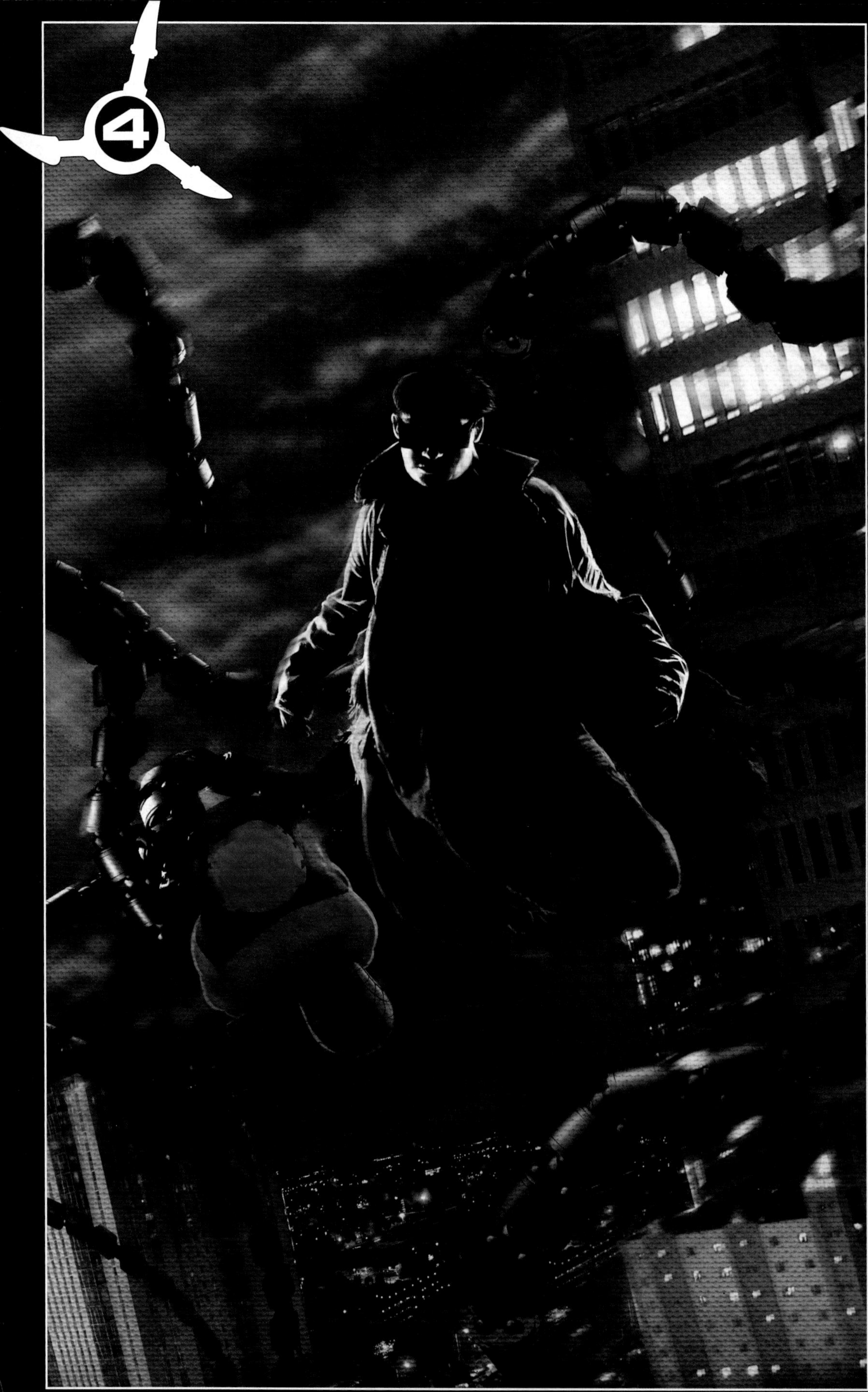
4

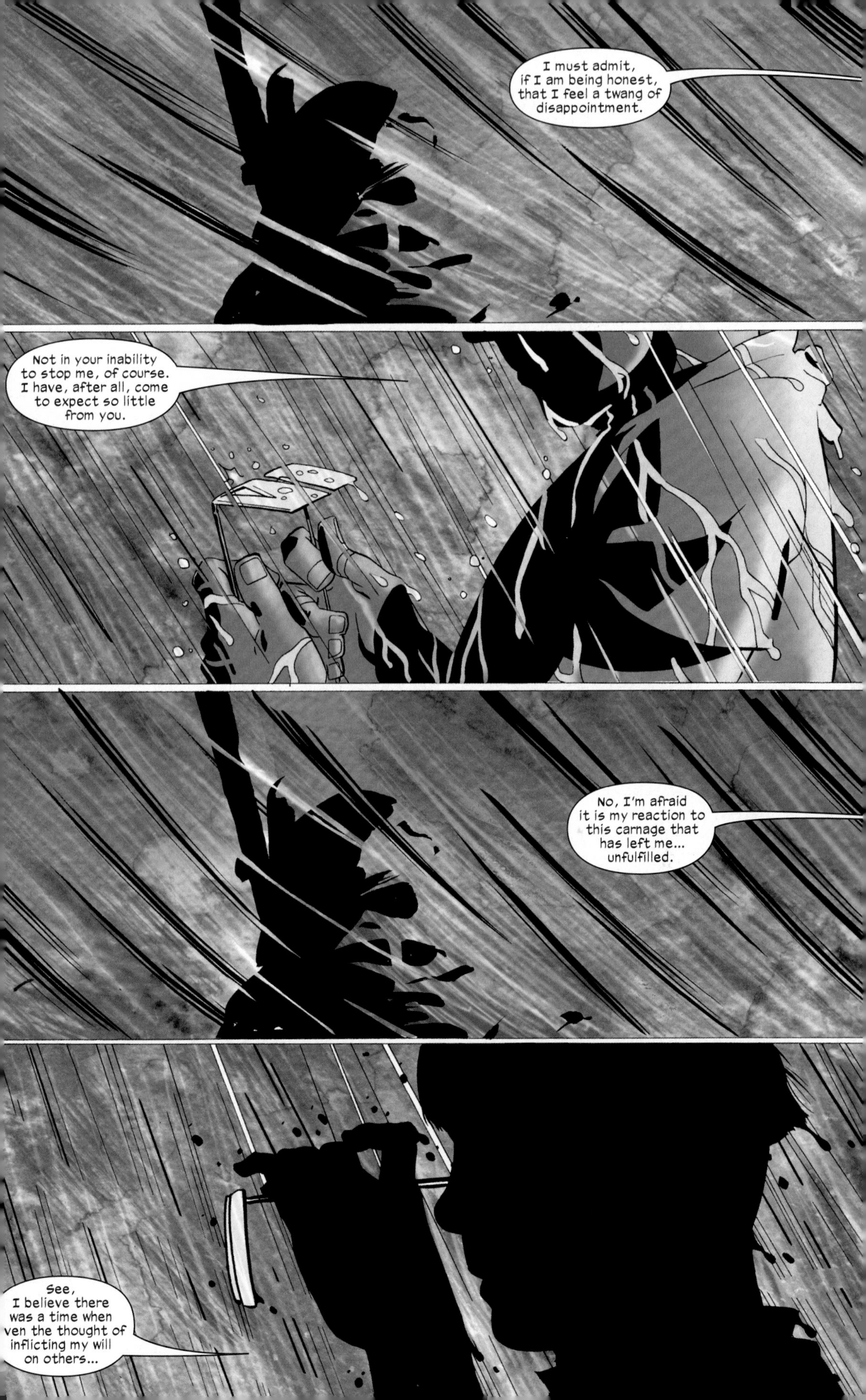
I must admit, if I am being honest, that I feel a twang of disappointment.
Not in your inability to stop me, of course. I have, after all, come to expect so little from you.
No, I'm afraid it is my reaction to this carnage that has left me... unfulfilled.
See, I believe there was a time when ven the thought of inflicting my will on others...

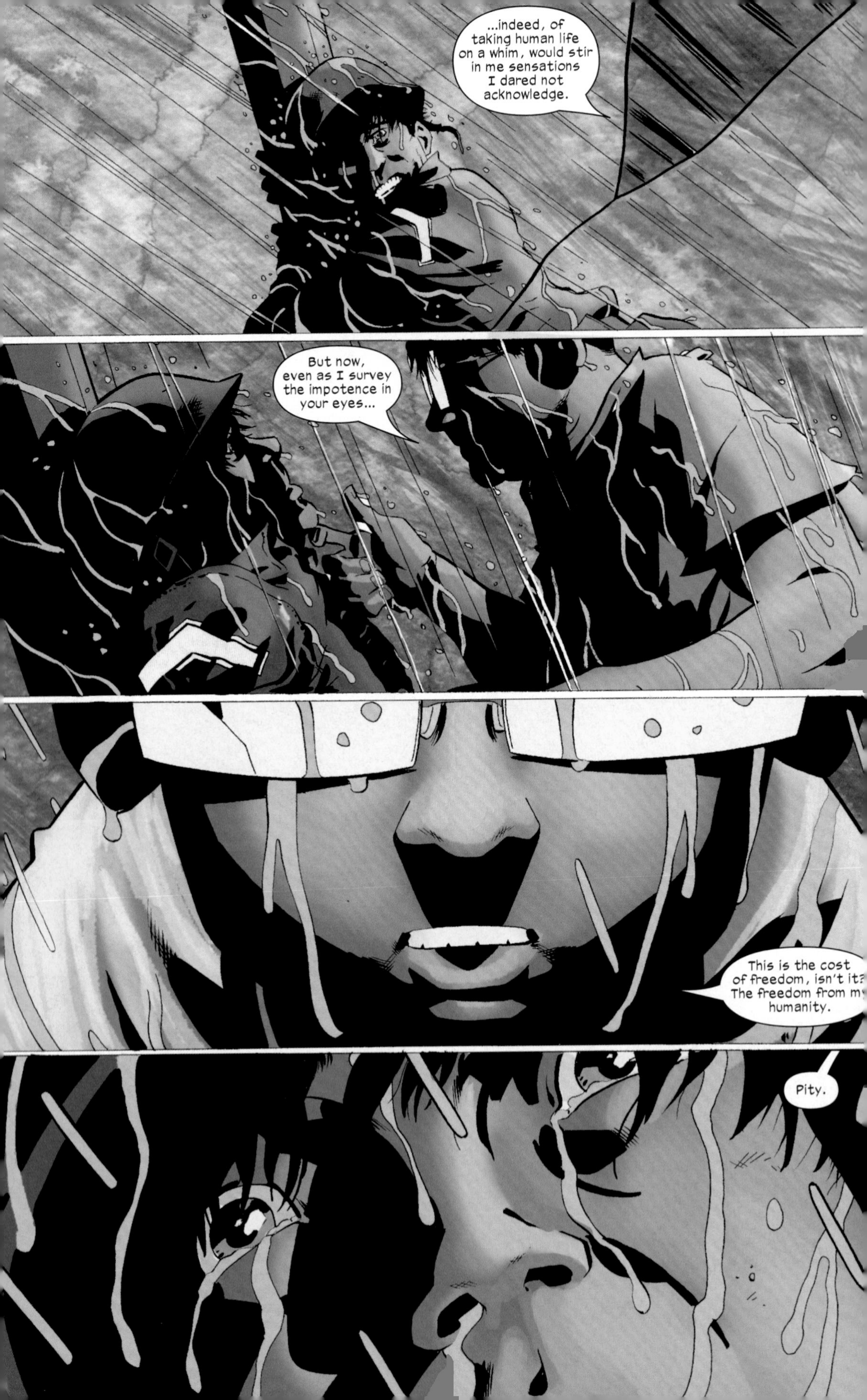
...indeed, of taking human life on a whim, would stir in me sensations I dared not acknowledge.
But now, even as I survey the impotence in your eyes...
This is the cost of freedom, isn't it? The freedom from my humanity.
Pity.

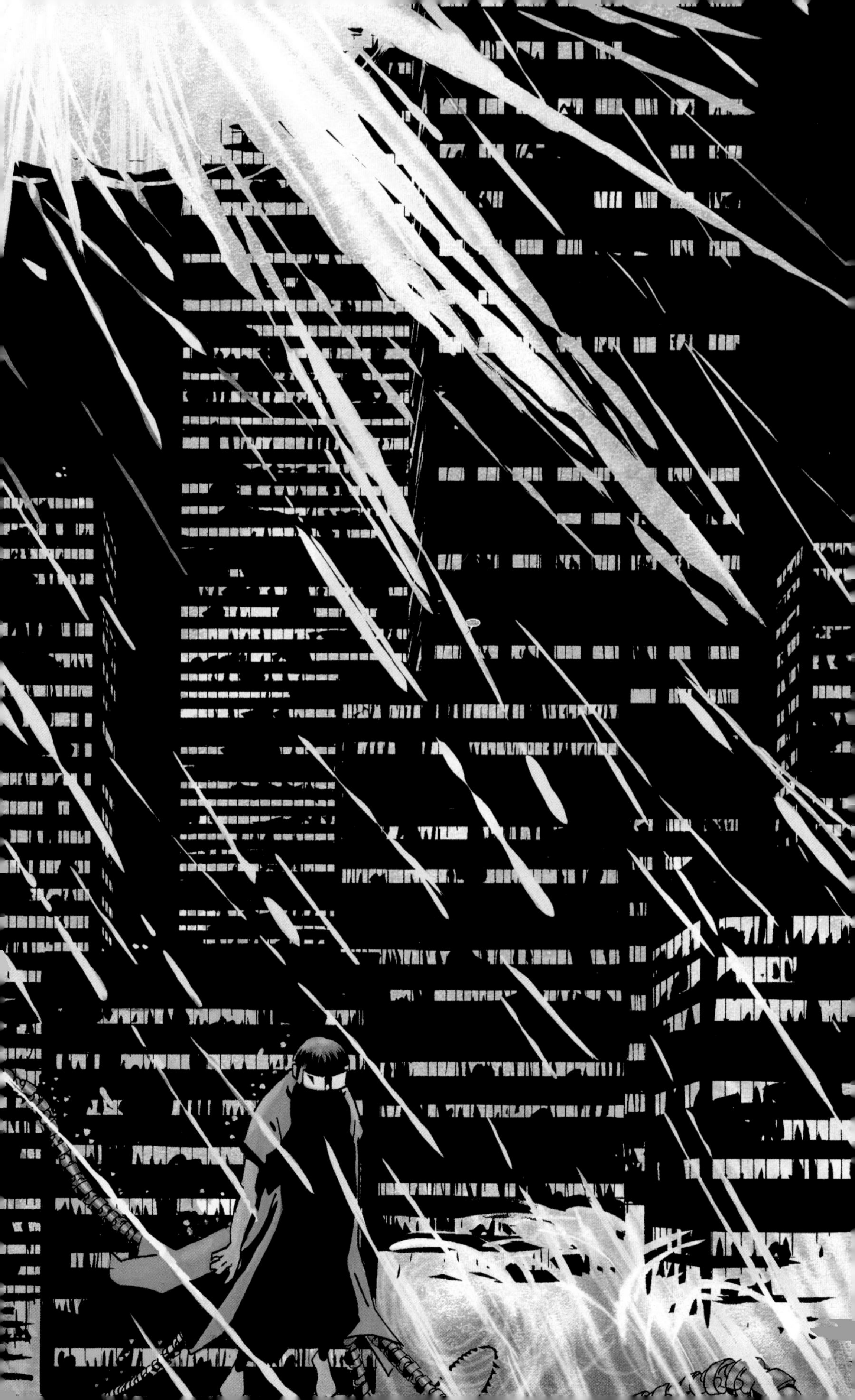

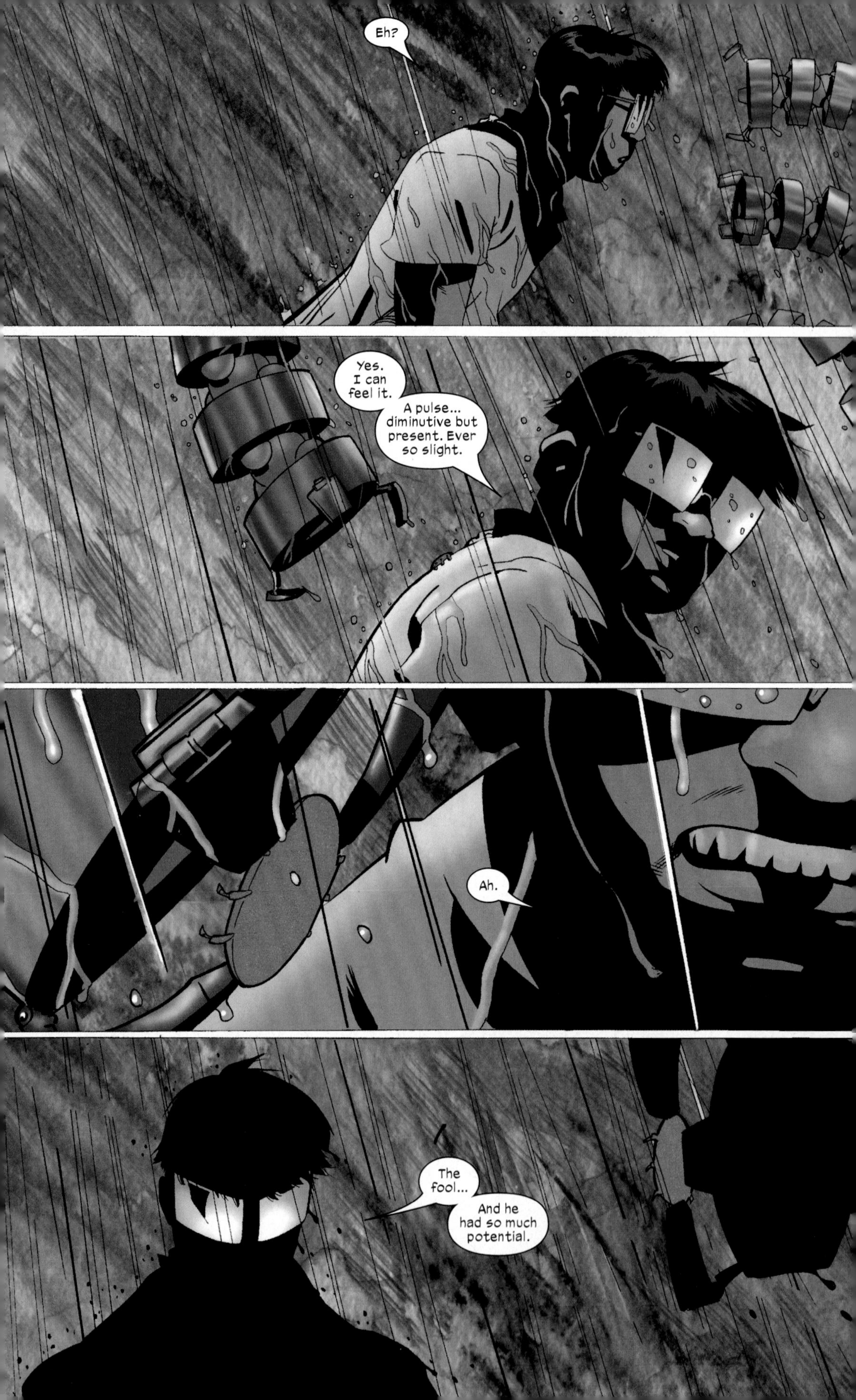
Eh?
Yes. I can feel it.
A pulse... diminutive but present. Ever so slight.
Ah.
The fool...
And he had so much potential.

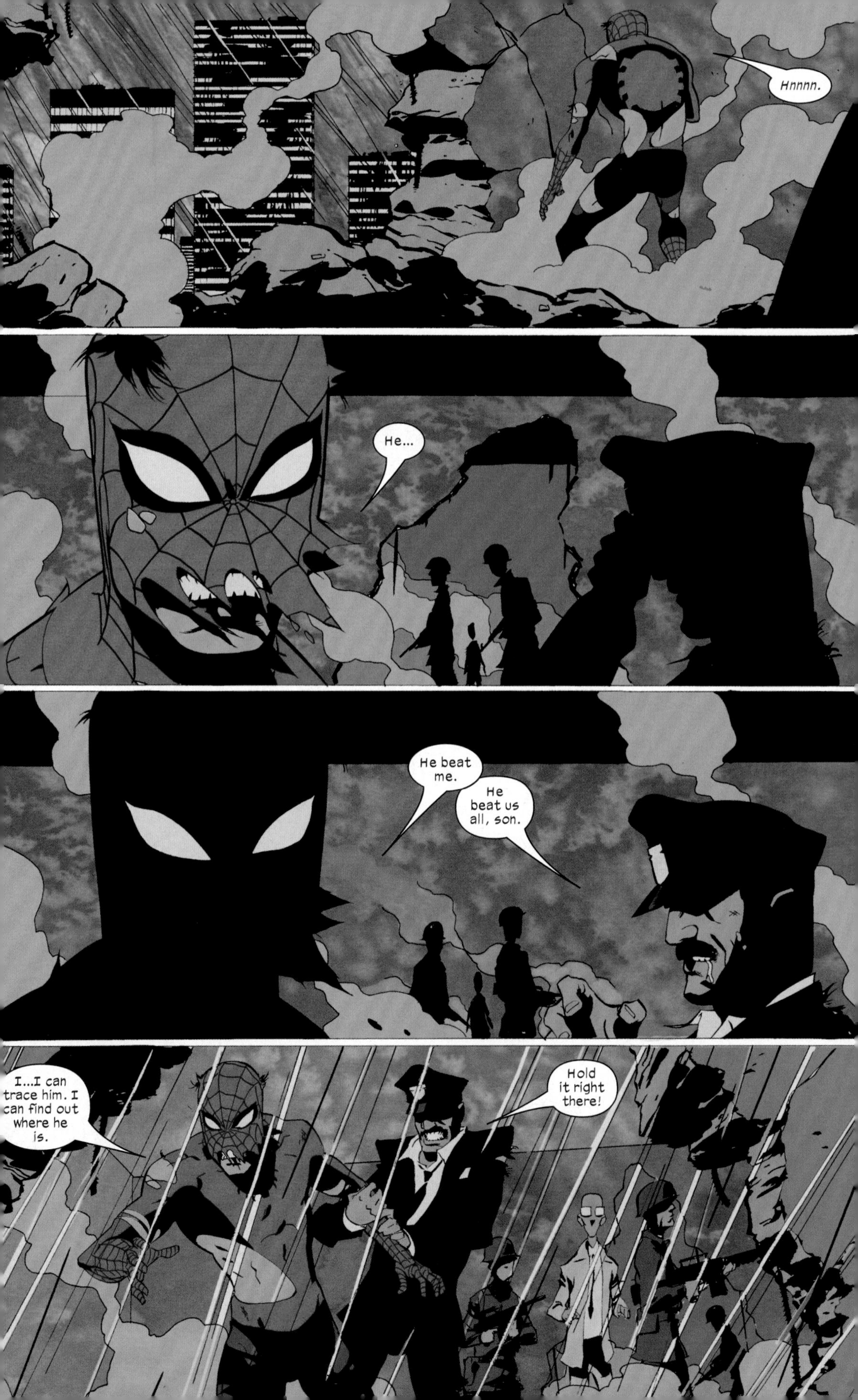
Hnnnn.
He...
He beat me.
He beat us all, son.
I...I can trace him. I can find out where he is.
Hold it right there!

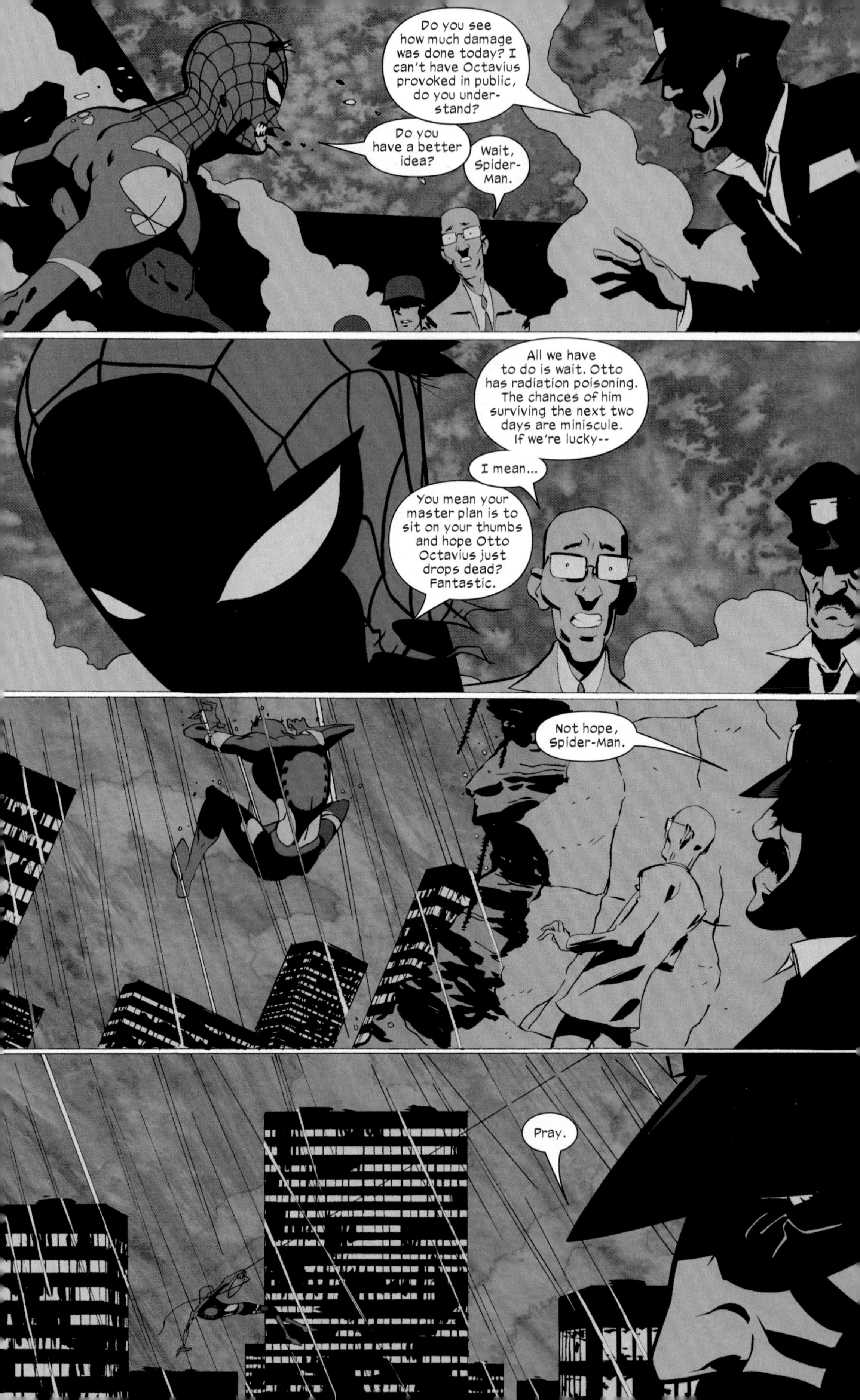
Do you see how much damage was done today? I can't have Octavius provoked in public, do you understand?
Do you have a better idea?
Wait, Spider-Man.
All we have to do is wait. Otto has radiation poisoning. The chances of him surviving the next two days are miniscule. If we're lucky--
I mean...
You mean your master plan is to sit on your thumbs and hope Otto Octavius just drops dead? Fantastic.
Not hope, Spider-Man.
Pray.

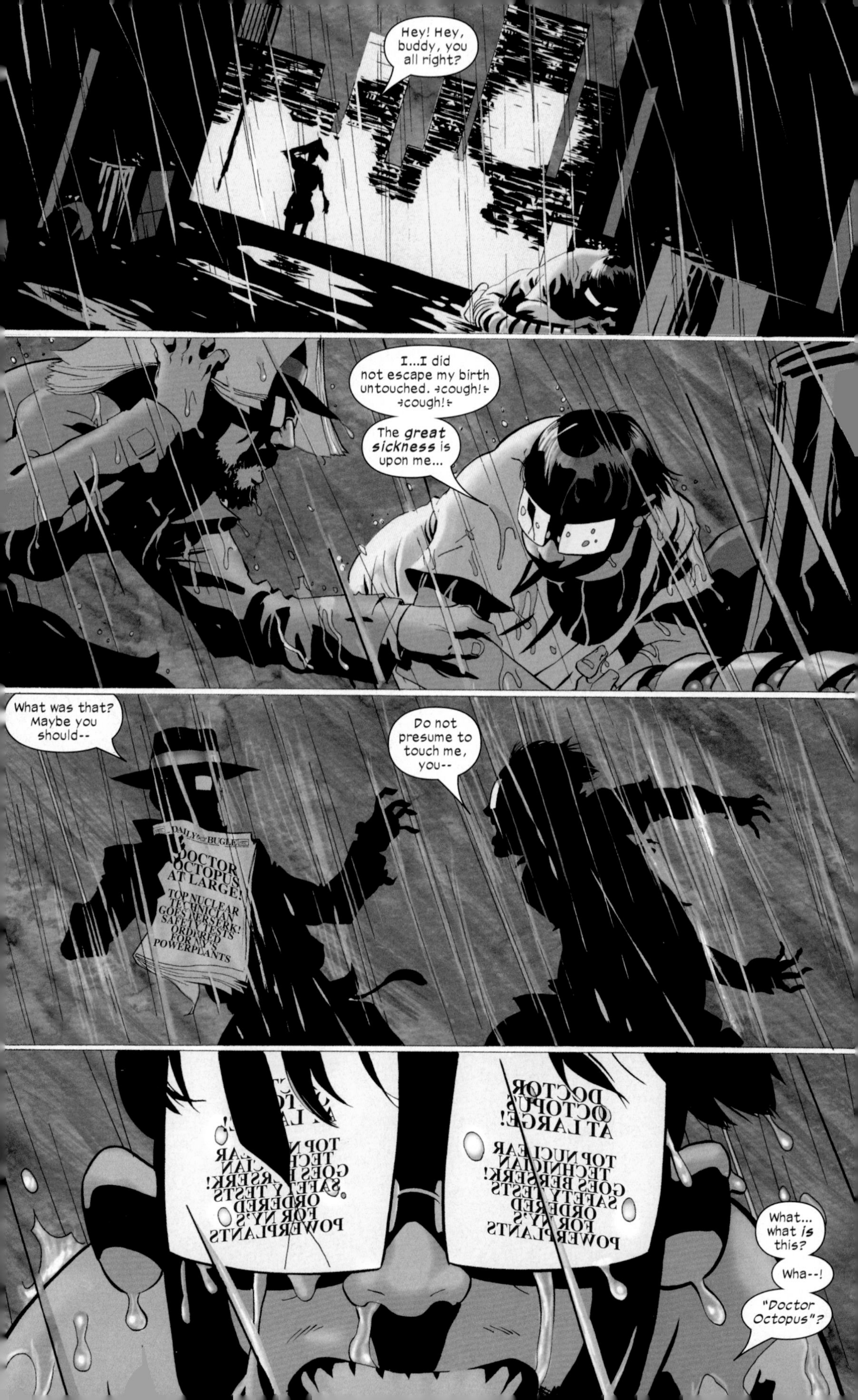
Hey! Hey, buddy, you all right?
I...I did not escape my birth untouched. ∻cough!∻ ∻cough!∻
The *great sickness* is upon me...
What was that? Maybe you should--
Do not presume to touch me, you--
DAILY BUGLE
DOCTOR OCTOPUS AT LARGE!
TOP NUCLEAR TECHNICIAN GOES BERSERK! SAFETY TESTS ORDERED FOR NY'S POWERPLANTS
What... what *is* this?
Wha--!
"*Doctor Octopus*"?

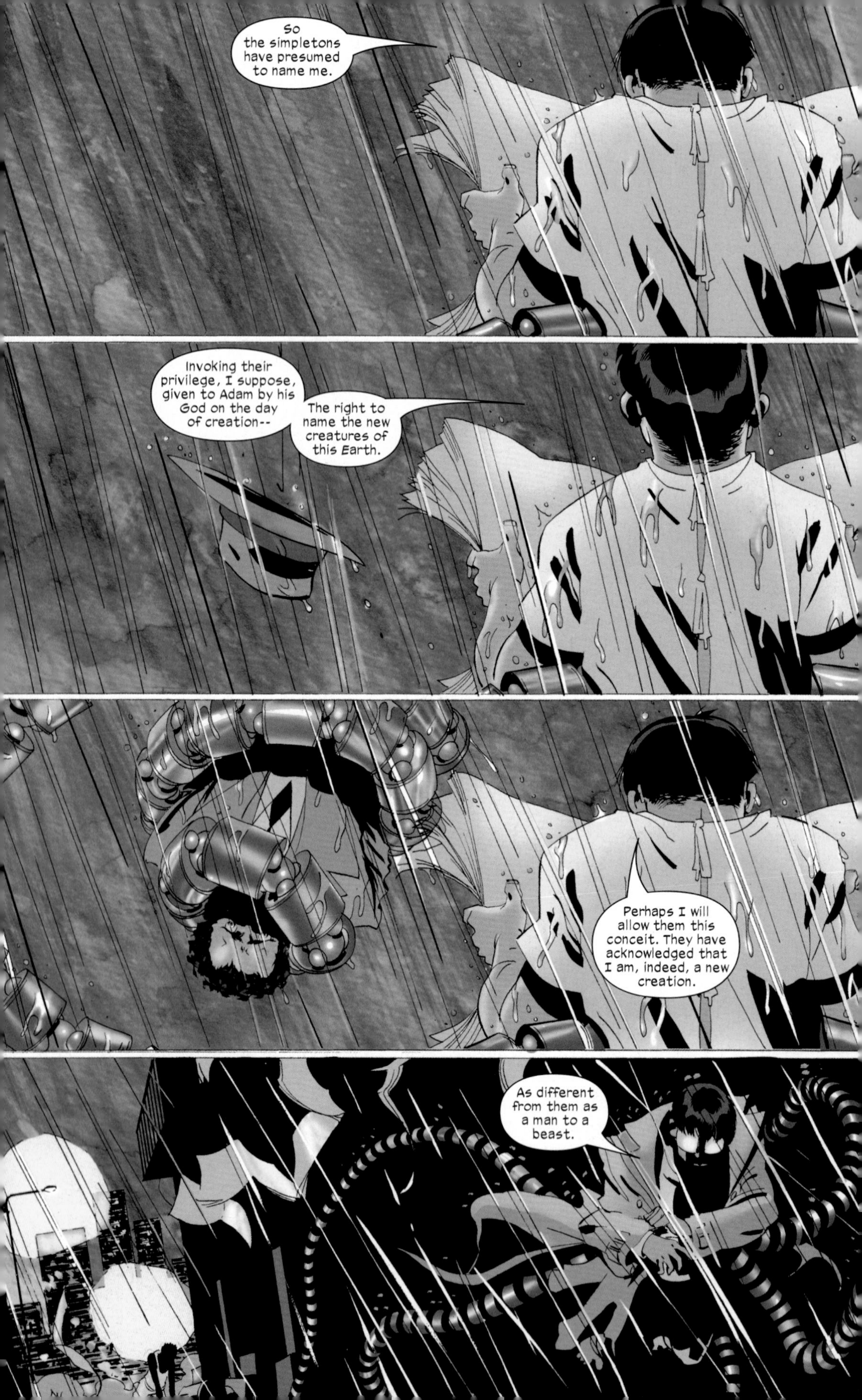
So the simpletons have presumed to name me.
Invoking their privilege, I suppose, given to Adam by his God on the day of creation--
The right to name the new creatures of this Earth.
Perhaps I will allow them this conceit. They have acknowledged that I am, indeed, a new creation.
As different from them as a man to a beast.

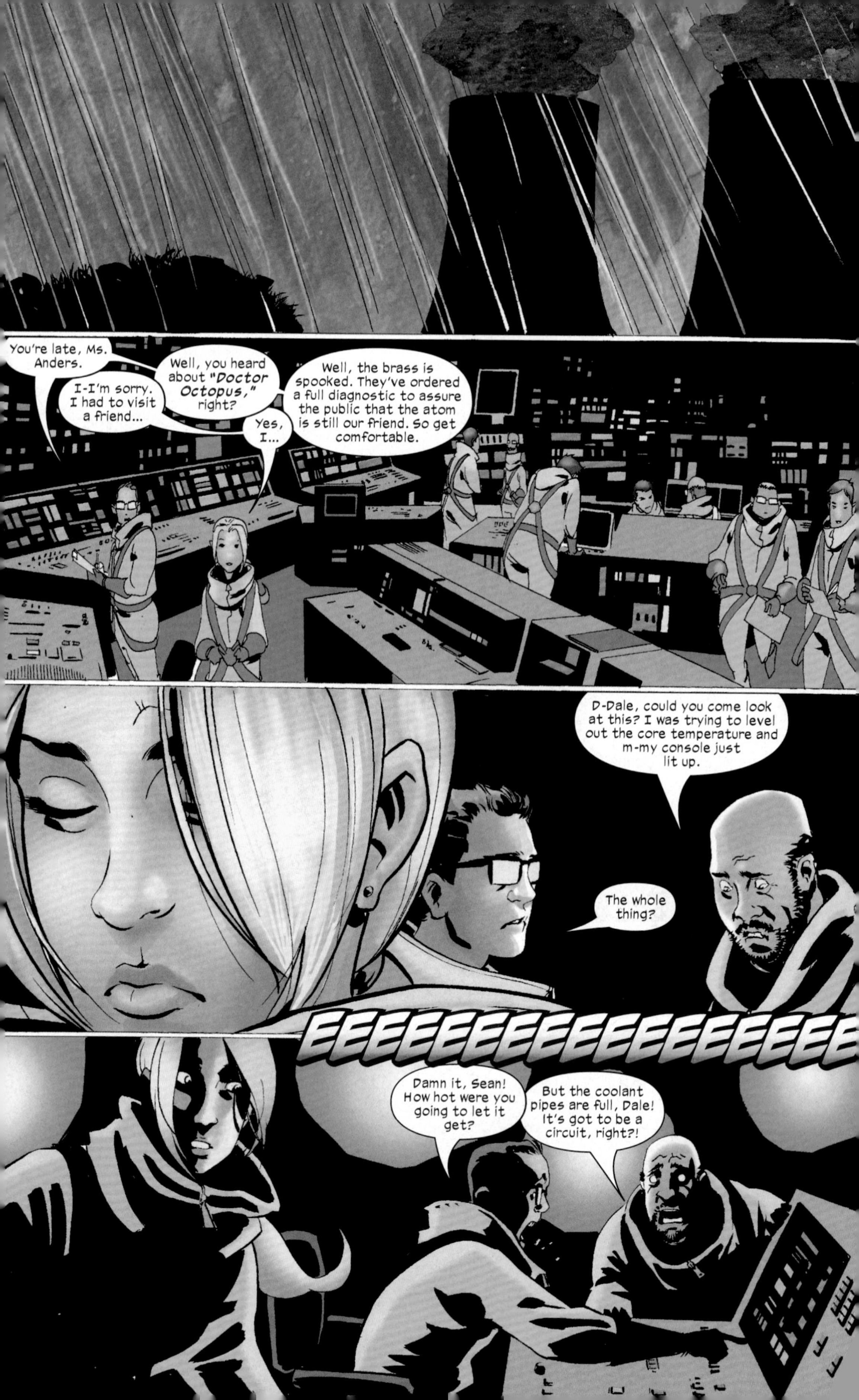
You're late, Ms. Anders.
I-I'm sorry. I had to visit a friend...
Well, you heard about "Doctor Octopus," right?
Yes, I...
Well, the brass is spooked. They've ordered a full diagnostic to assure the public that the atom is still our friend. So get comfortable.
D-Dale, could you come look at this? I was trying to level out the core temperature and m-my console just lit up.
The whole thing?
EEEEEEEEEEEEEEEEEEE
Damn it, Sean! How hot were you going to let it get?
But the coolant pipes are full, Dale! It's got to be a circuit, right?!

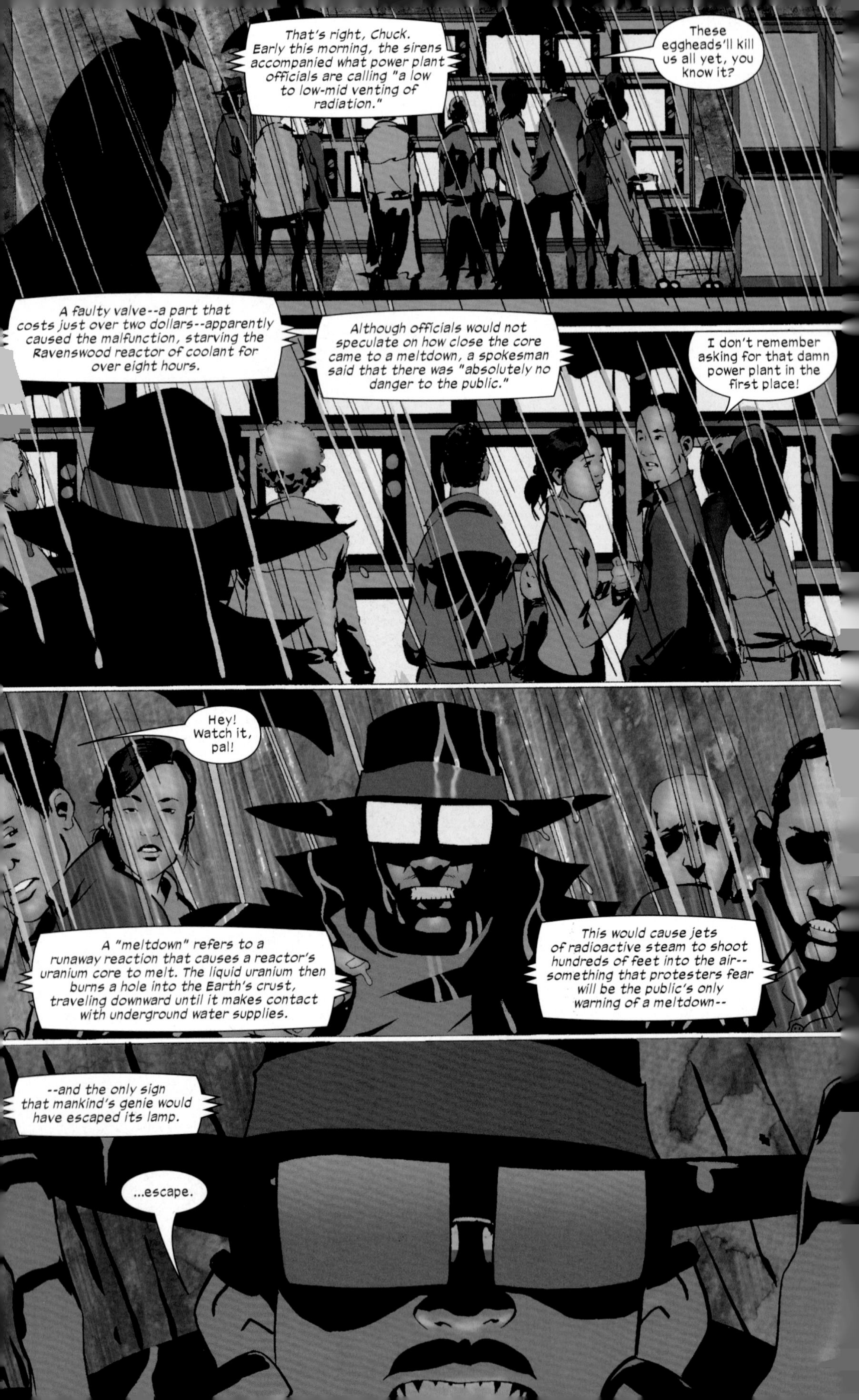
That's right, Chuck. Early this morning, the sirens accompanied what power plant officials are calling "a low to low-mid venting of radiation."
These eggheads'll kill us all yet, you know it?
A faulty valve--a part that costs just over two dollars--apparently caused the malfunction, starving the Ravenswood reactor of coolant for over eight hours.
Although officials would not speculate on how close the core came to a meltdown, a spokesman said that there was "absolutely no danger to the public."
I don't remember asking for that damn power plant in the first place!
Hey! Watch it, pal!
A "meltdown" refers to a runaway reaction that causes a reactor's uranium core to melt. The liquid uranium then burns a hole into the Earth's crust, traveling downward until it makes contact with underground water supplies.
This would cause jets of radioactive steam to shoot hundreds of feet into the air--something that protesters fear will be the public's only warning of a meltdown--
--and the only sign that mankind's genie would have escaped its lamp.
...escape.

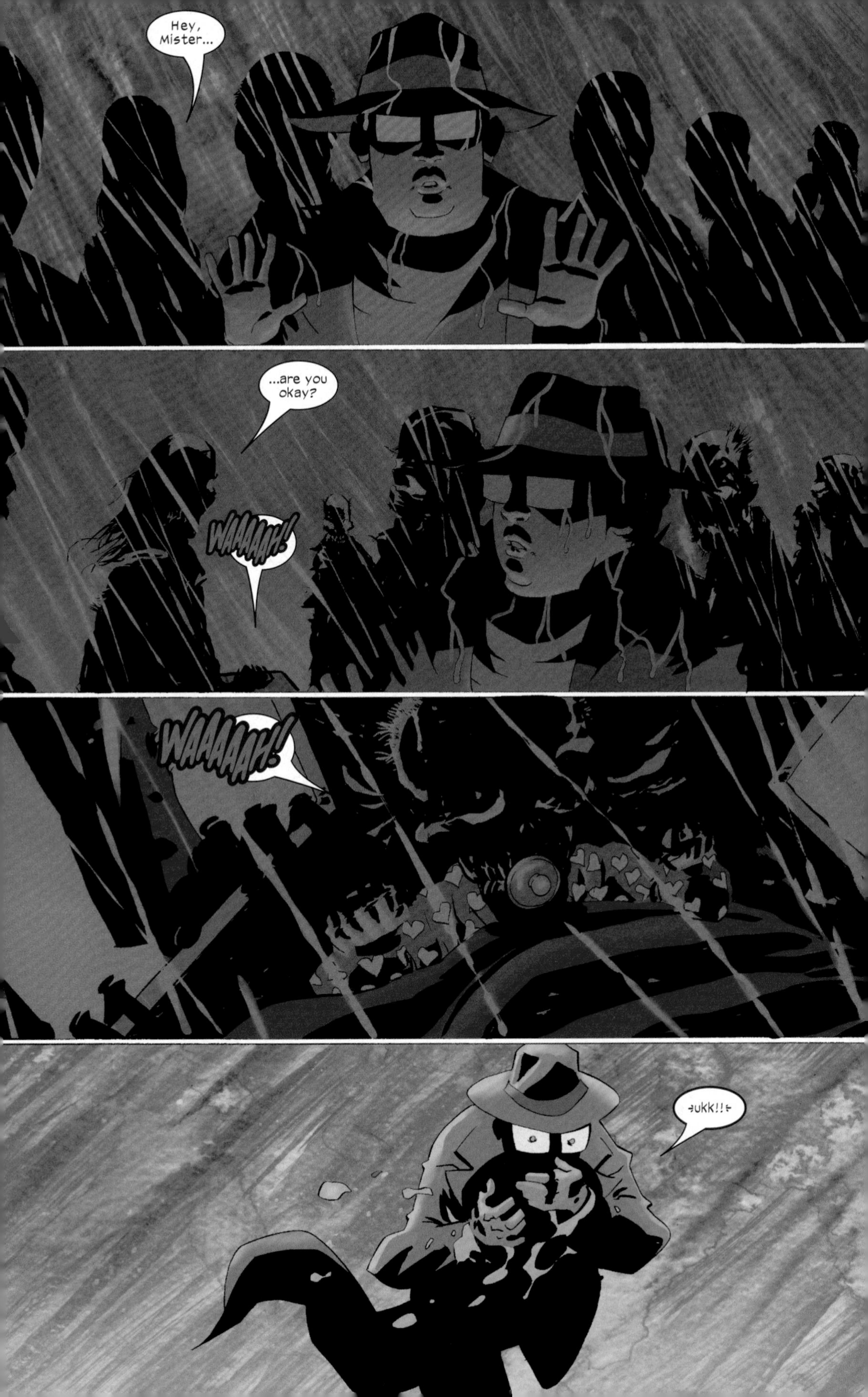

Hey, Mister...
...are you okay?
WAAAAAH!
WAAAAAH!
ukk!!

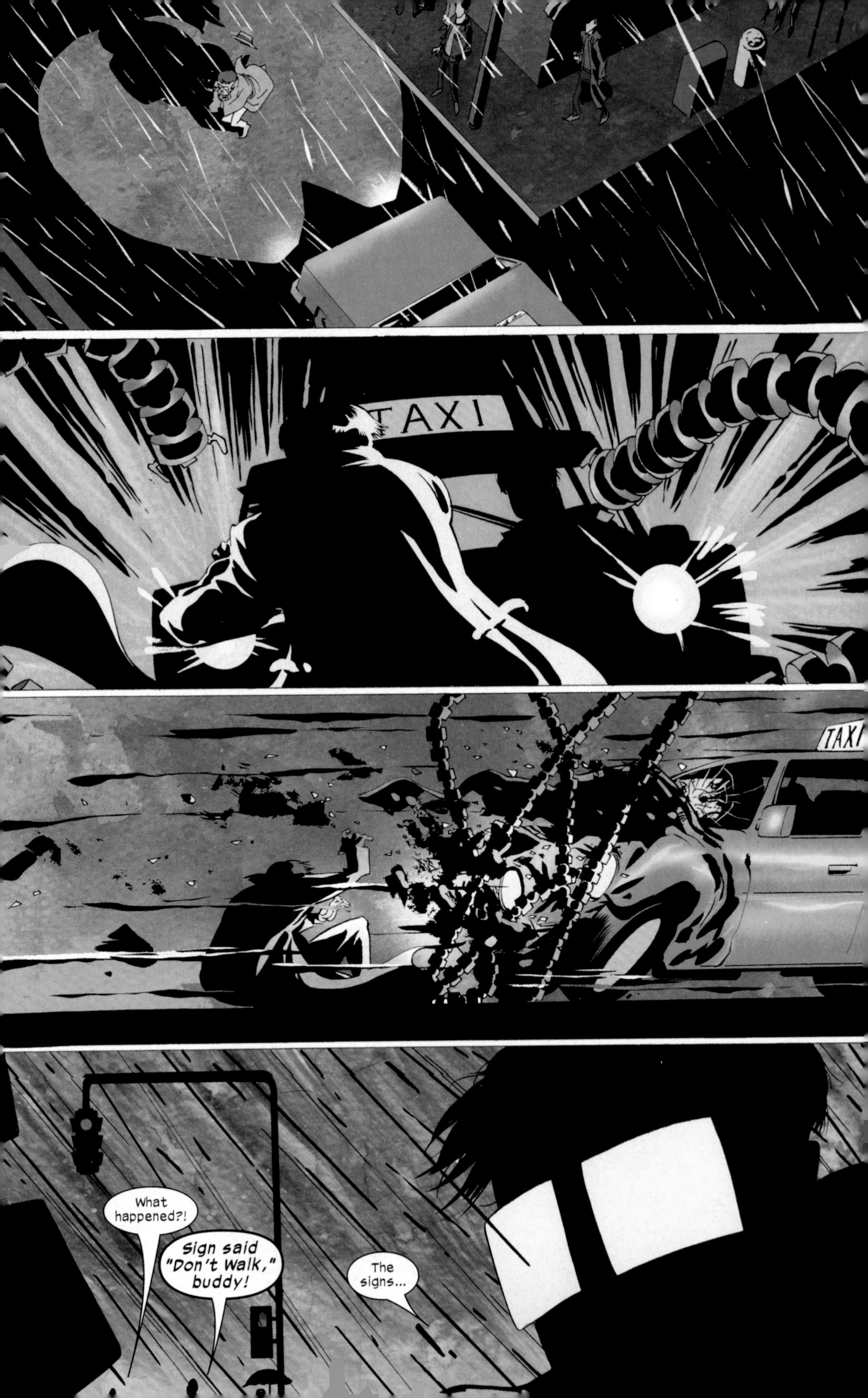
TAXI
TAXI
What happened?!
Sign said "Don't Walk," buddy!
The signs...

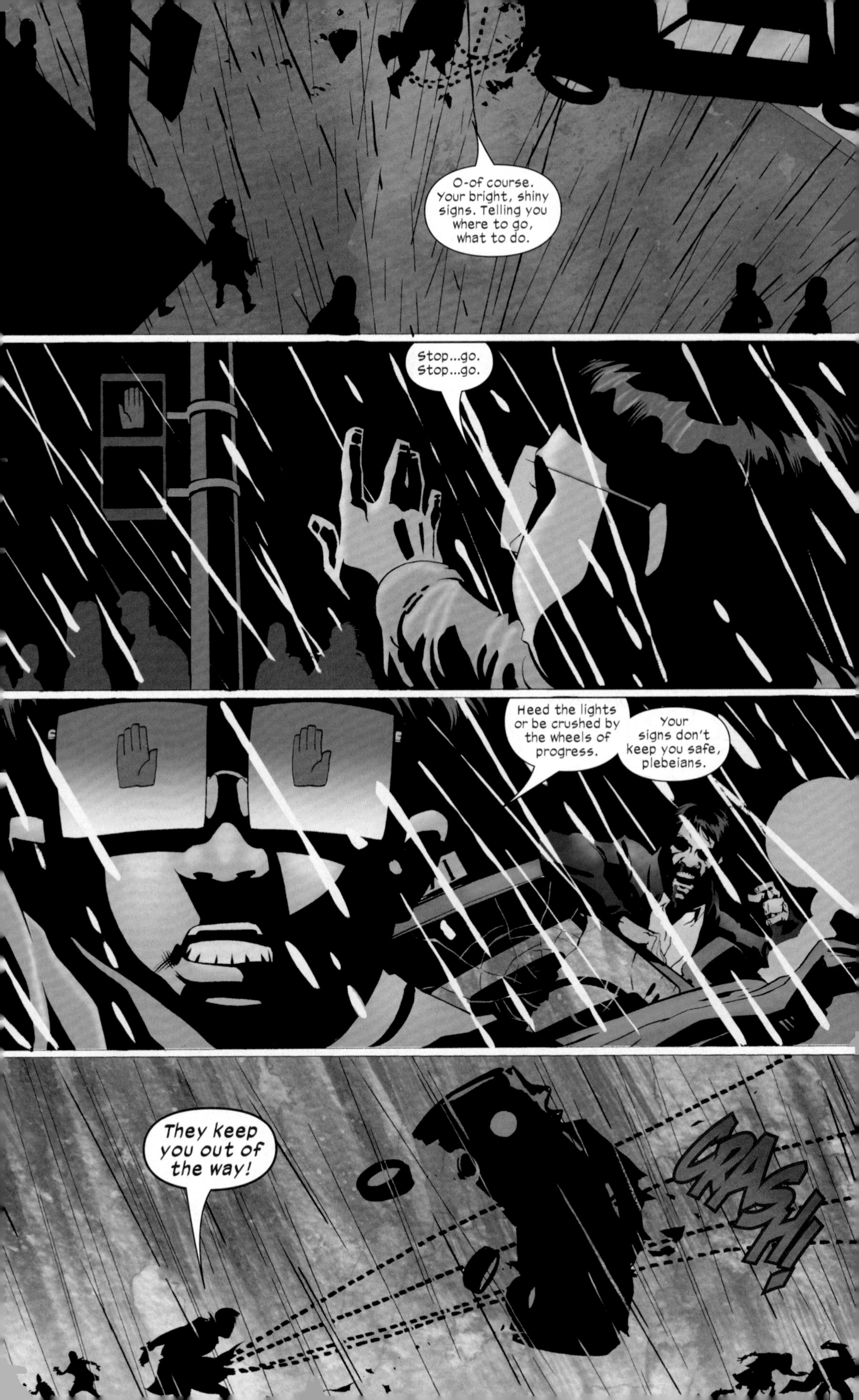
O-of course. Your bright, shiny signs. Telling you where to go, what to do.
Stop...go. Stop...go.
Heed the lights or be crushed by the wheels of progress.
Your signs don't keep you safe, plebeians.
They keep you out of the way!
CRASH!

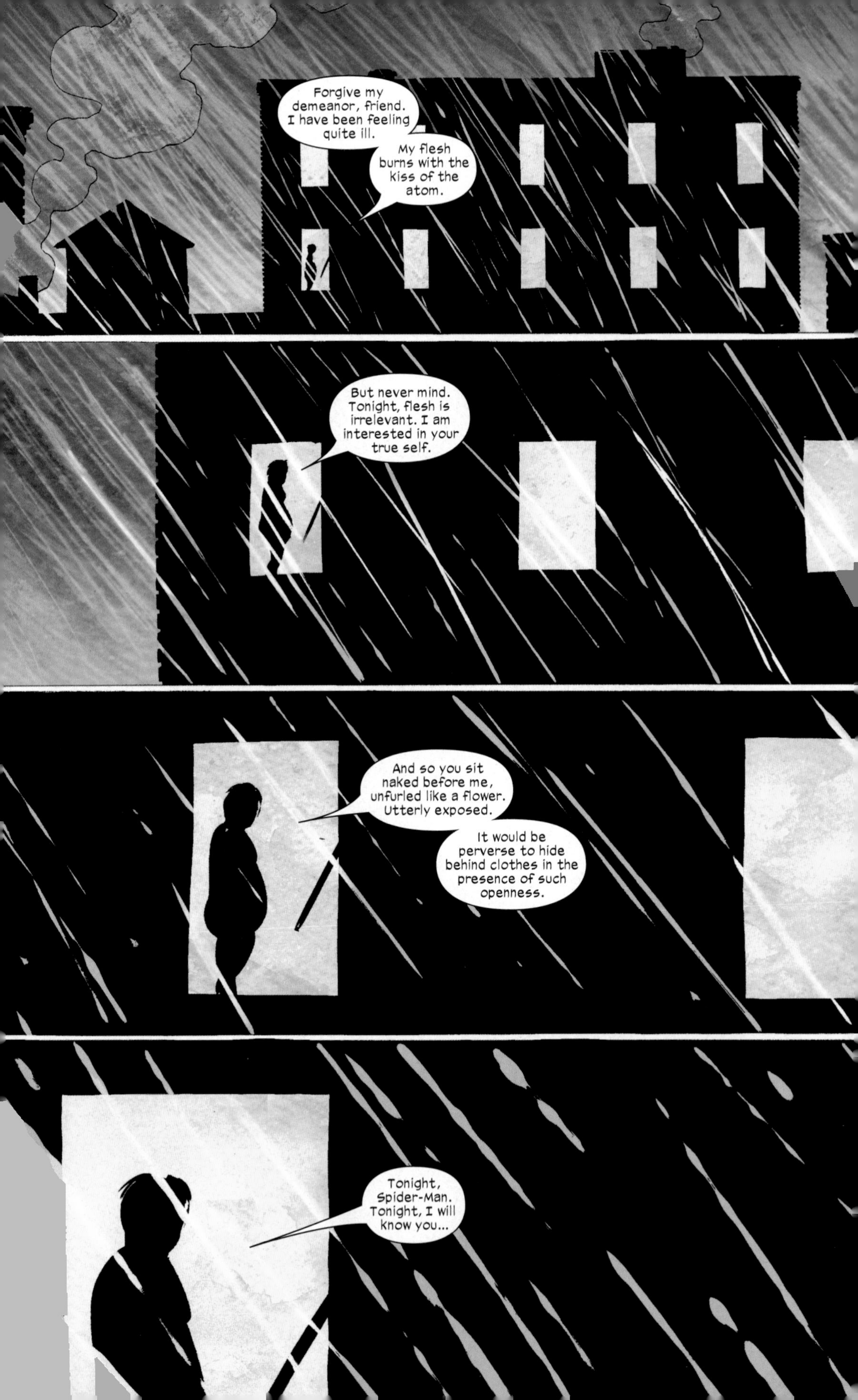
Forgive my demeanor, friend. I have been feeling quite ill.
My flesh burns with the kiss of the atom.
But never mind. Tonight, flesh is irrelevant. I am interested in your true self.
And so you sit naked before me, unfurled like a flower. Utterly exposed.
It would be perverse to hide behind clothes in the presence of such openness.
Tonight, Spider-Man. Tonight, I will know you...

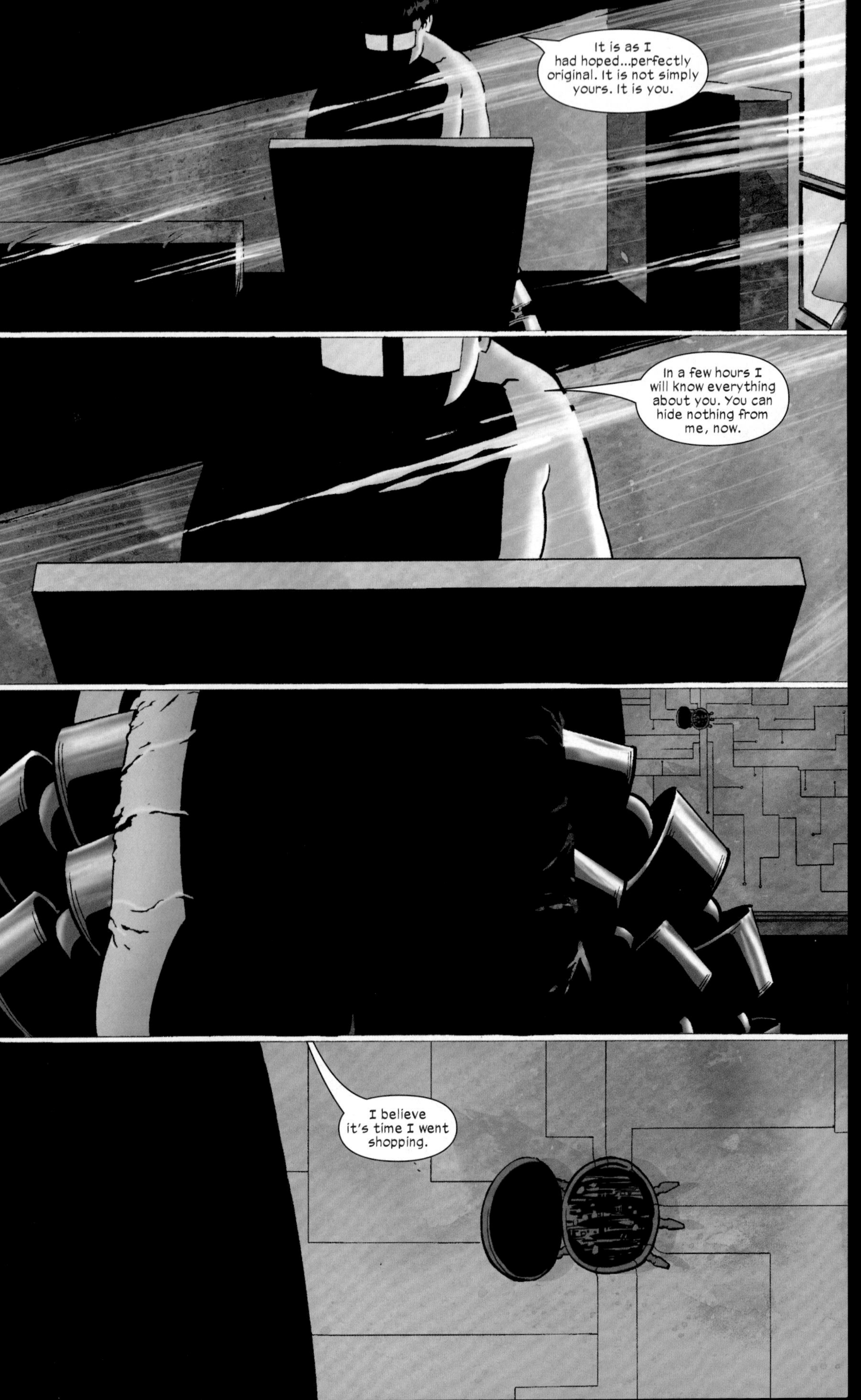
It is as I had hoped...perfectly original. It is not simply yours. It is you.
In a few hours I will know everything about you. You can hide nothing from me, now.
I believe it's time I went shopping.

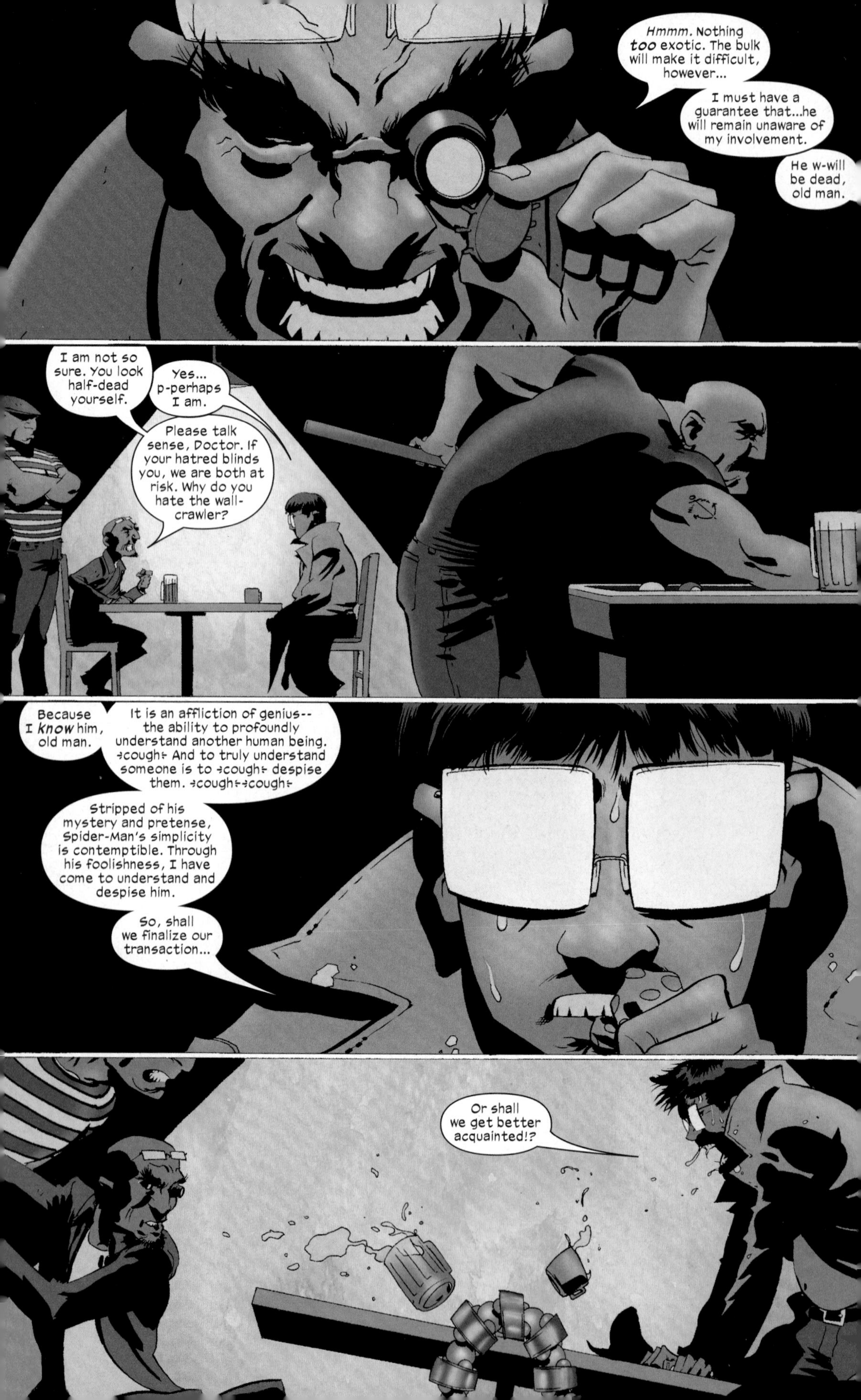
Hmmm. Nothing *too* exotic. The bulk will make it difficult, however...
I must have a guarantee that...he will remain unaware of my involvement.
He w-will be dead, old man.
I am not so sure. You look half-dead yourself.
Yes... p-perhaps I am.
Please talk sense, Doctor. If your hatred blinds you, we are both at risk. Why do you hate the wall-crawler?
Because I *know* him, old man.
It is an affliction of genius-- the ability to profoundly understand another human being. ‹cough› And to truly understand someone is to ‹cough› despise them. ‹cough›‹cough›
Stripped of his mystery and pretense, Spider-Man's simplicity is contemptible. Through his foolishness, I have come to understand and despise him.
So, shall we finalize our transaction...
Or shall we get better acquainted!?

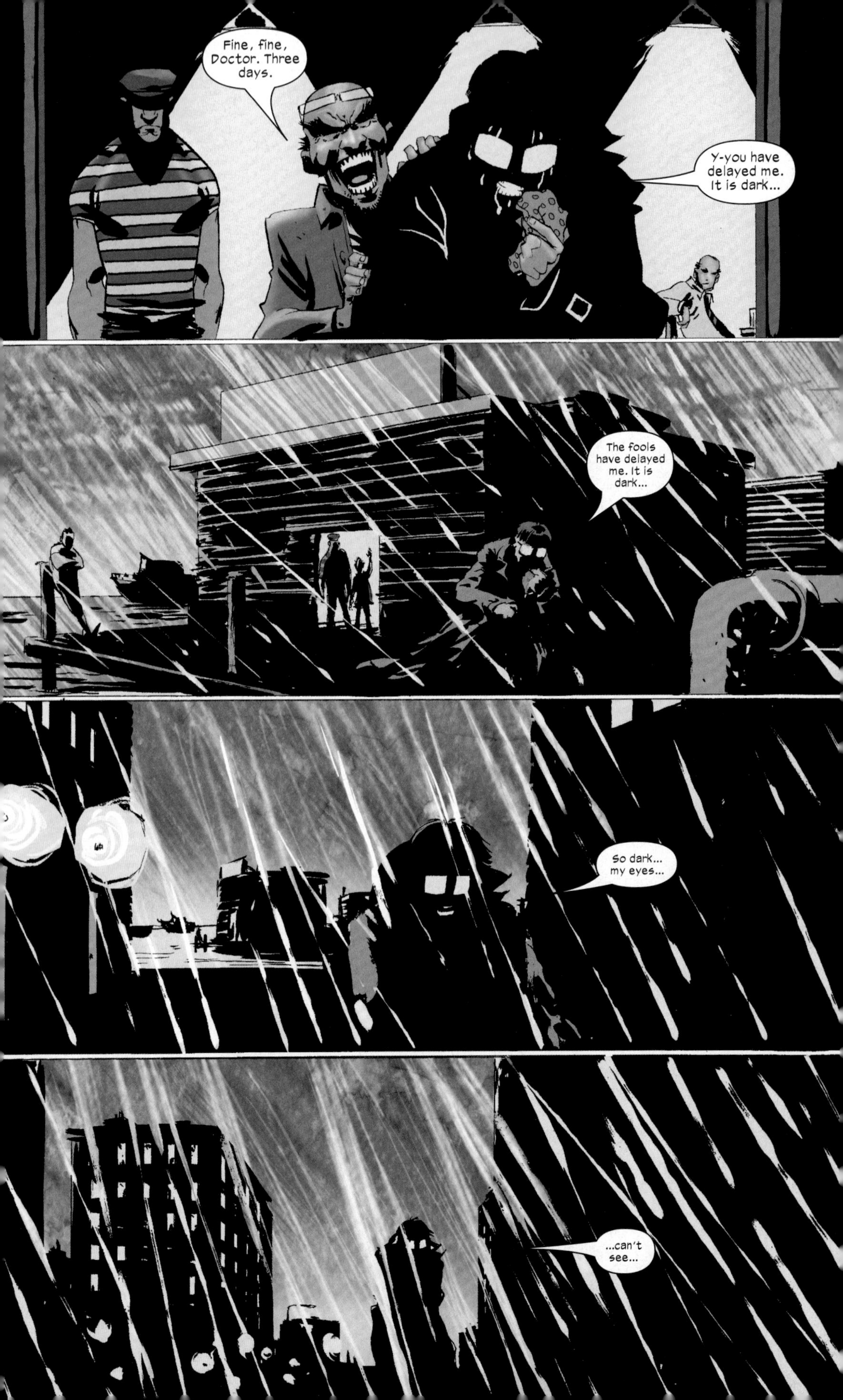
Fine, fine, Doctor. Three days.
Y-you have delayed me. It is dark...
The fools have delayed me. It is dark...
So dark... my eyes...
...can't see...

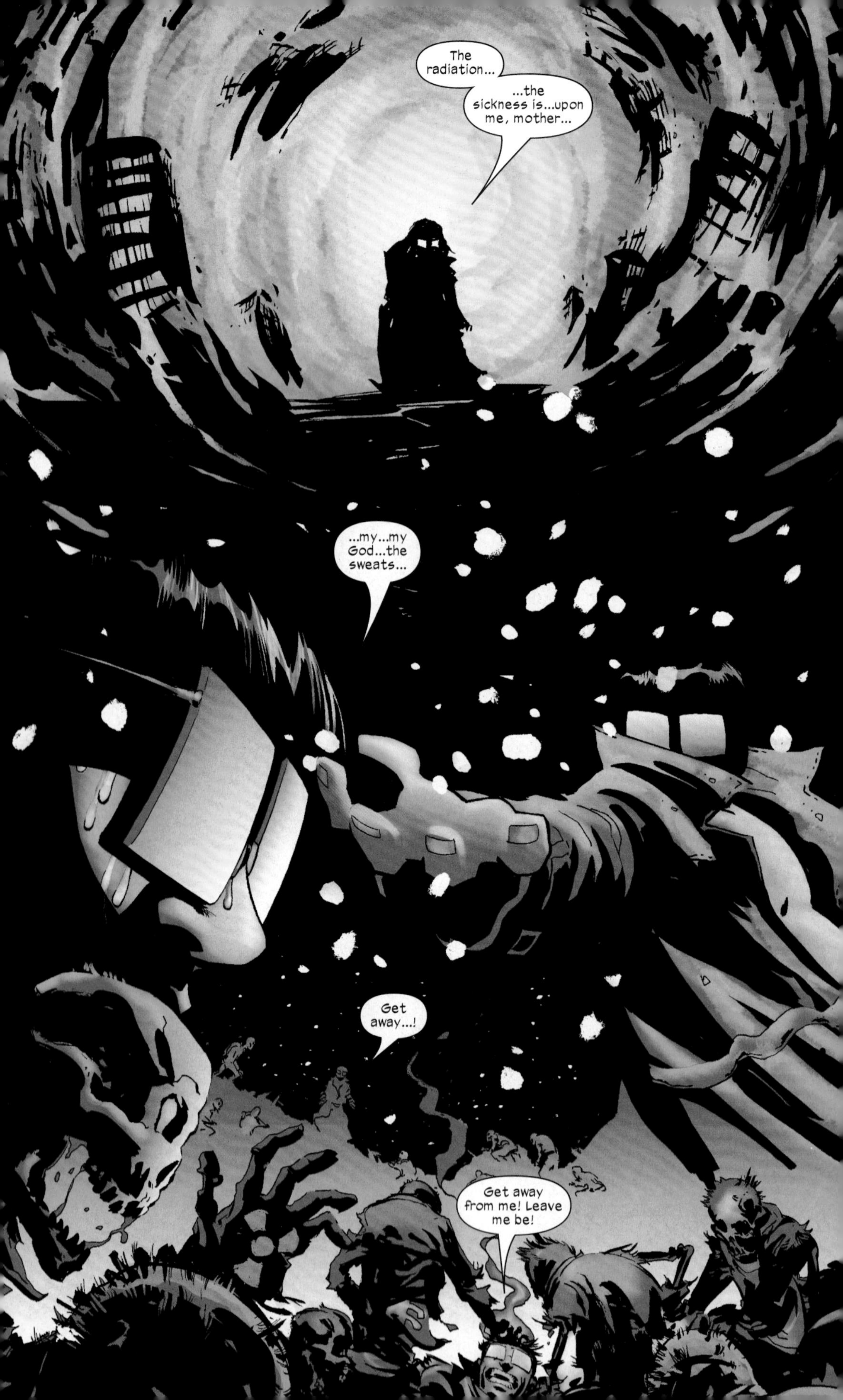
The radiation...
...the sickness is...upon me, mother...
...my...my God...the sweats...
Get away...!
Get away from me! Leave me be!

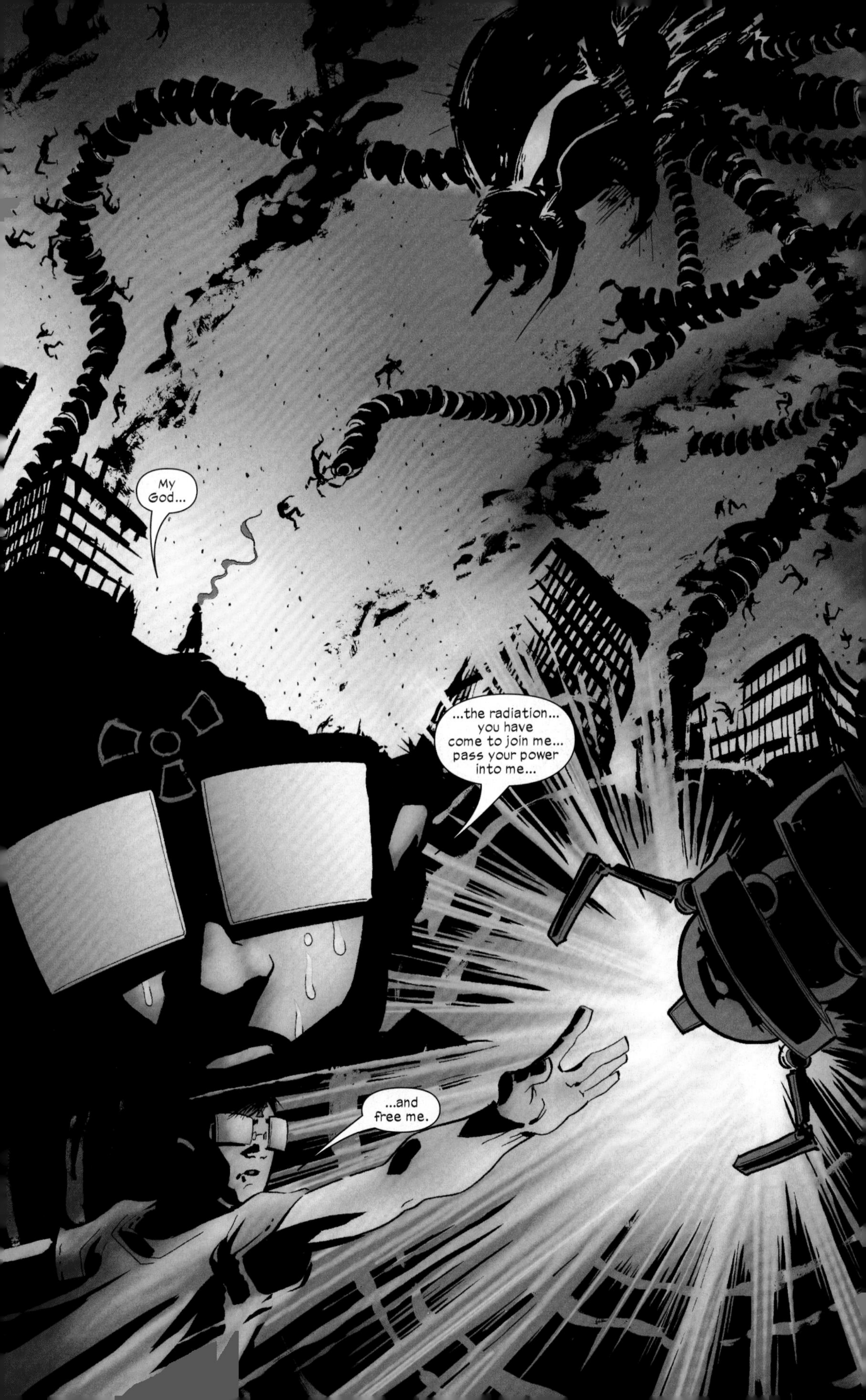
My God...
...the radiation... you have come to join me... pass your power into me...
...and free me.

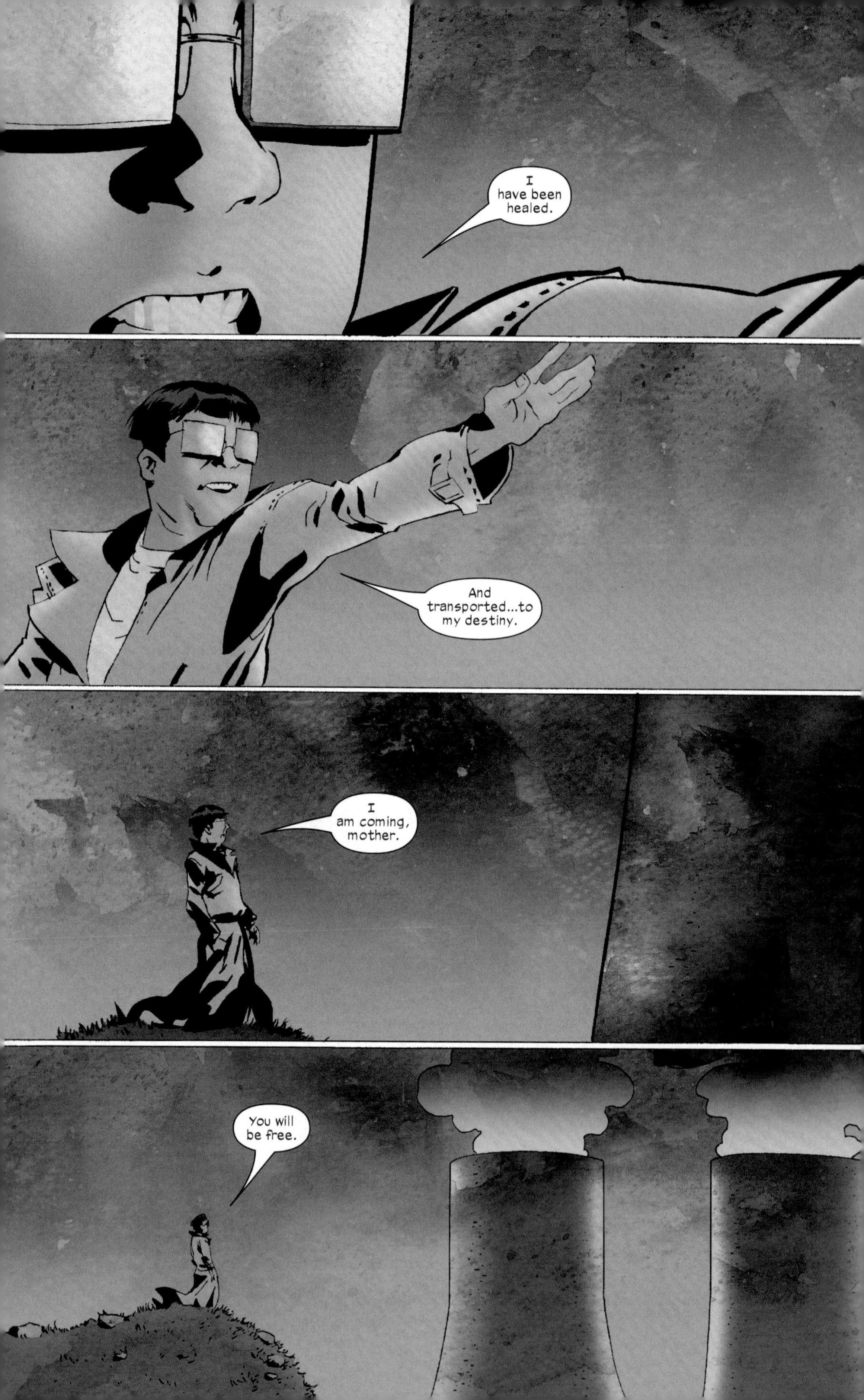
I have been healed.
And transported...to my destiny.
I am coming, mother.
You will be free.

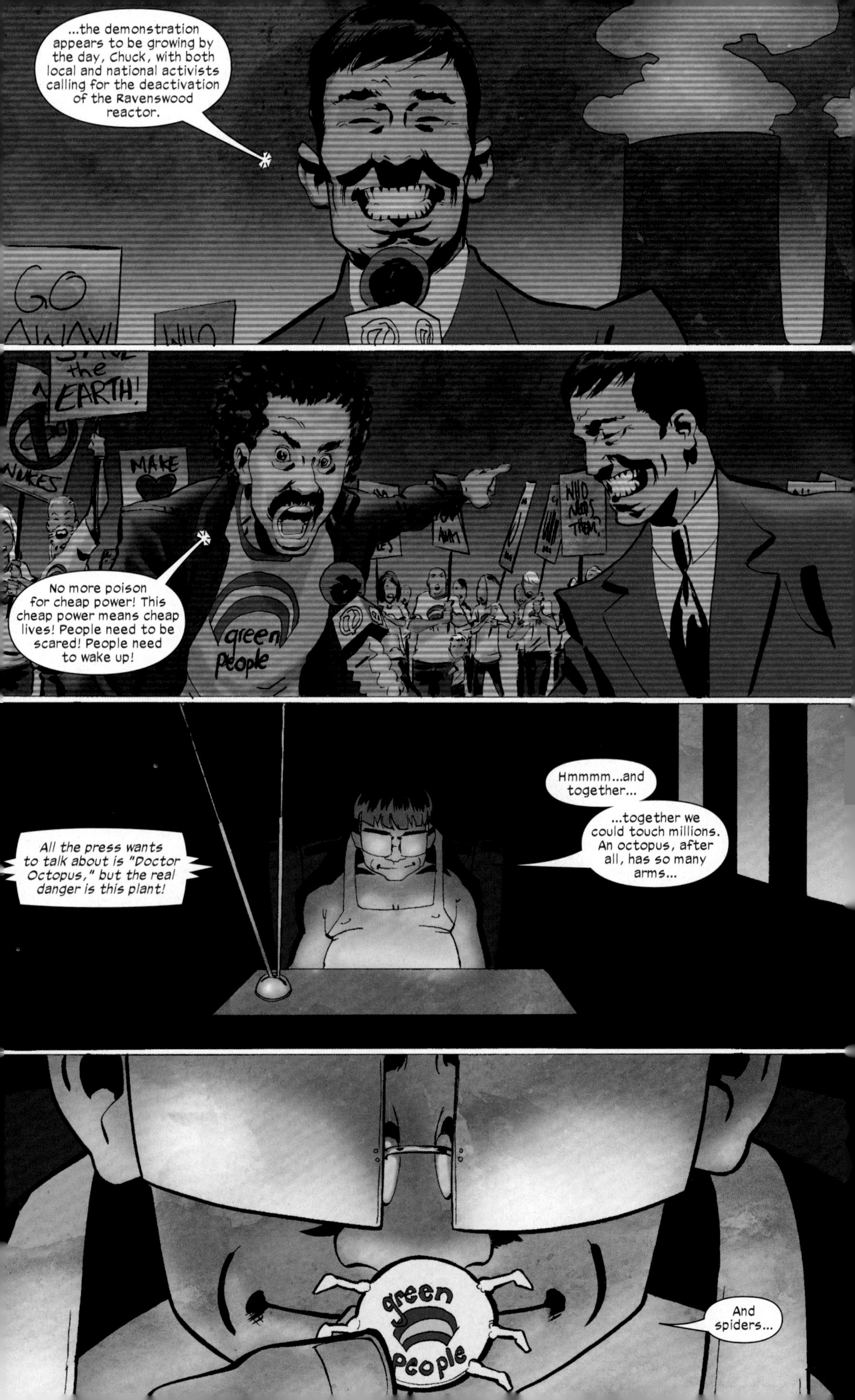
...the demonstration appears to be growing by the day, Chuck, with both local and national activists calling for the deactivation of the Ravenswood reactor.
GO AWAY!
SAVE the EARTH!
NUKES
MAKE
No more poison for cheap power! This cheap power means cheap lives! People need to be scared! People need to wake up!
green people
WHO NEEDS THEM?
All the press wants to talk about is "Doctor Octopus," but the real danger is this plant!
Hmmmm...and together...
...together we could touch millions. An octopus, after all, has so many arms...
green people
And spiders...

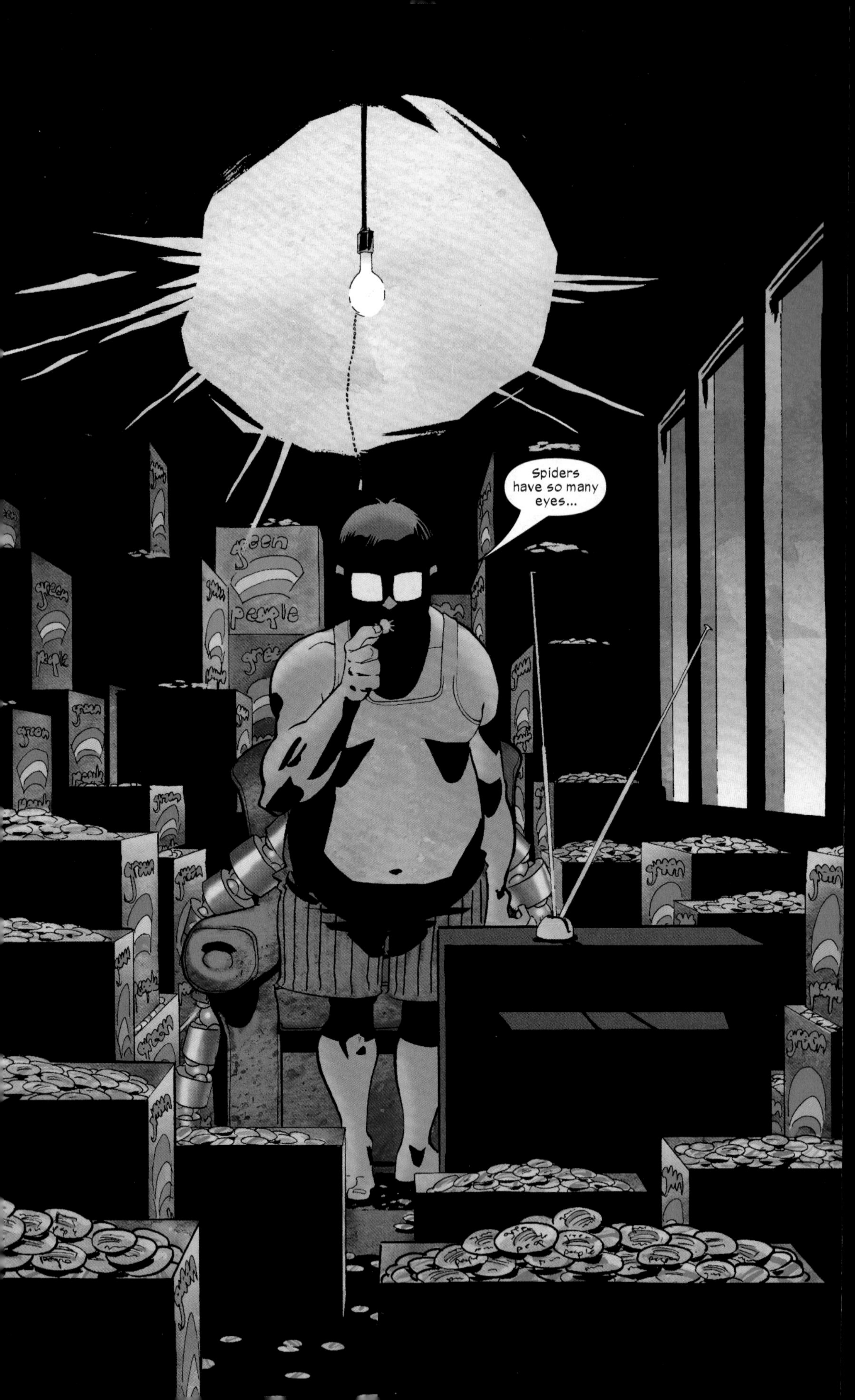
Spiders have so many eyes...
green people

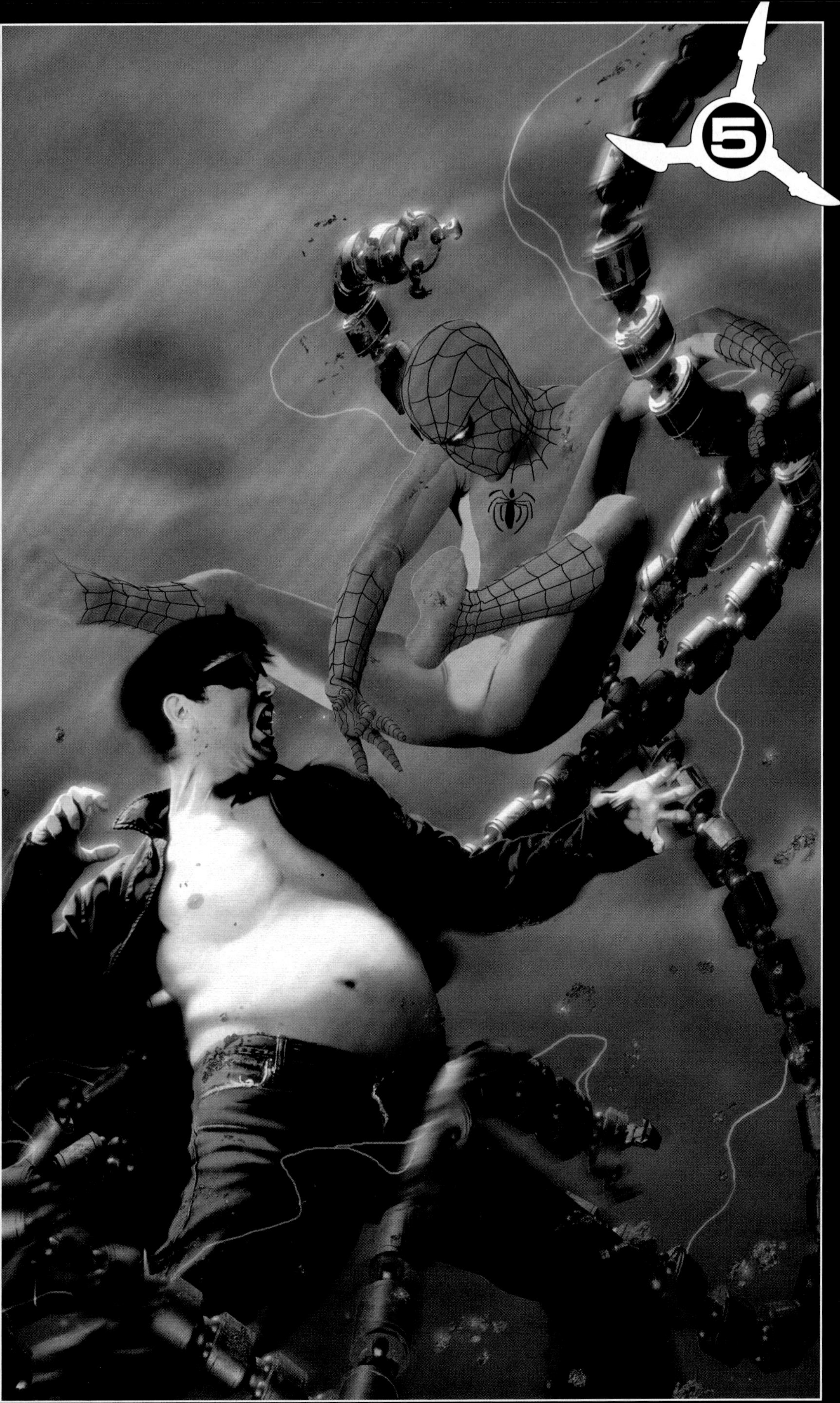
5

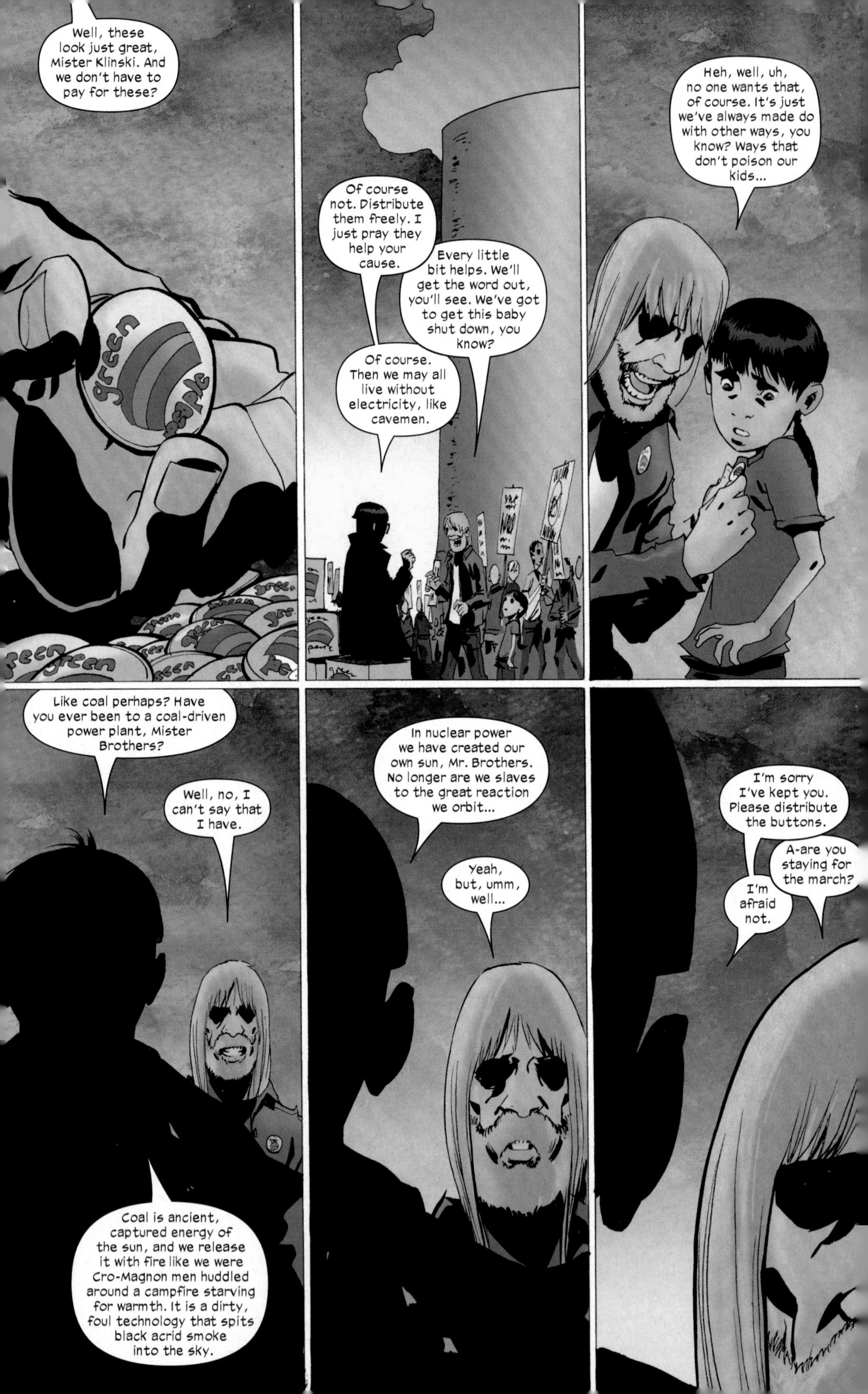
Well, these look just great, Mister Klinski. And we don't have to pay for these?
green people
Of course not. Distribute them freely. I just pray they help your cause.
Every little bit helps. We'll get the word out, you'll see. We've got to get this baby shut down, you know?
Of course. Then we may all live without electricity, like cavemen.
Heh, well, uh, no one wants that, of course. It's just we've always made do with other ways, you know? Ways that don't poison our kids...
Like coal perhaps? Have you ever been to a coal-driven power plant, Mister Brothers?
Well, no, I can't say that I have.
Coal is ancient, captured energy of the sun, and we release it with fire like we were Cro-Magnon men huddled around a campfire starving for warmth. It is a dirty, foul technology that spits black acrid smoke into the sky.
In nuclear power we have created our own sun, Mr. Brothers. No longer are we slaves to the great reaction we orbit...
Yeah, but, umm, well...
I'm sorry I've kept you. Please distribute the buttons.
A-are you staying for the march?
I'm afraid not.

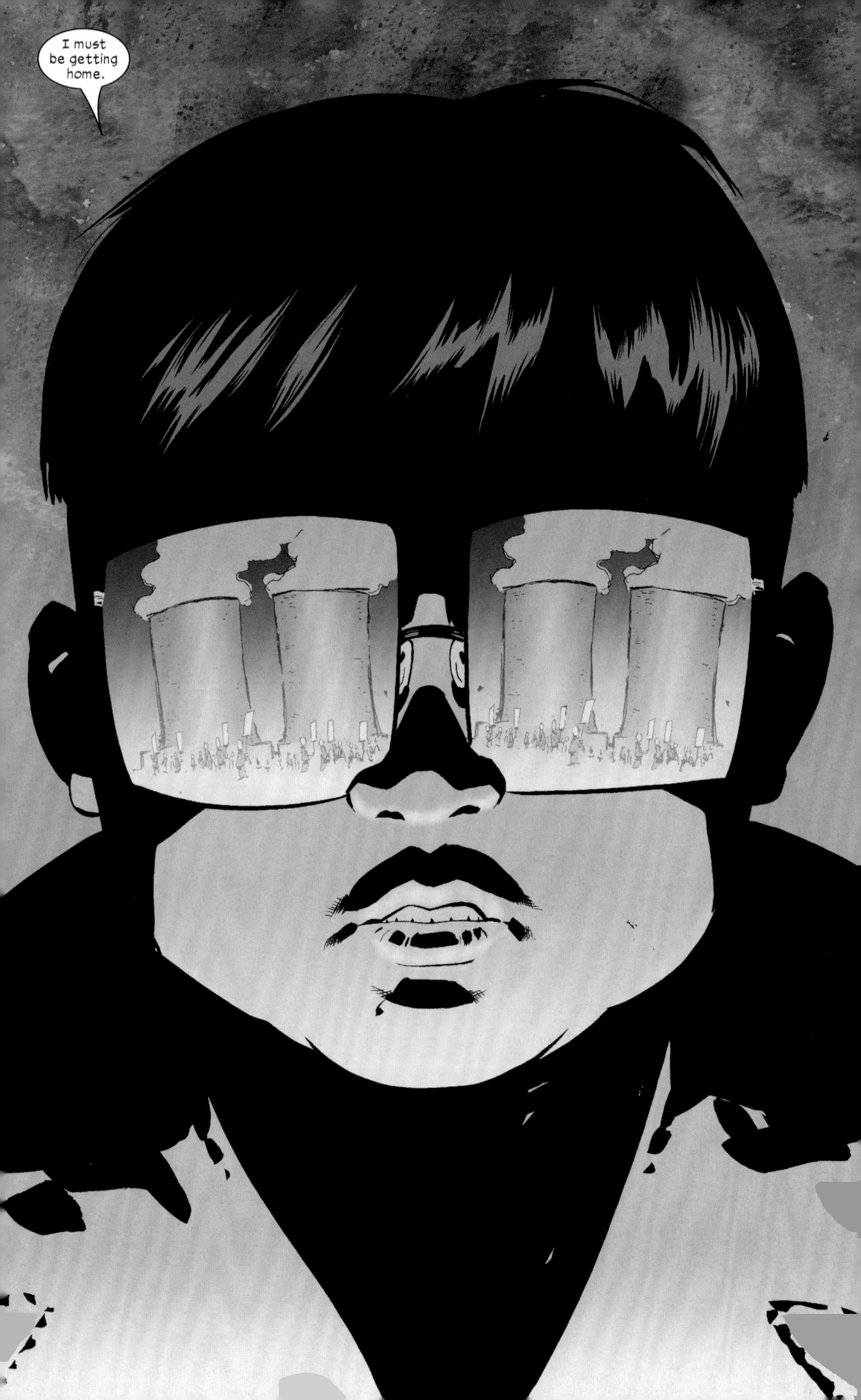
I must be getting home.

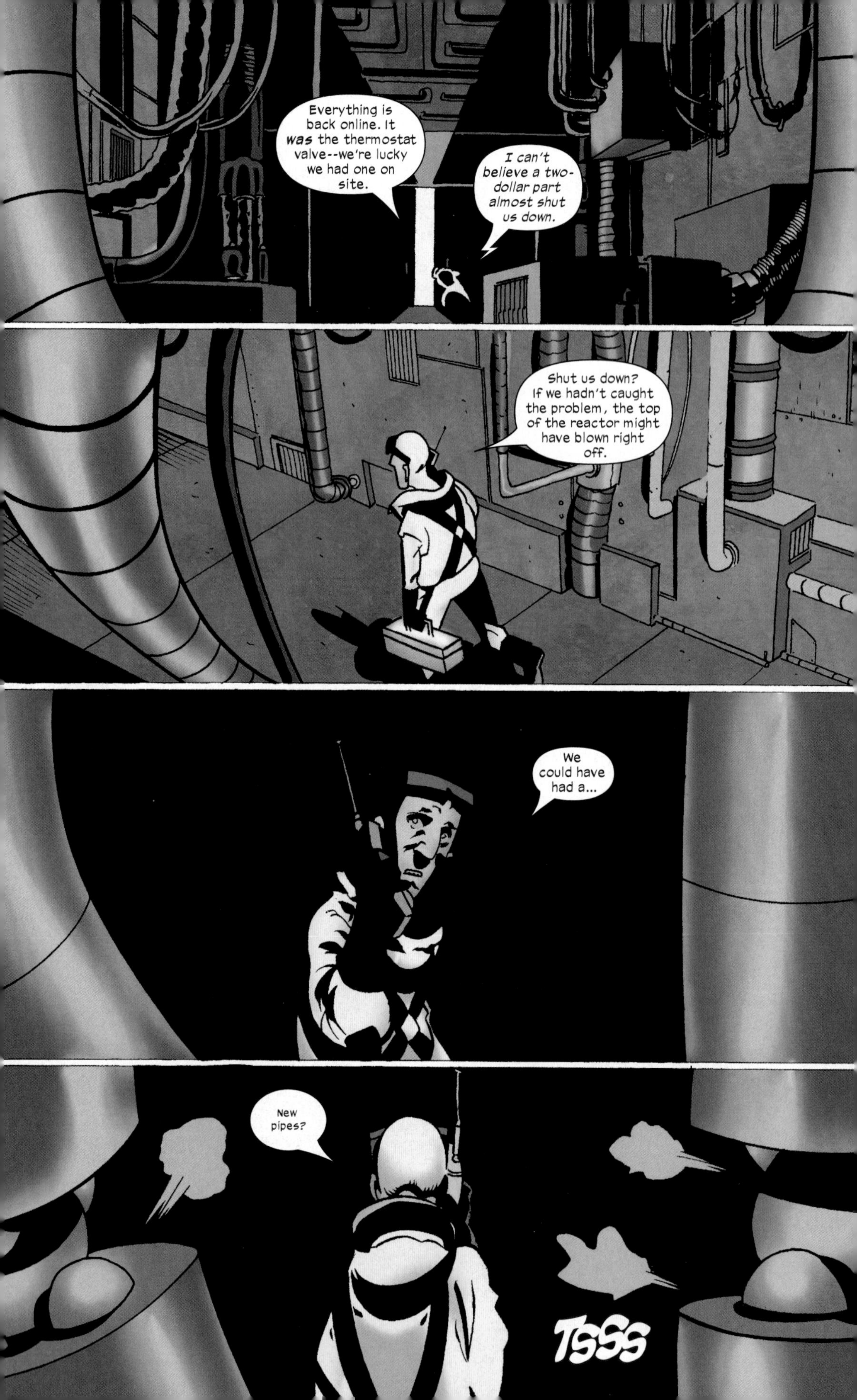
Everything is back online. It *was* the thermostat valve--we're lucky we had one on site.
I can't believe a two-dollar part almost shut us down.
Shut us down? If we hadn't caught the problem, the top of the reactor might have blown right off.
We could have had a...
New pipes?
TSSS

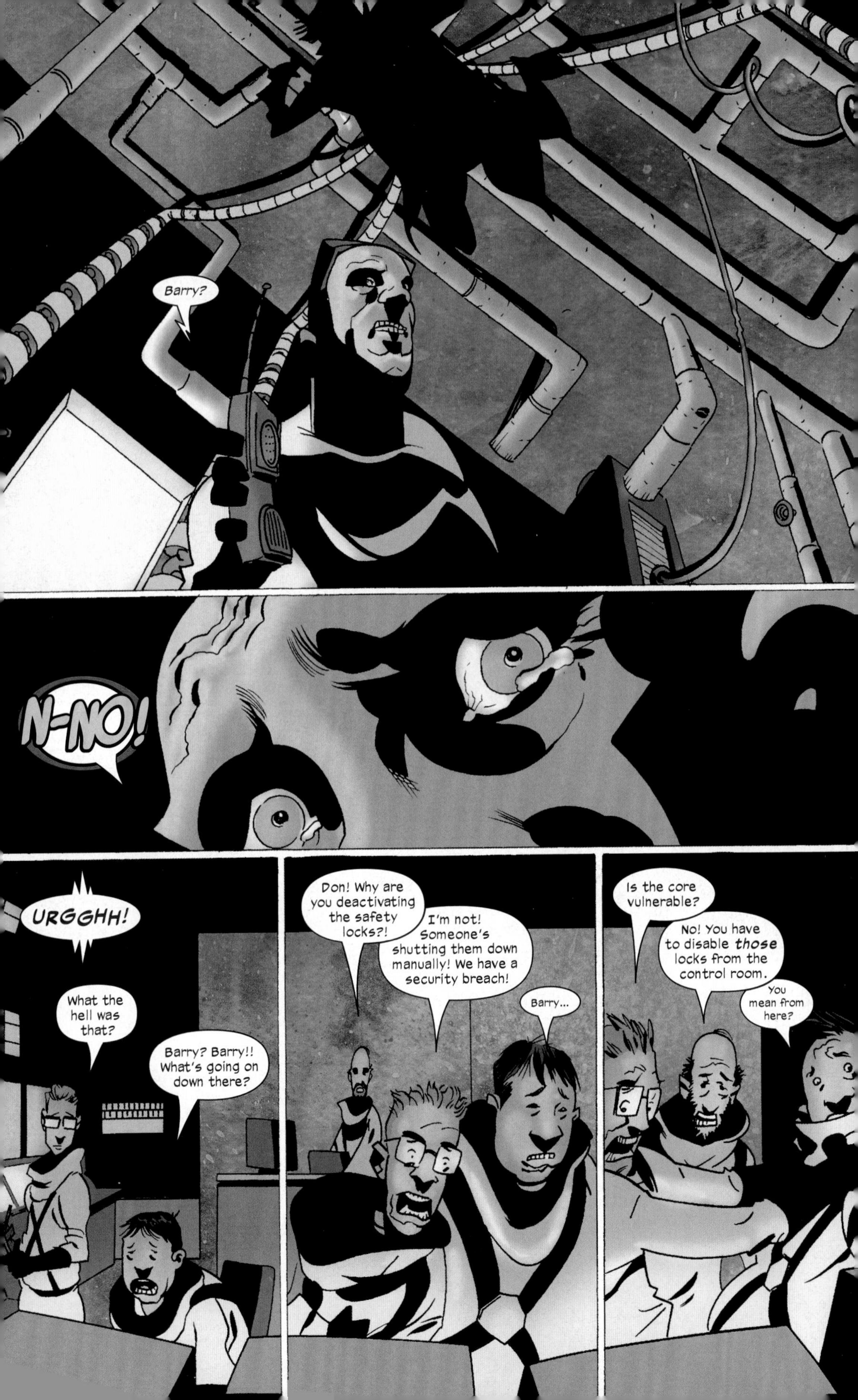

Barry?
N-NO!
URGGHH!
What the hell was that?
Barry? Barry!! What's going on down there?
Don! Why are you deactivating the safety locks?!
I'm not! Someone's shutting them down manually! We have a security breach!
Barry...
Is the core vulnerable?
No! You have to disable *those* locks from the control room.
You mean from here?

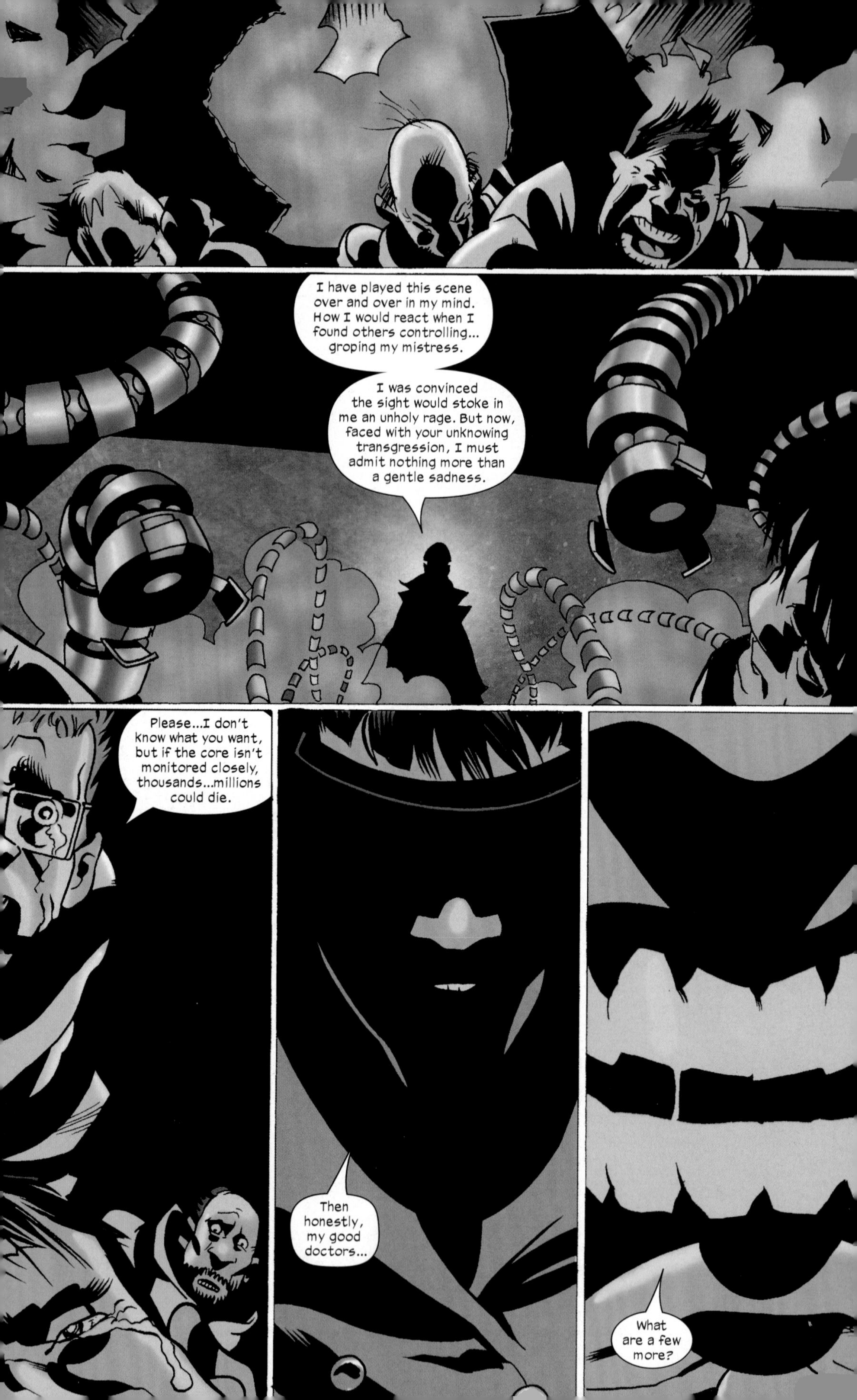

I have played this scene over and over in my mind. How I would react when I found others controlling... groping my mistress.
I was convinced the sight would stoke in me an unholy rage. But now, faced with your unknowing transgression, I must admit nothing more than a gentle sadness.
Please...I don't know what you want, but if the core isn't monitored closely, thousands...millions could die.
Then honestly, my good doctors...
What are a few more?

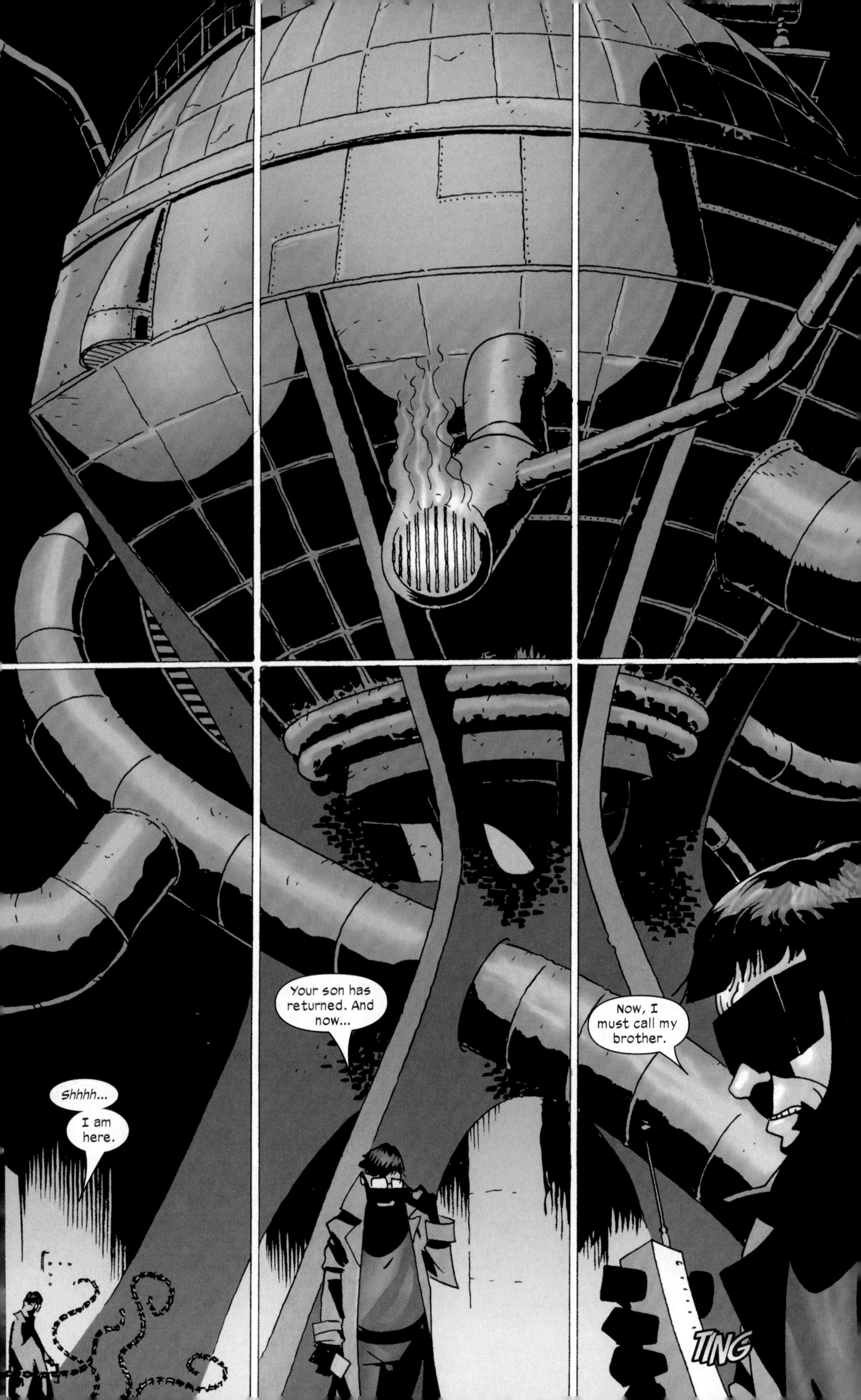
Shhhh...
I am here.
Your son has returned. And now...
Now, I must call my brother.
TING

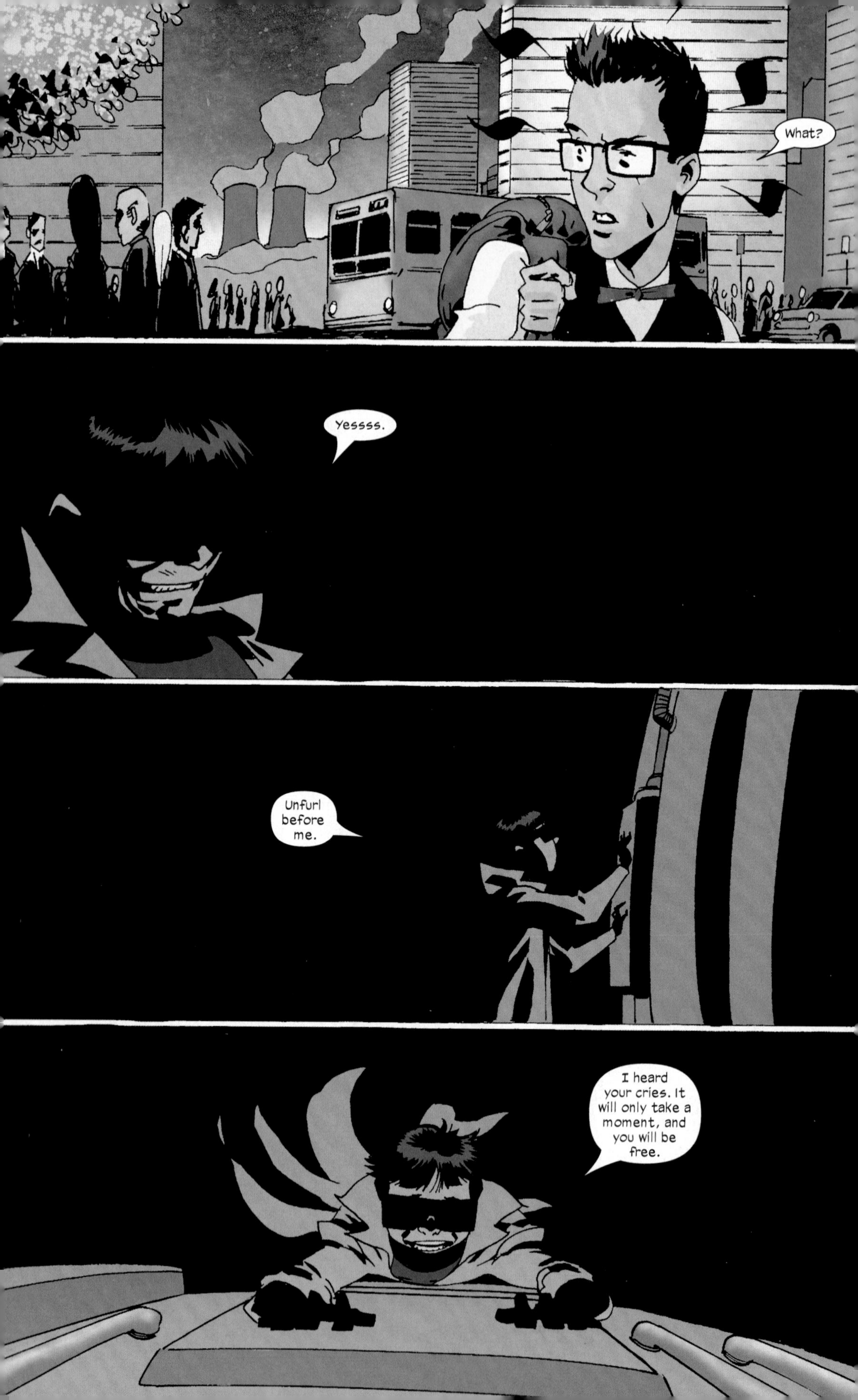
What?
Yessss.
Unfurl before me.
I heard your cries. It will only take a moment, and you will be free.

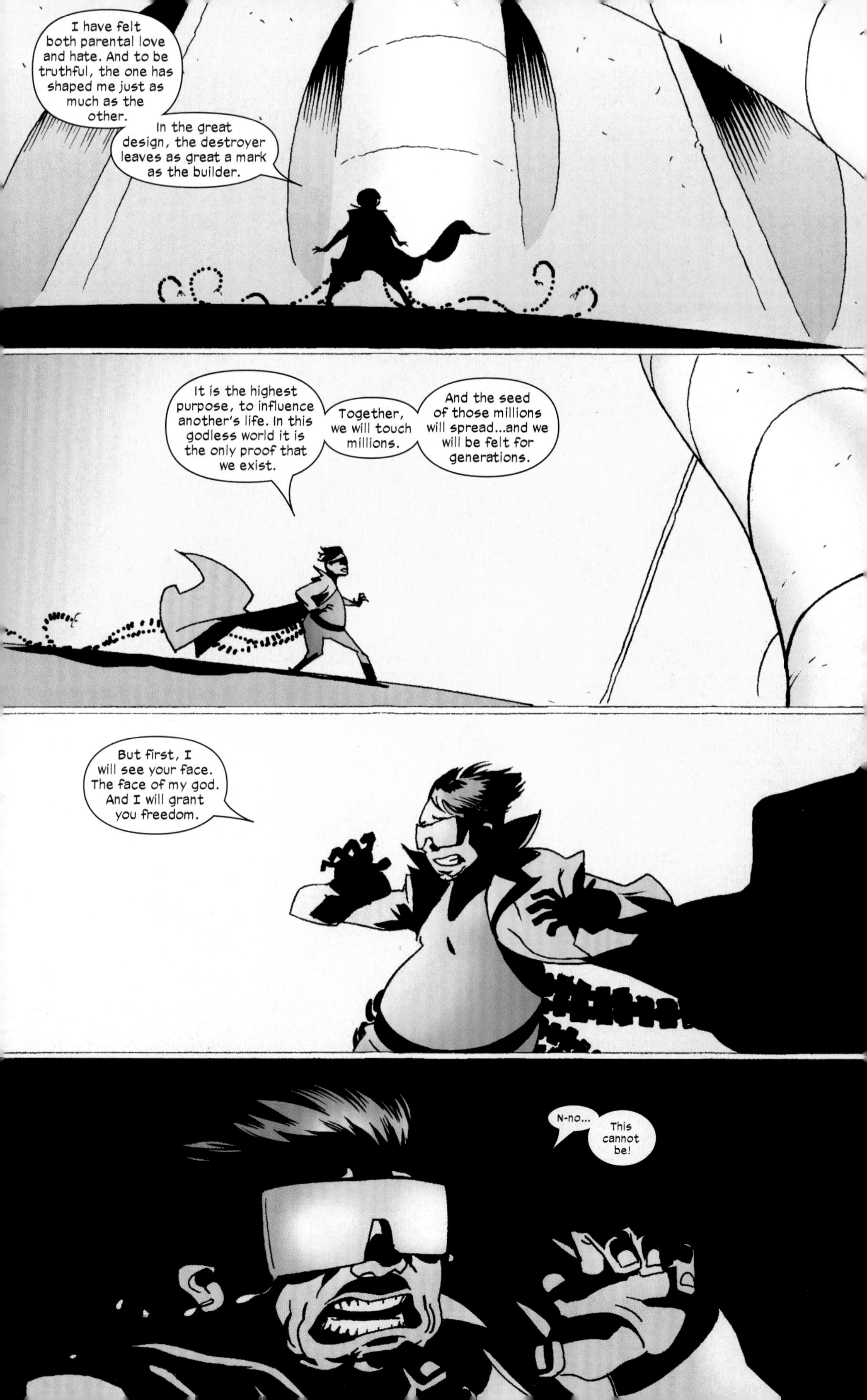
I have felt both parental love and hate. And to be truthful, the one has shaped me just as much as the other.
In the great design, the destroyer leaves as great a mark as the builder.
It is the highest purpose, to influence another's life. In this godless world it is the only proof that we exist.
Together, we will touch millions.
And the seed of those millions will spread...and we will be felt for generations.
But first, I will see your face. The face of my god. And I will grant you freedom.
N-no...
This cannot be!

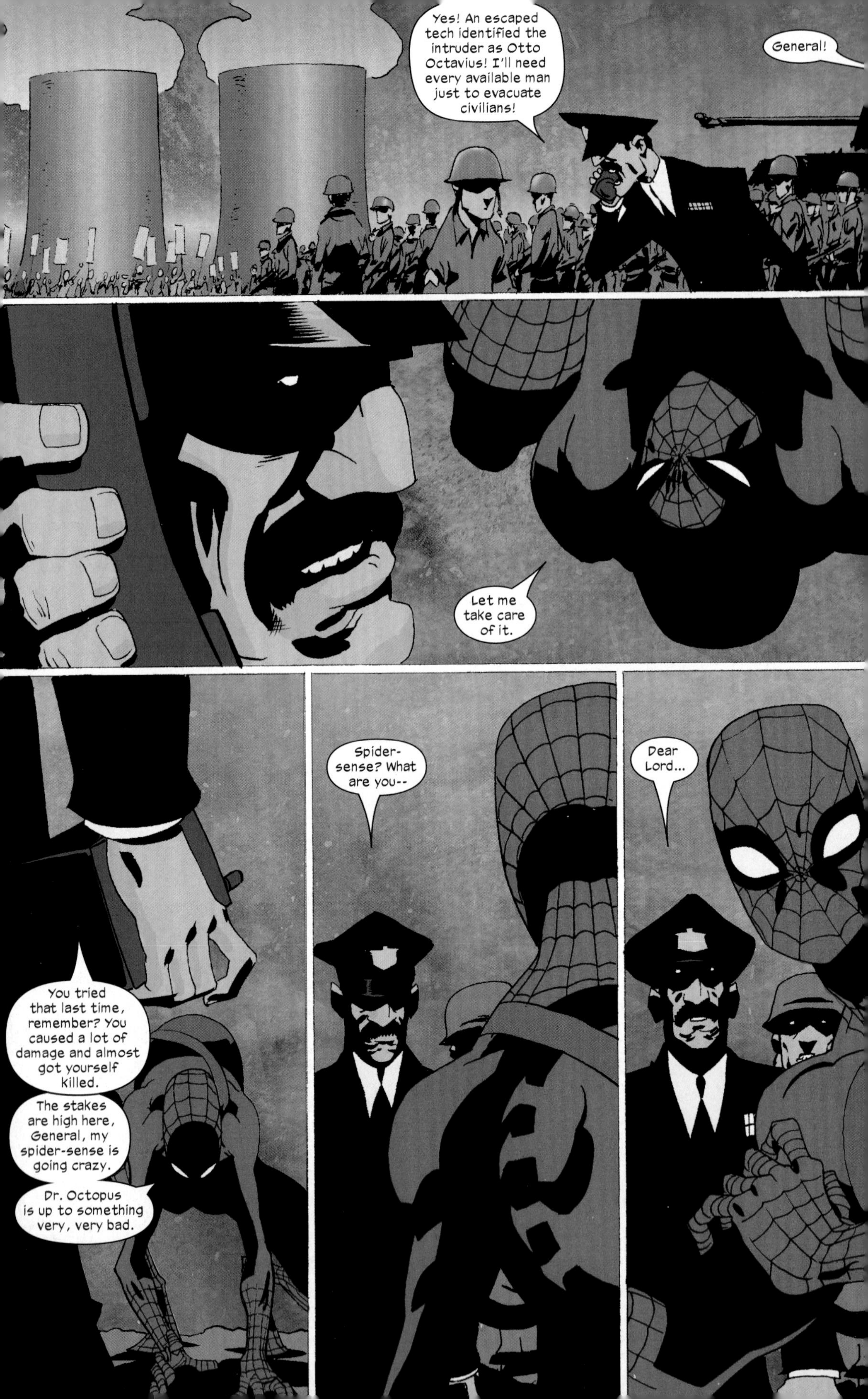

Yes! An escaped tech identified the intruder as Otto Octavius! I'll need every available man just to evacuate civilians!
General!
Let me take care of it.
You tried that last time, remember? You caused a lot of damage and almost got yourself killed.
The stakes are high here, General, my spider-sense is going crazy.
Dr. Octopus is up to something very, very bad.
Spider-sense? What are you--
Dear Lord...

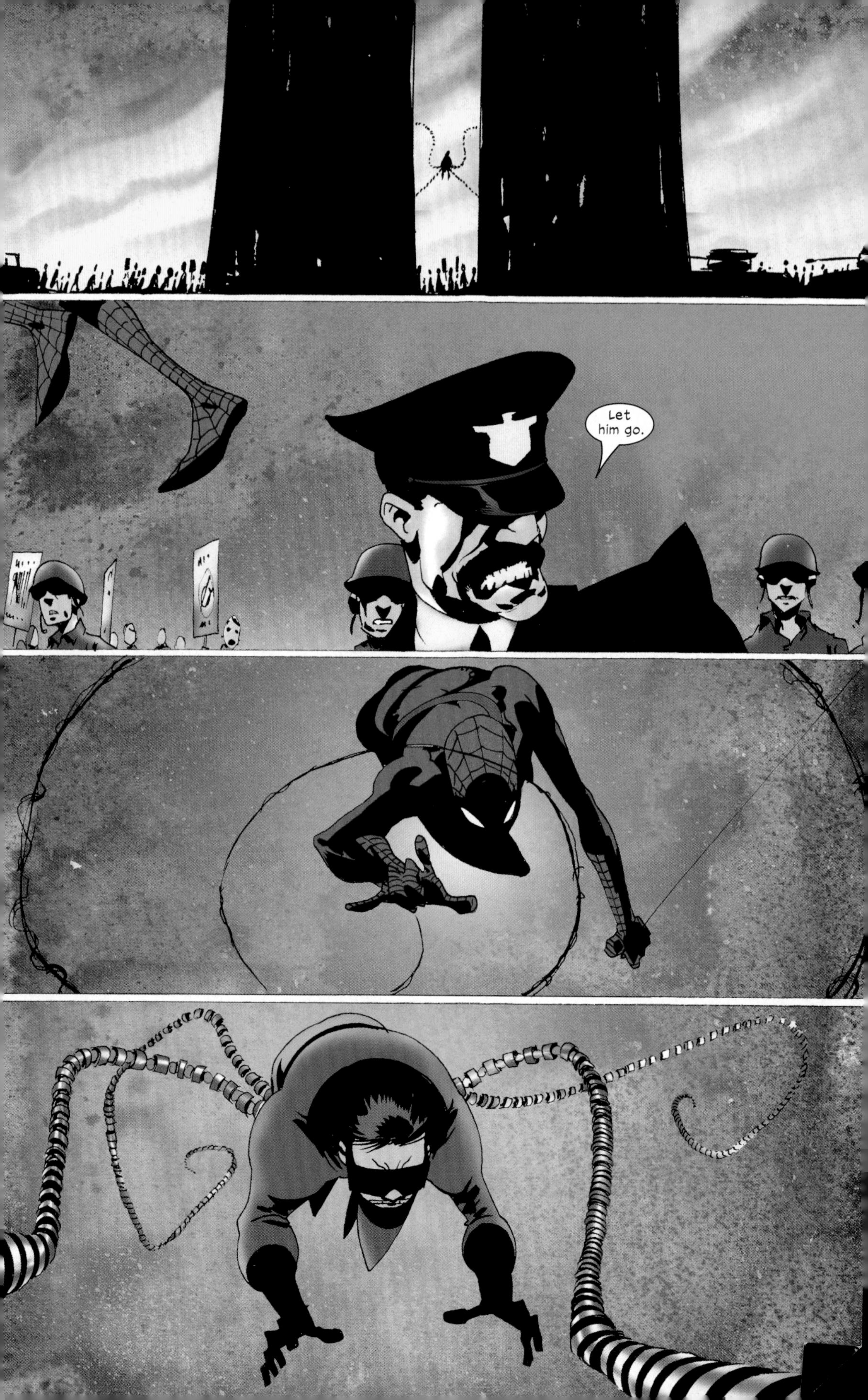
Let him go.

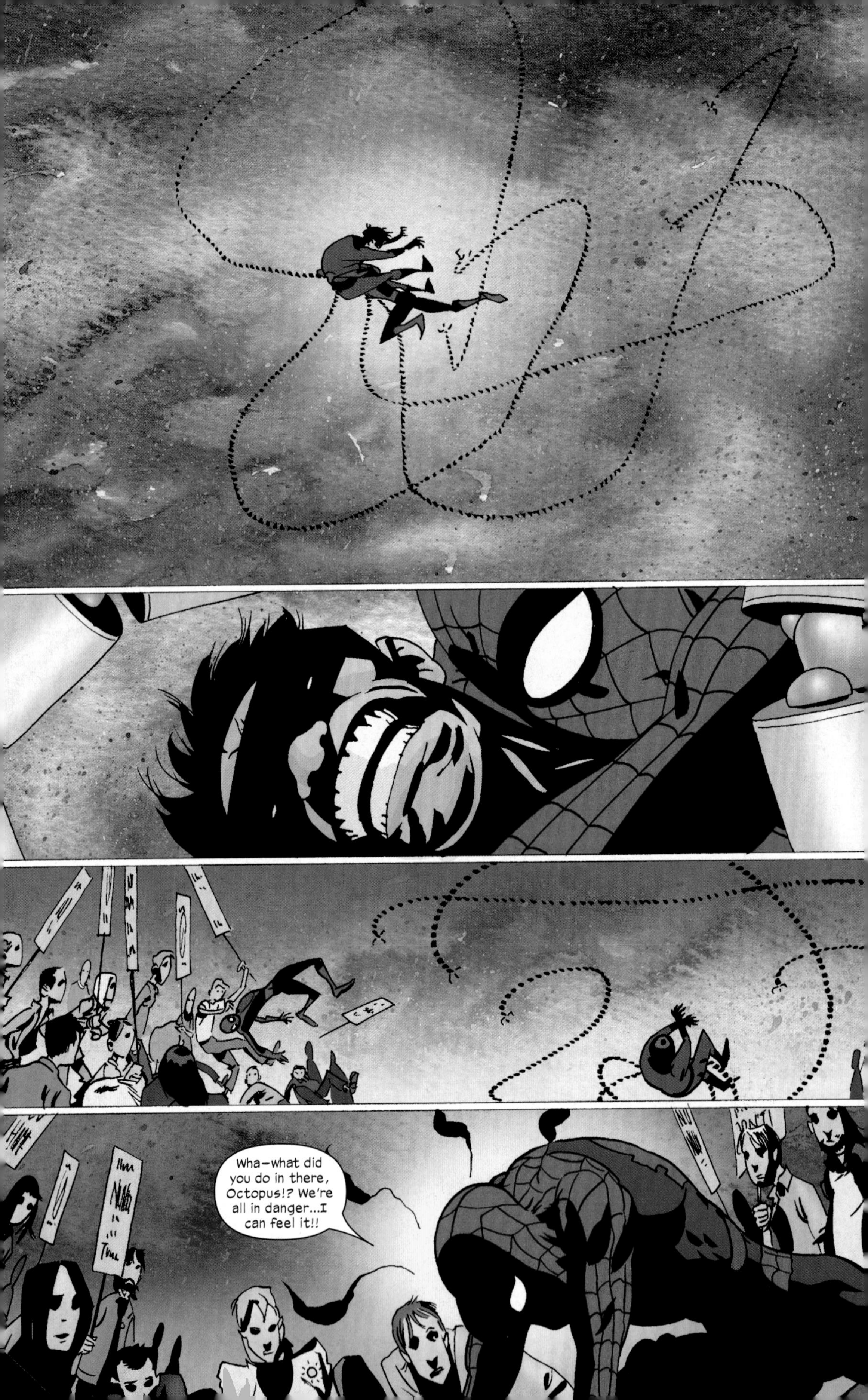
Wha–what did you do in there, Octopus!? We're all in danger...I can feel it!!

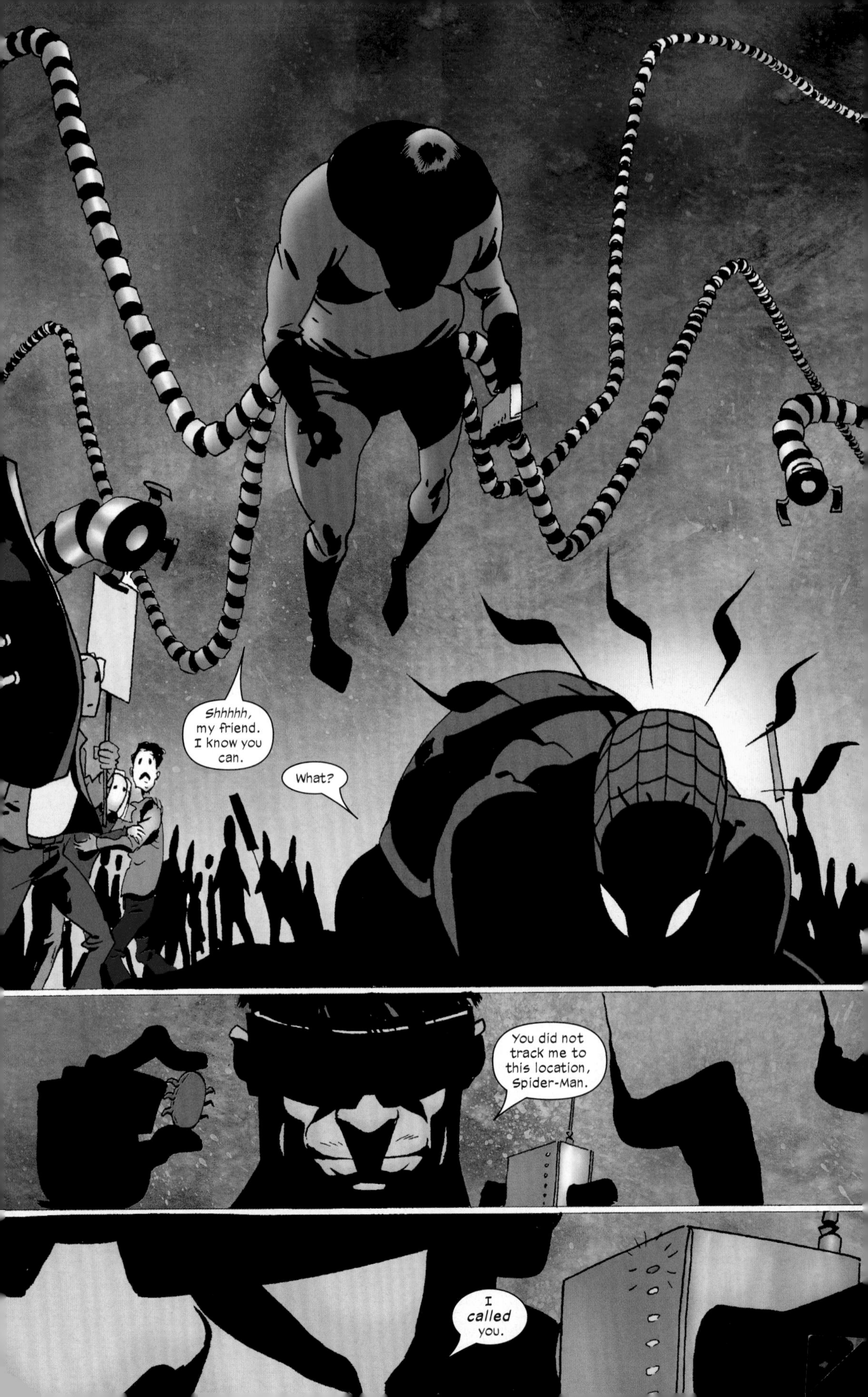
Shhhhh, my friend. I know you can.
What?
You did not track me to this location, Spider-Man.
I called you.

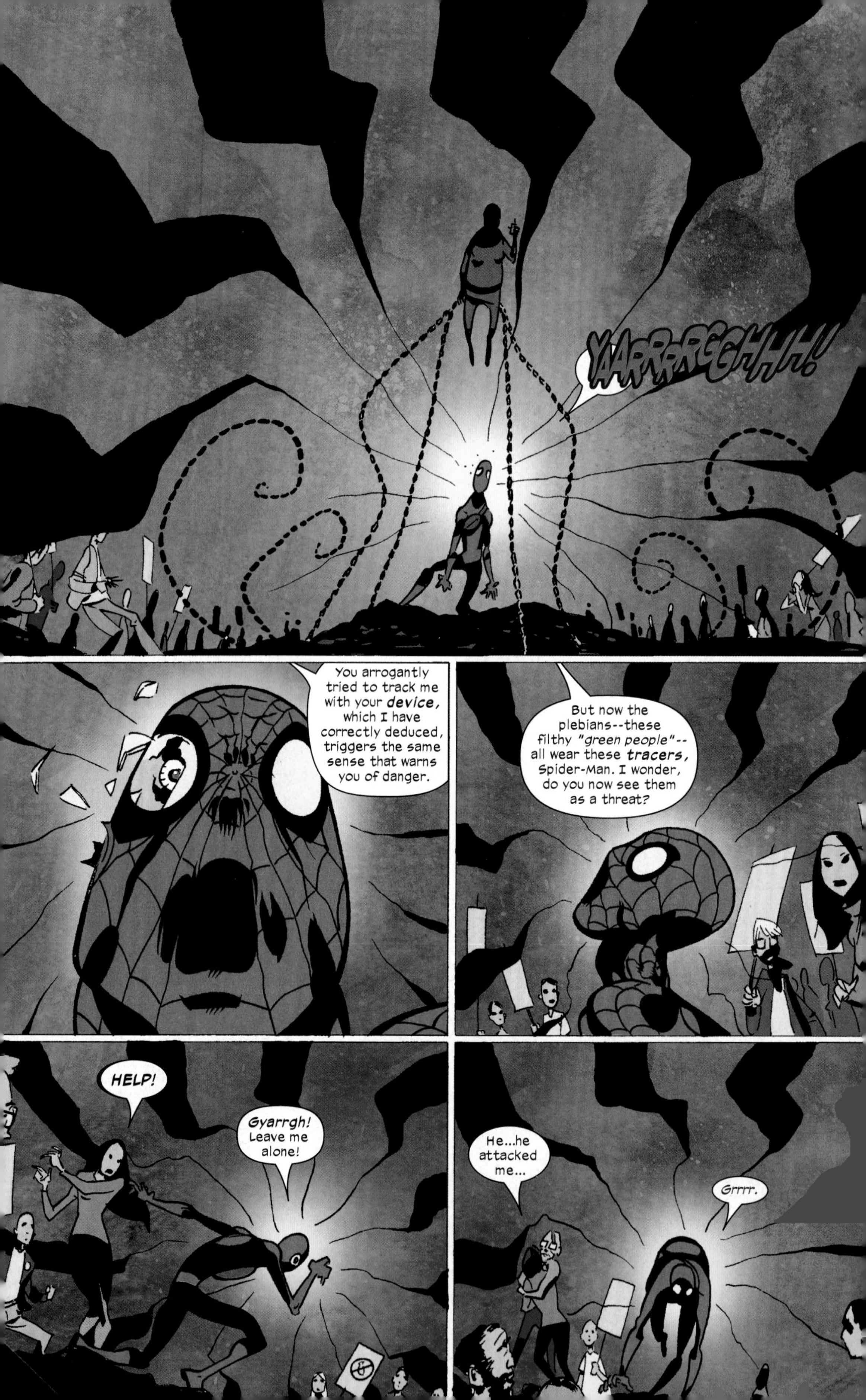
YAARRRRGGHHH!
You arrogantly tried to track me with your *device,* which I have correctly deduced, triggers the same sense that warns you of danger.
But now the plebians--these filthy *"green people"*--all wear these *tracers,* Spider-Man. I wonder, do you now see them as a threat?
HELP!
Gyarrgh! Leave me alone!
He...he attacked me...
Grrrr.

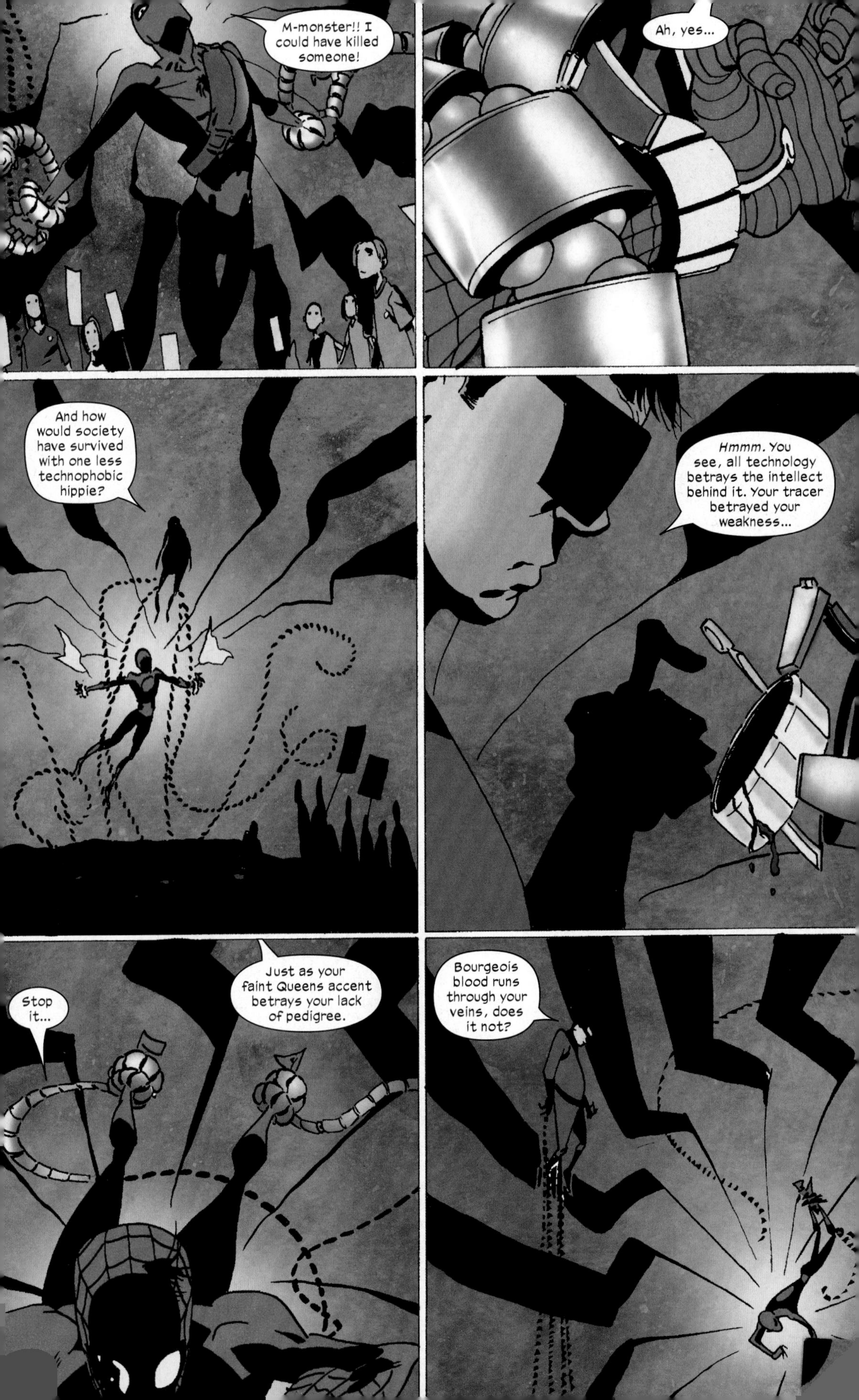
M-monster!! I could have killed someone!
Ah, yes...
And how would society have survived with one less technophobic hippie?
Hmmm. You see, all technology betrays the intellect behind it. Your tracer betrayed your weakness...
Stop it...
Just as your faint Queens accent betrays your lack of pedigree.
Bourgeois blood runs through your veins, does it not?

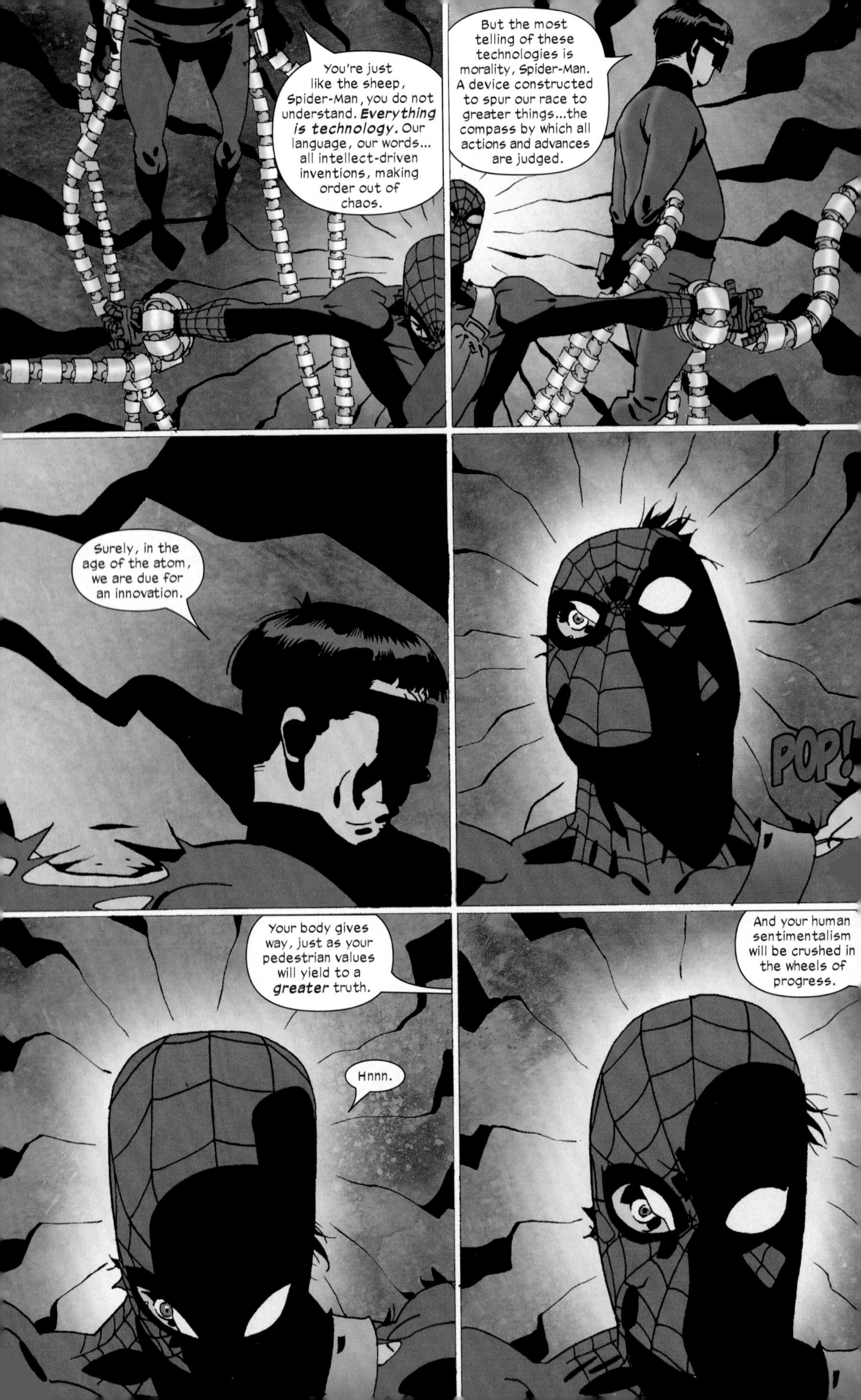
You're just like the sheep, Spider-Man, you do not understand. *Everything is technology.* Our language, our words... all intellect-driven inventions, making order out of chaos.
But the most telling of these technologies is morality, Spider-Man. A device constructed to spur our race to greater things...the compass by which all actions and advances are judged.
Surely, in the age of the atom, we are due for an innovation.
POP!
Your body gives way, just as your pedestrian values will yield to a *greater* truth.
Hnnn.
And your human sentimentalism will be crushed in the wheels of progress.

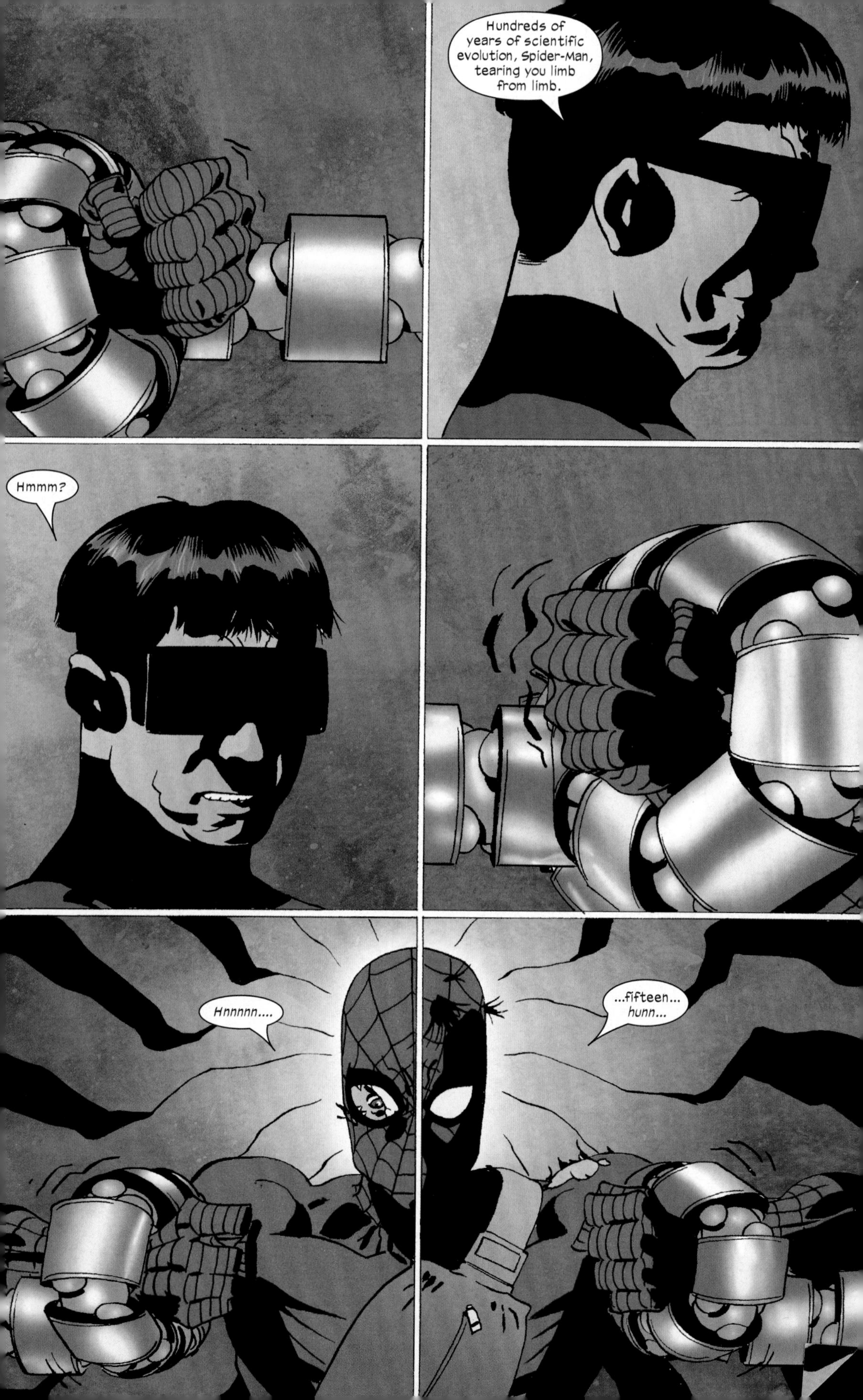
Hundreds of years of scientific evolution, Spider-Man, tearing you limb from limb.
Hmmm?
Hnnnnn....
...fifteen... hunn...

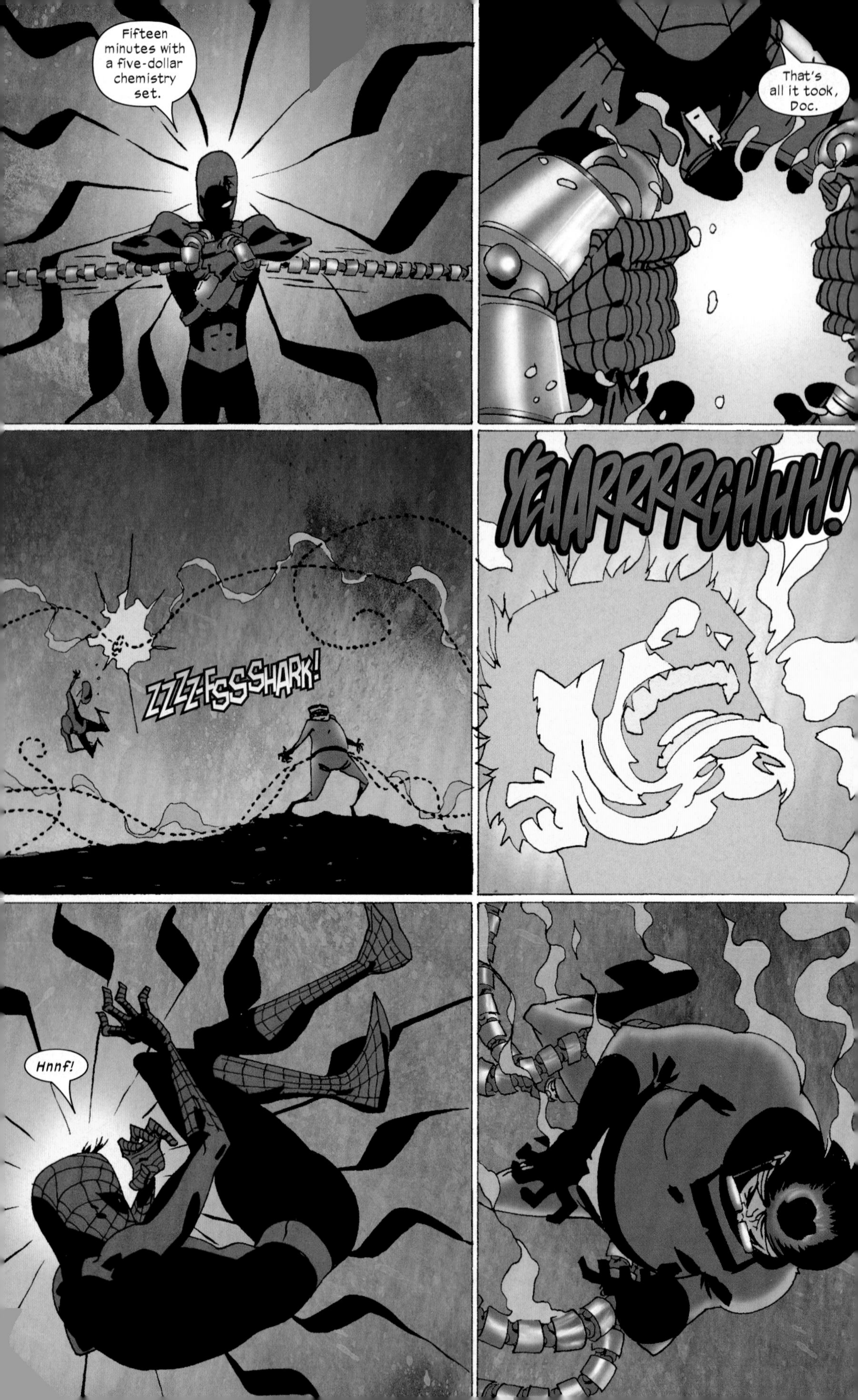
Fifteen minutes with a five-dollar chemistry set.
That's all it took, Doc.
ZZZZ-FSSSHARK!
YEAARRRRRGHHH!
Hnnf!

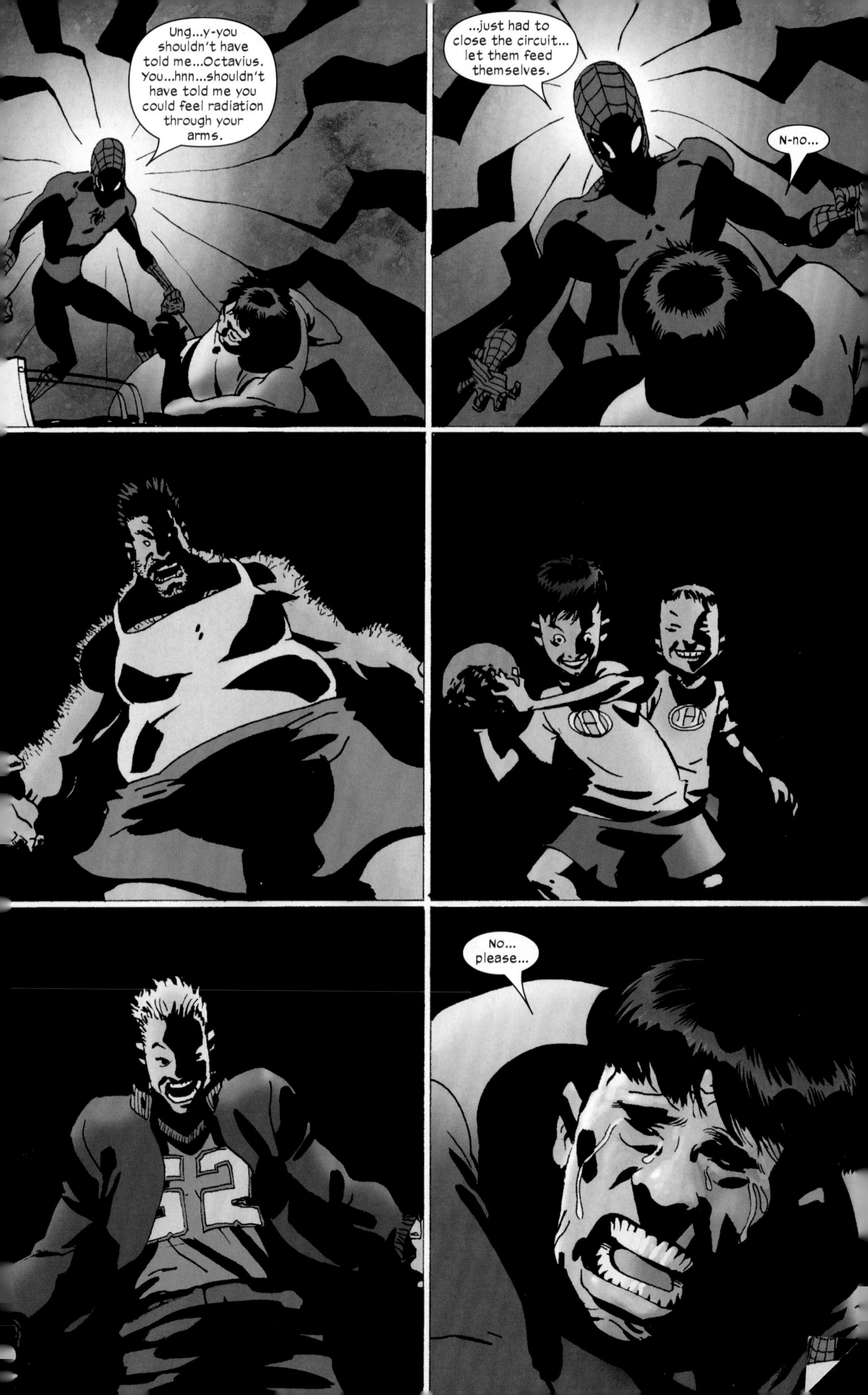
Ung...y-you shouldn't have told me...Octavius. You...hnn...shouldn't have told me you could feel radiation through your arms.
...just had to close the circuit... let them feed themselves.
N-no...
No... please...

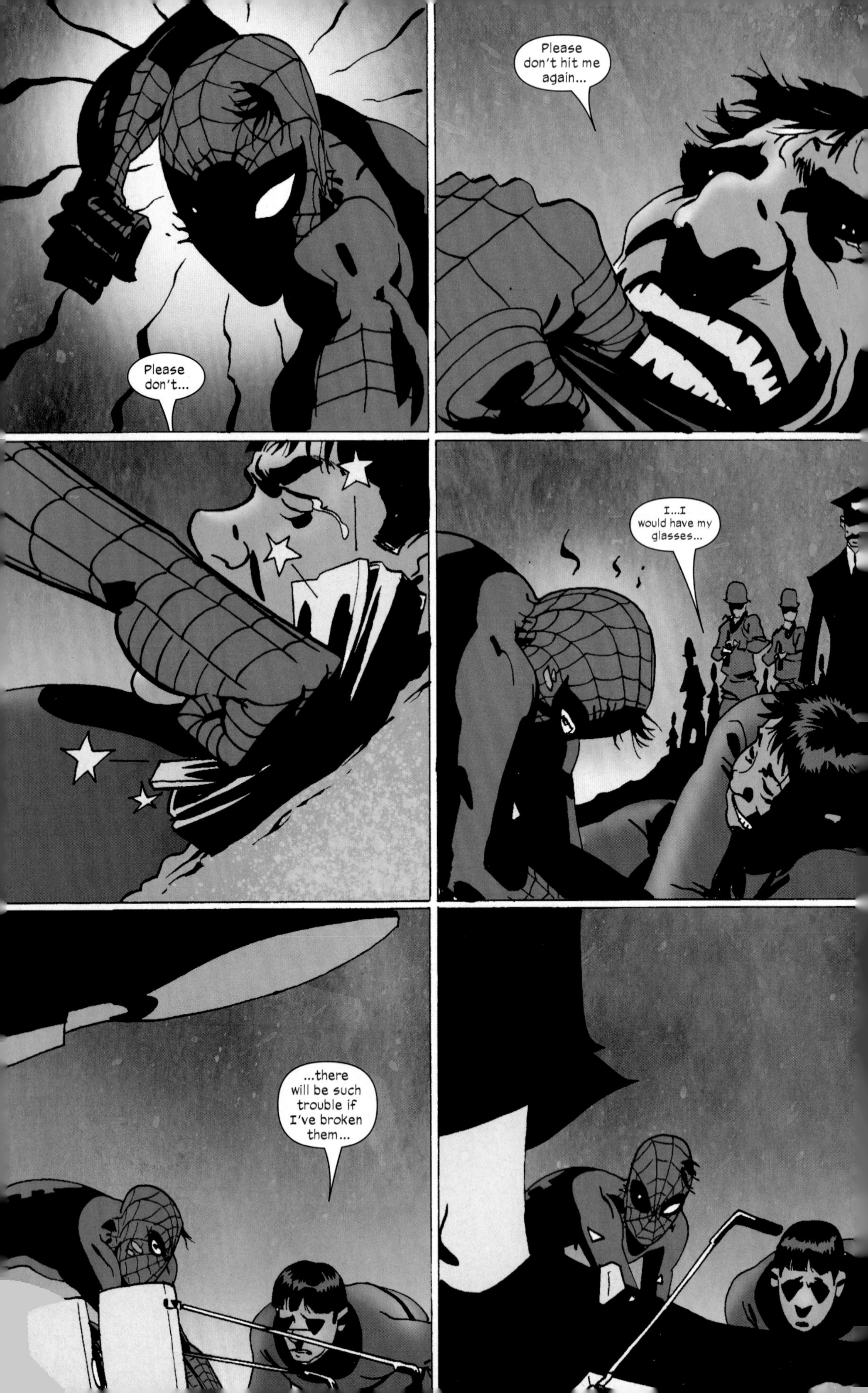
Please don't...
Please don't hit me again...
I...I would have my glasses...
...there will be such trouble if I've broken them...

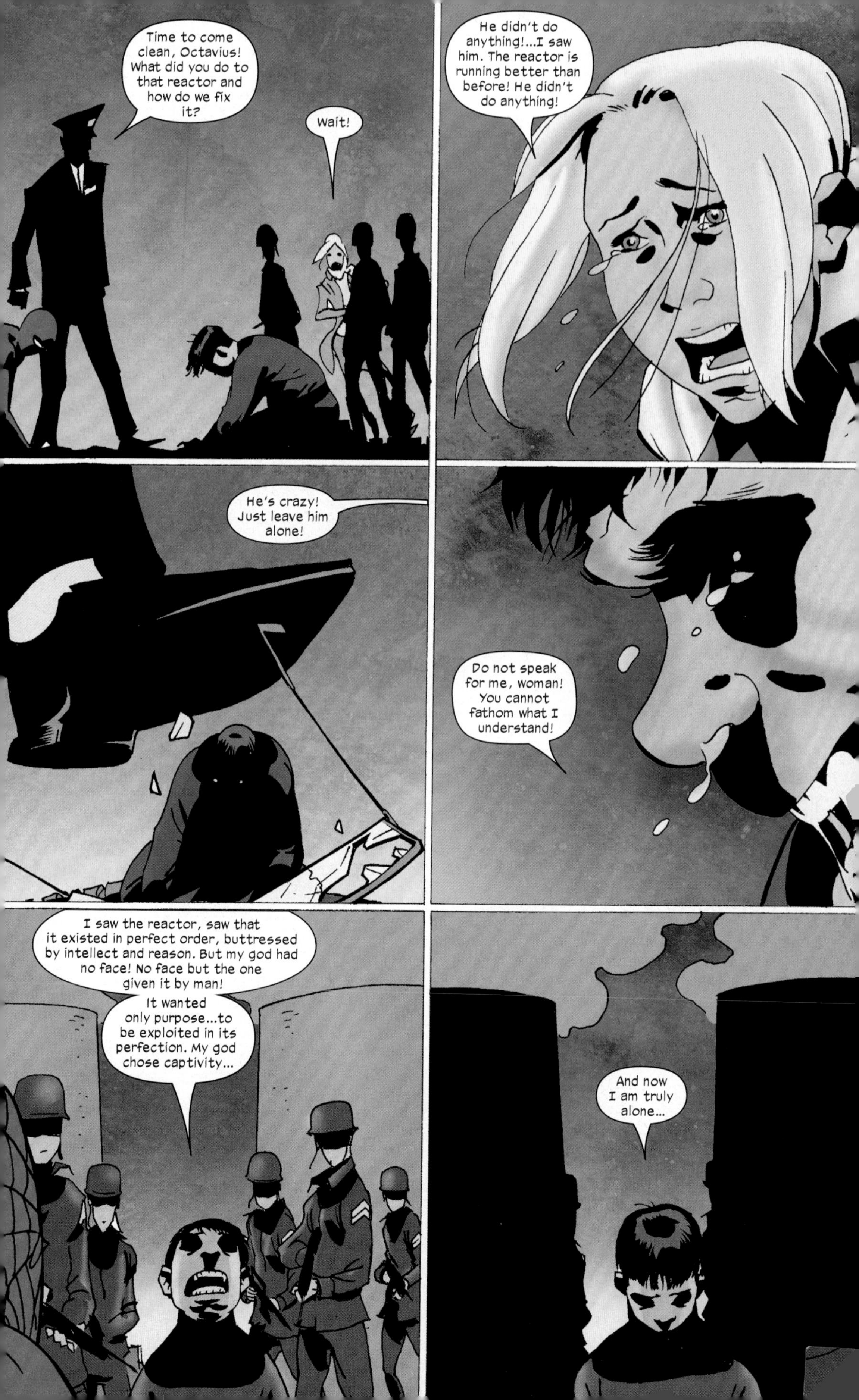
Time to come clean, Octavius! What did you do to that reactor and how do we fix it?
Wait!
He didn't do anything!...I saw him. The reactor is running better than before! He didn't do anything!
He's crazy! Just leave him alone!
Do not speak for me, woman! You cannot fathom what I understand!
I saw the reactor, saw that it existed in perfect order, buttressed by intellect and reason. But my god had no face! No face but the one given it by man!
It wanted only purpose...to be exploited in its perfection. My god chose captivity...
And now I am truly alone...

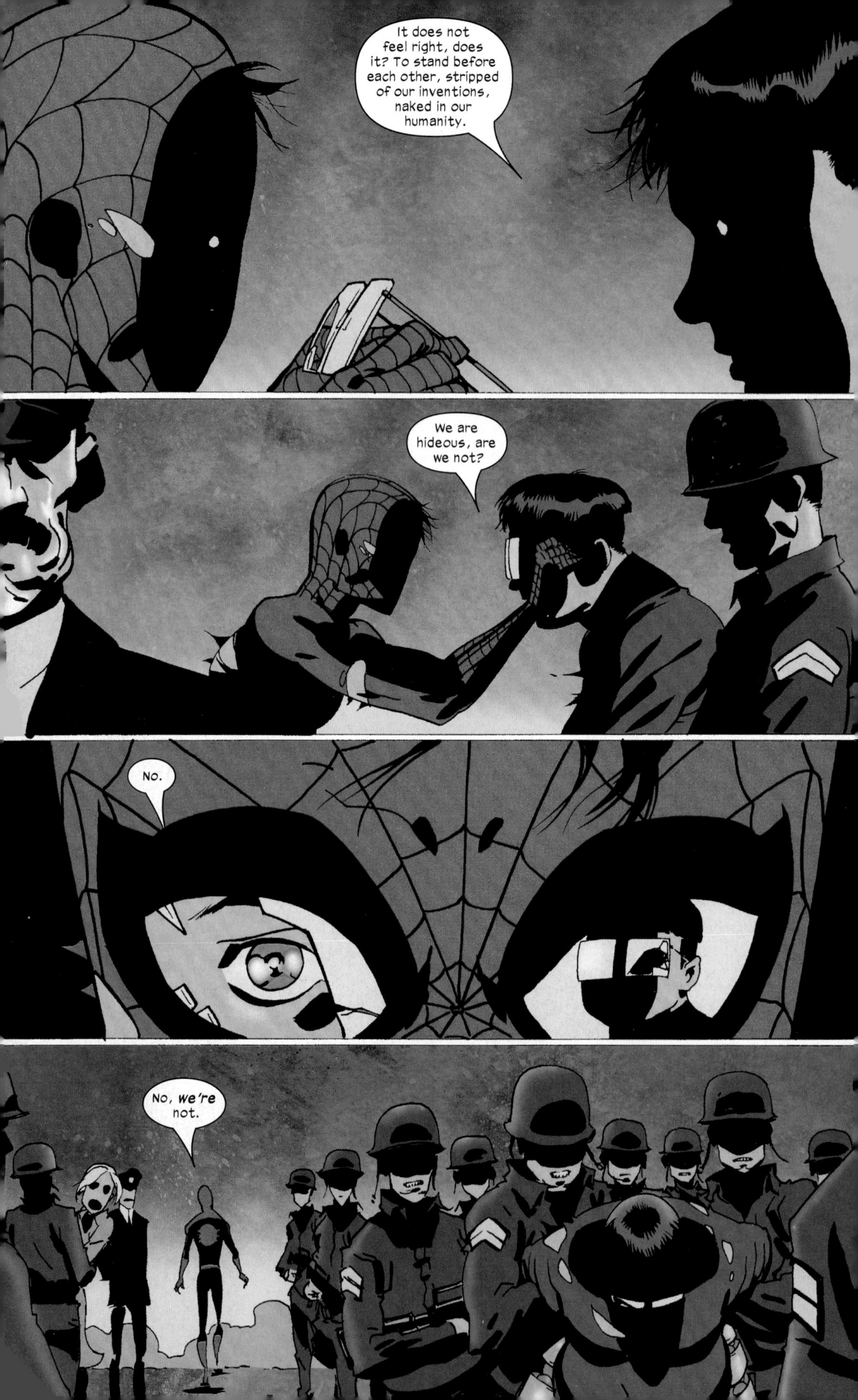
It does not feel right, does it? To stand before each other, stripped of our inventions, naked in our humanity.
We are hideous, are we not?
No.
No, *we're* not.

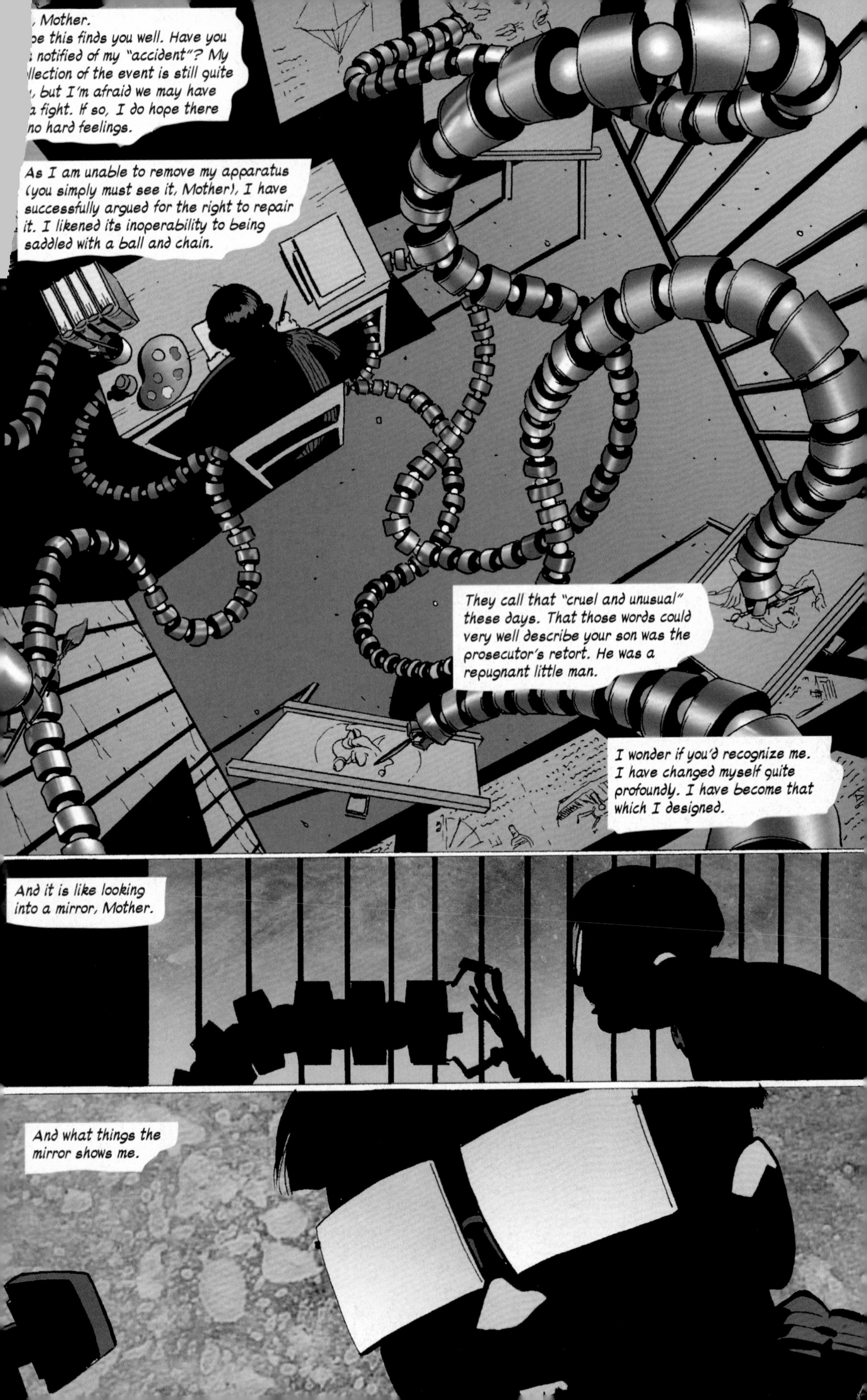
, Mother.
pe this finds you well. Have you
notified of my "accident"? My
llection of the event is still quite
, but I'm afraid we may have
a fight. If so, I do hope there
no hard feelings.
As I am unable to remove my apparatus (you simply must see it, Mother), I have successfully argued for the right to repair it. I likened its inoperability to being saddled with a ball and chain.
They call that "cruel and unusual" these days. That those words could very well describe your son was the prosecutor's retort. He was a repugnant little man.
I wonder if you'd recognize me. I have changed myself quite profoundly. I have become that which I designed.
And it is like looking into a mirror, Mother.
And what things the mirror shows me.

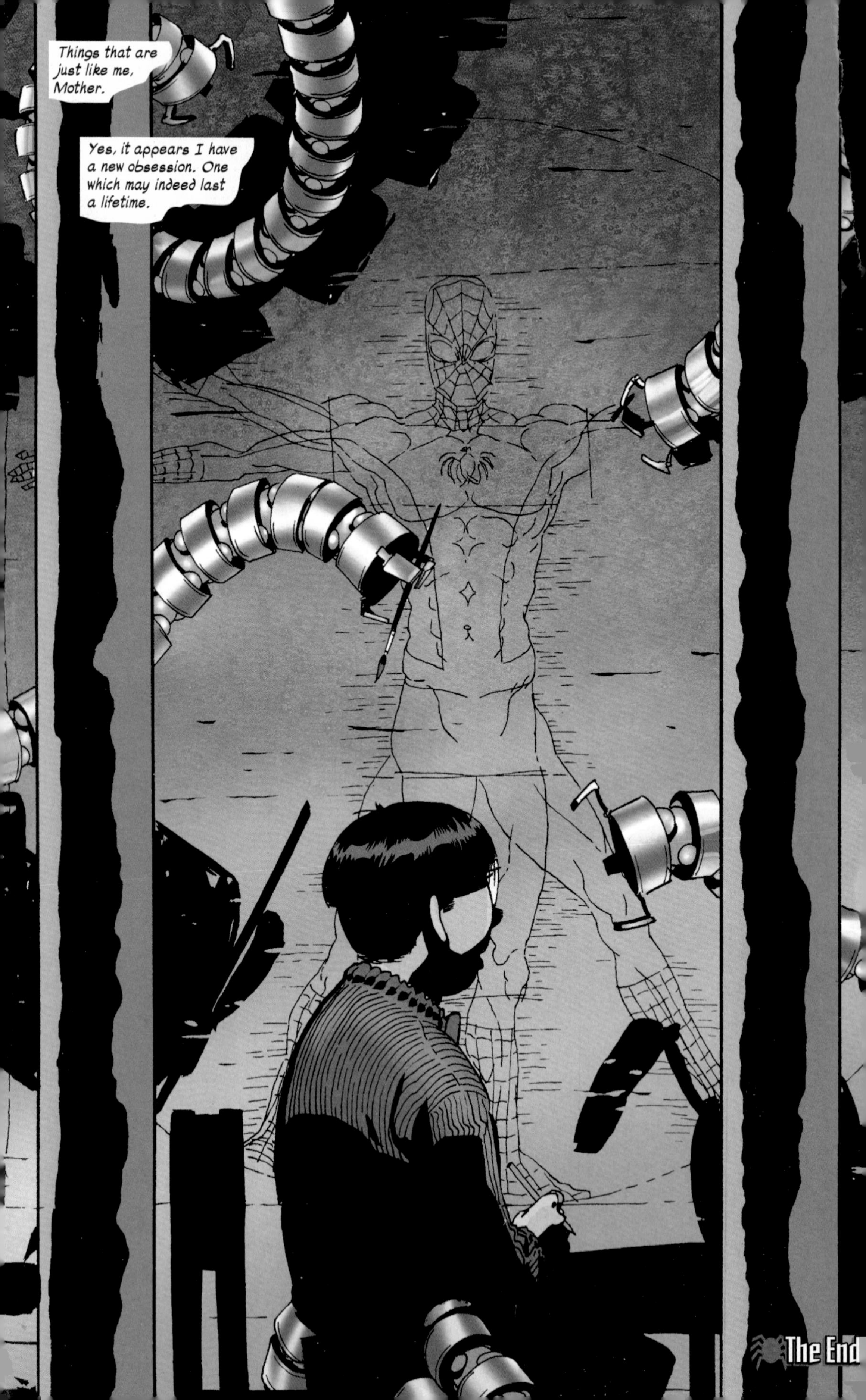
Things that are just like me, Mother.
Yes, it appears I have a new obsession. One which may indeed last a lifetime.
The End